Social Psychology
of Emotion

SAGE was founded in 1965 by Sara Miller McCune to support the dissemination of usable knowledge by publishing innovative and high-quality research and teaching content. Today, we publish more than 750 journals, including those of more than 300 learned societies, more than 800 new books per year, and a growing range of library products including archives, data, case studies, reports, conference highlights, and video. SAGE remains majority-owned by our founder, and after Sara's lifetime will become owned by a charitable trust that secures our continued independence.

Los Angeles | London | Washington DC | New Delhi | Singapore

Social Psychology
of Emotion

Darren Ellis
Ian Tucker

Los Angeles | London | New Delhi
Singapore | Washington DC | Boston

Los Angeles | London | New Delhi
Singapore | Washington DC

SAGE Publications Ltd
1 Oliver's Yard
55 City Road
London EC1Y 1SP

SAGE Publications Inc.
2455 Teller Road
Thousand Oaks, California 91320

SAGE Publications India Pvt Ltd
B 1/I 1 Mohan Cooperative Industrial Area
Mathura Road
New Delhi 110 044

SAGE Publications Asia-Pacific Pte Ltd
3 Church Street
#10-04 Samsung Hub
Singapore 049483

Editor: Chris Rojek
Assistant editor: Gemma Shields
Production editor: Katherine Haw
Copyeditor: Catja Pafort
Marketing manager: Michael Ainsley
Cover design: Shaun Mercier
Typeset by: C&M Digitals (P) Ltd, Chennai, India
Printed and bound by CPI Group (UK) Ltd,
Croydon, CR0 4YY

© Darren Ellis and Ian Tucker 2015

First published 2015

Apart from any fair dealing for the purposes of research
or private study, or criticism or review, as permitted under
the Copyright, Designs and Patents Act, 1988, this
publication may be reproduced, stored or transmitted in
any form, or by any means, only with the prior permission
in writing of the publishers, or in the case of reprographic
reproduction, in accordance with the terms of licences
issued by the Copyright Licensing Agency. Enquiries
concerning reproduction outside those terms should be
sent to the publishers.

Library of Congress Control Number: 2014954698

British Library Cataloguing in Publication data

A catalogue record for this book is available from
the British Library

MIX
Paper from
responsible sources
FSC
www.fsc.org   FSC® C013604

ISBN 978-1-4462-5478-3
ISBN 978-1-4462-5479-0 (pbk)

At SAGE we take sustainability seriously. Most of our products are printed in the UK using FSC papers and boards.
When we print overseas we ensure sustainable papers are used as measured by the Egmont grading system.
We undertake an annual audit to monitor our sustainability.

Table of Contents

List of Figures and Tables

Figures

Tables

About the Authors

Darren Ellis is Senior Lecturer and Programme Leader in Psychosocial Studies at the University of East London. Darren has been interested in ways in which emotion, affect and feeling are experienced, expressed and constructed. These interests have influenced his writings on psychotherapy, the emotional disclosure paradigm, theorising police stop and search activity, surveillance studies, conspiracy theory studies, and understandings of social media interactivity.

Ian Tucker is Reader in Social Psychology at the University of East London. He has a long standing interest in the social psychological aspects of emotion and affect, which has theoretically informed empirical work in the areas of mental distress, social media and surveillance. He has conducted research for the Mental Health Foundation and EPSRC Communities and Culture Network+, and is currently working on a project exploring the impact of social media on psychological support in mental health communities. Ian has published numerous articles in the areas of mental health, space and place, embodiment, surveillance and social media.

Acknowledgments

We would first like to thank SAGE for all their support throughout the making of this book (Gemma Shields and Katherine Haw in particular). Special mention must be made of Dave Harper, who has supported us through all aspects of this book, and provided much valued and welcomed company on our 'writing weekends' in Glastonbury!

Dr Ian Tucker

I would like to thank my co-author Darren for his unremitting commitment to this book, and huge effort to bring it to press! Thanks also to all my colleagues in the Psychology and Social Change Research Group at UEL, who have provided much needed intellectual support and nourishment. I would also like to thank all the students that have provided very useful questions regarding, and contributions towards, my thinking. Finally I would like to express a huge gratitude to my wonderful family, Katherine, Noah and Isaac, who have been with me all the way, and who I would be completely lost without.

Dr Darren Ellis

Many thanks to Ian who is a great pleasure to work with; he has been both a great friend and a rich source of inspiration. I'd also like to thank my colleagues in the area of Psychosocial Studies at UEL who encouraged me to develop this project (particularly David Jones, Candida Yates, Angie Voela, Heather Price, Corinne Squire, Nicola Diamond, Cigdem Esin and Lurraine Jones). Also thanks to the students who helped me shape some of this book through the emotion lecture series. I am very lucky also to have such a supportive and loving family, so a special thanks to Nicola, Lily, Otto and Arthur.

Introduction:
The social context
of emotion

As we write this, there is widespread coverage of the passing away of Nelson Mandela. This significant historical event has elicited a major outpouring of emotion, with people across the world expressing individual and collective emotional reactions to the news. Psychologically analysing the emotion in this event is no straightforward exercise. Would one try to operationalize it at the level of the individual, framing emotional expressions as reactions emanating from cognitive processes? Alternatively, would it be better analysed as some kind of instinctual biological response? Social psychology has the potential to address emotion as produced through multi-levelled processes, moving through people and societies, so it is not always easy to separate these out as clearly distinct realms. Emotion can come to act as a signifier, for instance in the case of Mandela as someone of huge importance. Not only this, but emotion can be expressed in hugely diverse and varied forms, for instance the media reports people crying outside the South African embassy in the UK, whilst people dance and celebrate Mandela's life in South Africa. This is because there are so many things bound up in his passing away: for example, the long history of racial discrimination, not only in South Africa itself, but in countries around the world. The emotional outpourings remind us of the great achievements of an individual, but can also remind us of the derogatory forms of social stratification that can come about simply based upon the colour of one's skin. Consequently emotion can feature as simultaneously joyful and sad, merging in individual expressions, rather than experienced as distinct feelings.

Nelson Mandela's death also shows how quickly emotion can spread as a social phenomenon, as emotional communication no longer simply occurs at a face to face level, but spreads through modern digital and social media e.g. the Twitter hashtag #Mandela. Here emotion can pass through bodies and technologies in an instant, moving through biological, social and technological realms with a speed that renders any attempt to separate them out as potentially unhelpful, if not a futile endeavour. Discipline-specific approaches can miss the multiple and complex ways that emotion travels. This is not to say that there is never value to single disciplinary approaches, but that when addressing the social psychology of emotion we are dealing with the messier and complicated realities of people's everyday lives, a study of which is likely to incorporate crossing disciplinary boundaries, and therefore take aspects from a variety of fields of study.

Social Psychology, Emotion and Interdisciplinarity

In this book we look at some of the many ways that emotion has been theorised. As we will discover, it has had many incarnations, from early Greek notions of pathos to more recent post-structuralist theories of affect. One thing we are sure of is that simply claiming one definition over others in an attempt to encapsulate an essence, in no way does justice to the historic and contemporary expressions of emotion. Indeed, it is easy to ask whether a 'thing' called emotion actually exists. This is not an invalid question given the remarkable amount of differing opinions regarding what it is and what it does. For instance, we may think of it as reification: another empty category or a term that has so many meanings that it becomes useless in distinguishing anything at all. In our opinion, there is no individual concept that encapsulates a sufficiently wide denotation of 'emotion', but rather a variety of assemblages that give it meaning and existence. As social scientists we are better equipped to gain some insight into phenomena when we take account of the context of their emergence. And yet this is a thoroughly, perhaps, impossible business, for where do we draw lines as to what to include and what to exclude from 'context'? For social scientists this may become more of a practical concern rather than a philosophical one. It concerns the resources that one has. Thinking about the social psychology of emotion therefore, as our project, is limited in its scope by the resources we have available to us (for example, in terms of limited time). Nevertheless, we did not want to limit the project, as is often the case in psychology, by only thinking of the social psychology of emotion as rooted in the modern era through figures such as Charles Darwin and William James. Instead we seek to do something a bit different in terms of tracing roots back to very early conceptualisations and follow those through to contemporary views in an attempt to develop a relatively comprehensive account.

Social psychology as a specific term and field of study emerged in the early twentieth century not long after the development of psychology itself as a distinct discipline. The immense desire to develop psychology as a science, primarily through relying on dominant scientific theories of the time (e.g. evolution), as well as the 'scientific method' (e.g. experiments), meant that psychological accounts of emotion were heavily focused on developing theories that could be used to support psychology's claim to scientific status. One consequence of this was that earlier philosophies of emotion have not featured in psychological theories of emotion. Early theories have of course come to be key constituents of contemporary histories of emotion, which has confounded the absence of pre-twentieth century thinking regarding emotion in psychology. One of the aims of this book is to address the relative lack of Ancient Greek and Medieval theological thinking in histories of emotion in psychology. Furthermore, in thinking about emotion from a social psychological perspective, we seek to explore historical accounts through a 'social' lens, which we argue, is valuable in terms of broadening contemporary psychological theories that often offer individualistic models of emotion (e.g. in terms of neurological or cognitive approaches). The fact that psychological theories have tended to be dominated by major theorists of the past 150 years (e.g. Charles Darwin, William James), means that histories often end up covering the same ground, which becomes self-fulfilling. This book is one attempt to broaden psychology's theoretical spectrum of emotion, both in terms of historical reach and disciplinary breadth. Whilst in recent times a number of broadly sociological accounts of emotion have emerged, there has yet to be a specific social psychological perspective offered. Given the importance of emotion to social relations and the ways people connect and communicate with one another, there is a vast swathe of human experience and activity that is potentially missed in the existing portfolio of psychological accounts of emotion, due to the dominance of individualistic biological and cognitive accounts therein.

Hence, one of the appeals of thinking about emotion through social psychology is that it includes both social and psychological processes. For instance, we might want to think of emotion as a signal, a psychic (embodied) signal to the self produced through sensations, feelings, affects, and moods. It can also be a social (external) signal to others from the self, or to the self from external objects (both human and non-human), e.g. through the means of facial expressions, voice tones, aesthetic appeal, and the vulgar. Yet just thinking about emotion in this way perhaps creates a false dichotomy between the inner and outer realms of individual experience. Indeed social psychology urges one to think about the dynamic, intimate and potentially indistinguishable relationship(s) between these two realms of experience. Consequently, exploring emotion socio-psychologically entails breaching frequently-imposed disciplinary boundaries.

Although we offer a variety of perspectives that are housed in particular fields, each of these tend to incorporate a degree of interdisciplinarity. For example, a feature of emotion that occurs in numerous chapters is a concern with the face or what has come to be known as the 'facial expression thesis'. This thesis is often understood as arising through the work of Darwin in his book 'The expression of emotion in humans and other animals' (otherwise known simply as 'the expressions') in relation to his theory of evolution. However, this does not do justice to what Darwin was arguing, as he was more concerned about emotional expression in humans as being vestigial (maladaptive features of human functioning). Additionally, theorists from Ancient philosophers (e.g. Plato) through to Enlightenment thinkers (e.g. Immanuel Kant) have been interested in associating facial expressions with emotion-related phenomena. There are also numerous contemporary considerations of the importance of facial expressions of emotion which have a variety of concerns; for example: sociological accounts of emotion have considered the relational aspects of the emotional face as performance; neurobiologists have researched the muscular activity of facial expressions; crowd psychologists have looked at the micro-activity of the face in relation to emotional contagion; developmental psychologists have investigated forms of affect regulation and attunement that occur as a result of the gaze between the primary carer and the neonate; and internet researchers have been interested in facial expressions through analysing topics such as emoticons and Skype interactivity.

Throughout this book we seek to chart some of the threads that weave through different disciplines and fields, and point to the value in thinking of them in social psychological terms. In this sense, we are keen to point to themes running in and across previous theories and accounts, rather than mapping only disciplinary-specific thinking regarding emotion. One way of doing this is to tack between contrasting poles in related fields. For example, there is a long history of thinking of emotions as biologically-determined phenomena as opposed to resulting from the rational activities of individuals as free and wilful actors. These traditionally feed into contemporary academic discourses focusing on the potential for people to be overcome by emotion and using it as an excuse for, for example, socially unacceptable behaviour. Hence there has been a prevalent view of emotions as relating to primitive aspects of the self, for example, as being basic, biological and irrational. However, some historical accounts contain a less prevalent perspective that at times views emotion as a form of intelligence, something that facilitates moral development, and which is the glue for social cohesion. Emotion has also been understood as something that can not always be consciously felt or perceived, and consequently difficult to empirically study at the level of the individual (e.g. recent 'turns to affect'). The desire for empiricism in psychology has led to a model that renders that which cannot be easily pointed to as individual behaviour and activity invalid as a theoretical or analytic concern. This is why we see so much talk of emotion in biological, cognitive and neurological terms, rather than a language of the soul, virtue or collective expressions of affect.

We can see then that a spectrum of accounts and questions of concern to the social psychologist in relation to emotion is not simply a recent phenomenon that has come about with the aid of the inductive methodologies that today shape much of the mainstream social sciences. Indeed both the mainstream and some of today's more experimental, less constrained (post-structural) social commentaries of emotion still, to some degree, mirror the forms of questions that have been in evidence for millennia. For example, can emotion be taught and tamed to enhance socially desirable behaviour and attitudes? Can it facilitate the enlightenment of individuals? Have its expressive manifestations come about through habit and learning? In what ways is it represented in the soul or body? Are aspects of it transcendent of human experience within a virtual realm? In what ways can it be used in decision making? What about the relationship between the embodied experience and the outer expression? What of the incongruence between these realms? Is the expression a real view of the soul or is it a socially constituted reflex incongruent to inner reality? Is it catching, a virus, a meme or a gene? In what ways should we think about it in relation to the good society, social cohesion and governmentality? In what ways may it be manipulated to obtain, remain in, or regain power? How does it influence societal structures, for example related to gender, class, religion and race?

These concerns have been around for millennia and there is still much to learn from the pre-empiricist histories to improve social psychological understandings of emotion, and therefore they should not be written out of contemporary accounts on the grounds of being outdated. We feel there are clear trajectories to be mapped from, for example, ancient Greek philosophies of emotion to emotional activity in digital media. Throughout there is a concern to point to the ways emotion works in relational terms to connect people, objects and places, and tack between individual and collective realms, shifting and morphing as it passes. This of course makes identifying and defining it a challenge, as, empirically at least, one can only ever point to one 'moment' of emotion, capturing a snapshot of the ongoing affective flow. Here we see the importance of not reifying emotion, and categorising it as a stable form with inherent properties, but instead theoretically setting out emotion as often slippery and complex phenomena, constituted in changing configurations of events that are at once biological, psychological, social, spatial, temporal and increasingly technical. Attempting to separate any one of these elements out seems to us to be an unhelpful simplification. Considering these elements as continually connected with one another, albeit subject to changing speeds and intensities, makes it important to frame them as social. Even those aspects deemed in the first instance to be internal and individual, e.g. biological activity, can take a social form, e.g. the physiological manifestation of fear or anger. For us then, taking a social view becomes an important tool for inclusivity in terms of addressing a wide range of theories and empirical approaches, as it immediately positions emotion as multi-factorial and relational. Our aim is to discuss theories and approaches throughout the history of emotion that we argue are important for social psychology of emotion. Additionally, we use a social lens to frame our coverage of emotion past and present because it facilitates understandings that do not get reduced and bogged down within disciplinary boundaries. Instead, being 'social' means adopting an inter-disciplinary approach throughout.

We have entitled the book 'Social Psychology of Emotion' rather than '.... of Emotions' for a number of reasons. Primarily because the term 'emotions' often divides emotion into a number of specified categorical forms that are familiar to all. However, there has always been, and still is today, dispute concerning what these actually are, how many of them exist, and from where do they arise? Additionally, we are not concerned with systematically looking at individual emotions. We are more concerned with overarching theories that more generally relate to what we conceive of as social psychology. So we are not attempting to answer the question posed by William James of 'what is emotion?' but are rather asking 'in what ways has emotion been conceptualised and how are these useful for a social psychology of emotion?' Furthermore our approach is not to take any individual theory or approach to task in a critical way, in terms of pointing to what it fails to address in emotion activity and experience. We are not seeking to 'put things right' in terms of current or past thinking on emotion. Instead, our approach is to navigate a journey through the vast range of emotion literature, from Ancient Greece to contemporary internet studies that are relevant and important for social psychological understandings of emotion. At times it is necessary to take a more critical view of previous accounts, particularly those featuring in secondary sources, in which primary materials have become skewed through the repetition of previously reductive and potentially misrepresenting narratives. The aforementioned tendency for psychological approaches to address single areas and disciplines often results in narrow and potentially simplistic accounts. Instead, our approach of looking through a 'social lens' to the variety of conceptualisations of emotion, past and present, becomes a narrative layering that emerges as its own form of criticality. Our approach is therefore critical, not in a traditional, but rather a narrative sense.

Chapter Summaries

We structure the book according to two overarching sections. Firstly, we cover four historical epochs of emotion, namely Ancient, Medieval, Enlightenment and Modern eras. In doing so, we draw out aspects of the various historical accounts of emotion that are important for social psychological understandings. This approach will of course not be exhaustive, but follows our own line of thinking regarding what we deem important for understanding emotion through a social psychological lens. Although some of the theories may not always appear to be immediately 'social', we argue it is important to discuss them as they have played a valuable contributory role to later theorisations. The second overarching section focuses on a number of key areas (sociology, biology, psychology) before addressing some contemporary issues of social psychology (text, post-structural, and digital technologies). We hope that structuring the book this way facilitates an understanding and discussion of emotion that takes in a variety of histories right through to modern day social realities.

We begin our exploration of social psychology of emotion in Chapter 1 with two of the most celebrated philosophers of all time, Plato and Aristotle. We spend some time detailing the philosophies of each of these theorists as they had much to say about issues pertinent to social psychological accounts of emotion today. They stand as bedrock upon which theorisations of emotion are built. Plato and Aristotle's theories of emotion have often been characterised, and subsequently stereotyped, as being in opposition to each other (almost in terms of being a villain and a hero of emotion). Both Plato and Aristotle develop understandings of emotion that are thoroughly social. Interestingly they have gone on to influence, for example, political theories, which necessarily include their understanding of emotion. And yet they tend to be left out of (social) psychological theorisations of emotion.

Chapter 2 discusses the influence Plato and Aristotle had on Stoic, Christian and Islamic theologies that concern emotion. The Stoics were not focused specifically on the utility of emotion but how it can be eradicated as a means to preserve well-being. They developed some complex conceptualisations of how emotions are experienced, which went on to influence theological thoughts that were prevalent throughout the Middle Ages. The chapter discusses these influences, with specific focus on how Stoic notions of controllability and eradicability can be seen to feed into Saint Augustine's pivotal writings on the nature of will. Plato was the prime influence here, with Aristotle relatively absent in Christian thought, although he was very influential in Arabic thought. Before going on to detailing Thomas Aquinas' very influential writings on the passions of the soul, we look at some Islamic thought on emotion.

Chapter 3 draws out key aspects of the Enlightenment and Modernist theories of emotion. We see the debates between monist and dualistic thinking (e.g. Spinoza and Descartes) as well as the broader movements of rationalism and empiricism. The first half of the chapter considers the rationalistic offerings of Descartes and Spinoza, and how each addressed the 'problem of the body' when thinking about emotion; for instance, whether mind and body exist as distinct entities (Descartes), or if just one 'substance' exists with different elements within (Spinoza). The second half of the chapter moves on from ontological rationalism to the empirical epistemology of David Hume's associationist thought. Here we see a plea for emotion to be core to ethical decision making practices, with understandings based upon empirical principles. Kant attempts to bring the schools of rationalism and empiricism together, through his conceptualisation of a synthetic a priori.

Chapter 4 discusses the emergence of social psychology as a distinct sub-discipline within the newly formed discipline of psychology in relation to emotion theories. We begin by sketching the context of the discipline, e.g. the work on William James and Walter Cannon. Interestingly, some of the foundational theoretical works that underpin this progression, most particularly the work of McDougall, are often missed in histories of social psychology. McDougall brought the discipline a complex account of emotion that was integral to his social psychology. We add to this coverage the lesser discussed Gestalt Psychology of Lewin, who urges us to think more holistically about emotional activity and experience, through developing a topological account of emotion that can speak to and analyse the micro spatialities of 'emotional units', and how these feature in everyday living.

A related development was to think about emotion of the group, or crowd. In Chapter 5 we focus on psychologists, such as Le Bon and Freud, who were concerned with how emotion was a fundamental driver of crowd experience and activity. A later, opposing, force to these notions within social psychology was the more rationalistic accounts that featured throughout social identity theory. Here there was a move away from seeing crowds as motivated by the irrationality of emotion to a focus on aspects of shared identity and other social structural factors. Emotional contagion since McDougall, Le Bon and Freud is, as we shall see, still very much a contemporary issue that we discuss through, for example, the work of Hatfield and colleagues and through Sampson's understanding of virality. The chapter concludes by turning back to psychoanalytic developments of group psychology that have been devised by such thinkers as Bion and Foulkes.

Chapter 6 begins with Darwin's understanding of emotion as being a vestigial aspect of human behaviour. Darwin of course is a pivotal figure in most mainstream accounts of the social psychology of emotion. He has gone on to influence 'the facial expression thesis' which, as we discussed above, is so prevalent within emotion theories (e.g. Ekman). Of course to understand the complexity of emotion, even from a social psychological perspective, the biological constituents of emotion are undeniable. Hence we give an account of theorists that have focused on both the function and structure of these constituents, through for example, McLean's 'Triune Brain' and various hemispheric accounts of emotion. Affective neuroscience and neuro-psychoanalysis are among the more contemporary biological accounts of emotion that are concerned with its relational aspects. This chapter concludes with Damasio's 'Somatic Marker' hypothesis which has been influential beyond the field of neuroscience, as its integral account of the relationship between individual and society has been taken up by a number of social theorists.

In Chapter 7 we draw attention more explicitly to sociological accounts of emotion. This involves discussing the dramaturgical theory of Goffman which leads into coverage of Hochschild's 'emotion work'. Following that we draw out the value of sociological theories for illuminating the issues associated with gender and emotion, particularly through the work of Shields and her colleagues. The sociology of emotion is a burgeoning sub-discipline of sociology, which is often valuably issue driven, focusing on categories of gender, sexuality, race and class. This approach crosses both macro and micro boundaries, with the latter being very close to social psychology. The chapter allows us to draw out these important influences, and contextualise our own coverage of social psychological approaches.

Chapter 8 focuses specifically on empirical approaches to the analysis of emotion, as featured in social psychology. The chapter begins with theories of verbal emotional expression, specifically the 'inhibition confrontation model' and the 'cognitive reappraisal model'. We discuss Bucci's understanding of referential activity before going on to discuss various forms of linguistic analysis that have been developed to look at emotion in speech, e.g. discourse analysis. This allows us to consider how emotion has been conceptualised as performative acts, through text and talk. We then go on to look at mixed methods emotion research that has married experimental and discursive methods to understand the links between embodied processes, talk, emotion and identity.

Chapter 9 addresses theories of affect, and facilitates a useful positioning of emotion in relation to affect. These terms have often been used interchangeably, and are commonly not distinguished in sufficient detail. We seek to address this in relation to social psychology, with specific focus on how affect has been conceptualised as a relational force, rather than an individual one. We chart a brief history of affect, beginning with the seminal work of Tomkins, and then how affect has been conceptualised through what has now become known as the 'affective turn', and the role of poststructuralist theory (e.g. Deleuze and Massumi). The chapter concludes with discussion of debates about the status of 'subjectivity' with theories of affect, which speak directly to social psychological concerns.

In Chapter 10 we address the role of emotion in the relationships between bodies and technologies, with specific reference to the increased impact of digital media on social life. The chapter covers Simondon's philosophy of technology, which has at its core, a concern with how people's relationships with technologies are fundamentally emotional. Simondon's work can speak usefully to a social psychological understanding of the ways people connect in and through digital media. The chapter concludes by pointing to the problems associated with views that present increased digital media usage with a likelihood of technological determinism. Instead, through Simondon, we see that emotion and affective activity are in no way lessened by an increase in digital media communication.

1

Two Ancient Theories of Emotion: Plato and Aristotle

Key Aims

In this chapter we will present the philosophies of Plato and Aristotle in relation to emotion. In doing so we will:

- Identify the initial theoretical split of emotion from reason
- Discuss their more nuanced and complex views of emotion
- Draw attention to their social psychologies of emotion

Introduction

We begin our historical exploration of emotion with Plato and then Aristotle. The Ancient Greek word that is customarily rendered as the English word 'emotion' was *pathos* (plural *pathê*). Terms such as 'psychopath' and 'pathology' derived from this. The term is distantly related to the Latin *patior* from which the English word 'passion' derives. Among the *pathê* were equivalent English emotion terms such as 'anger', 'fear', 'love', 'pity', 'indignation', 'envy' and so on. However, as one might imagine, Ancient understandings of the emotions can be quite different to contemporary conceptions. For example, the ordinary Greek term for 'love' is *philia*, but this has a much wider usage than the English equivalent of romantic love. It can also mean 'friendship' and 'business relationships'; the latter does not usually represent 'love' in the English speaking world! Yet, these early conceptualisations of emotion are of particular importance because they are the foundation of the many subsequent theorisations. Most psychological histories of emotion tend to start with Charles Darwin and William James, and neglect the earlier rich tapestry of thought that the Ancient philosophers have to offer. The twentieth century process philosopher, Alfred North Whitehead, famously stated that, 'the safest general characterization of the European philosophical tradition is that it consists of a series of footnotes to Plato' (Whitehead, 1927–8: 39).

One of the reasons that many ancient, medieval and enlightenment theories of emotion have tended to be forgotten within academic disciplines such as psychology is that they tended to include *metaphysical* understandings of the *soul* which concerned *theology* and *ethics*. Psychology as a discipline has set itself up as a *scientific* discipline and operates according to principles of modern *empiricism*. Theories that have derived from philosophical speculation associated with cosmologies and theologies are considered rather more *mythological* than *psychological*. However, the kinds of epistemological and ontological arguments that inform these understandings of emotion arguably still have much to offer contemporary approaches, and particularly social psychological perspectives. For instance, they provided some of the foundational understandings of relationships between emotions, individuals and society, which relate to key concerns of much contemporary psychosocial thought. They offer us archetypal discourses of emotion that subsume subsequent thought and everyday speech. Indeed, contemporary historians of emotion such as Thomas Dixon, Susan James, and Richard Sorabji would agree with Simo Knuuttila that 'ancient philosophy involves high-level debates on emotions in which rigorous philosophical analysis is wedded to philosophy as a way of life' (2004: 1); thus the contemporary thinker would do well to take note of these.

In this chapter then we seek to draw out some of the nuanced understandings of emotion that Plato and Aristotle offered, particularly to facilitate the contextualisation of contemporary approaches, and furthermore to provide a reengagement with these fundamental theories that potentially allow for something new to emerge. Common in the accounts that tend to distinguish Plato's and Aristotle's theories of emotion is the tendency to characterise Plato as prising the emotional from the intellectual, thus devising a split between the lower aspects of human nature from the more divine higher. In this account the emotion related aspects of the human are often determined by misguided evaluations and beliefs that have come about through sense perception, which is wholly unreliable and thus leads the person to the pursuit of things that are earthly, immoral and therefore damaging to the soul. Emotion then needs to be put under the control of the higher faculty of reason. Subsequently Aristotle is characterised as influenced by Plato's systematic account of emotion but not as seeing emotion as necessarily needing to be brought under the strict control of reason. Instead emotion is claimed to have a significant part to play in relation to the moral development of the individual. Emotional activities are aspects of human life that should be cultivated in the aid of civilising both the individual and society.

As we shall see, this account of Plato's model of the soul which polarised reason and emotion at opposite ends of the moral spectrum came to be very influential within subsequent theologies, psychologies and everyday discourses of emotion. However, this characterisation does not do justice to Plato's theorisation, particularly as he went on in his later dialogues to think about some of the more virtuous aspects of emotion and how some emotion based activity can induce transcendental visions of 'true beauty' and 'the good'. The more positive aspects of emotion are often shunned in discourses of emotion in which it is often allied to irrational processes that are only worthy of condemnation.

After a general discussion of how Plato's and Aristotle's philosophies are relevant to emotion we move on to draw out the social psychological aspects of these accounts. For example, Plato develops a theoretical tripartite division of the soul that positions emotion in the lower faculties, a psychosocial relationship between the types of soul that are related to aspects of society. Aristotle is concerned with how emotion can be socialised to facilitate the virtuous person and society. Moreover, Aristotle goes on to think about how emotion can be used by the orator to, for example, sway the opinions of others. Additionally he discusses how the rights of emotional expression are unequally socially distributed due to power imbalances.

Plato

Plato's (429–347 BC) writings are developed through a series of dialogues between Socrates and various other philosophers, commonly known as the Sophists. Plato's dialogues are often categorised into three periods: early, middle and late dialogues. The passage below (Box 1.1) is taken from one of Plato's later dialogues through which he describes Timaeus giving an account of Locrius' story of the origin of the universe (*kosmos*) to Socrates, Critias and Hermocrates. As many scholars, historians who analyse narratives, and psychologists who study memory will state, it is very difficult to know from stories (re-collections) what events actually took place and what has been added and taken away by the story-teller. Indeed, through looking at the below origin story, we are writing an account of an account of an account of an account which itself had been passed down orally for millennia! Although Plato is known to have attempted in his earlier writings to accurately depict the philosophies of his teacher Socrates (who, it is often surmised, never wrote anything down), Plato continued to develop his own philosophies through writing about Socrates' dialogues with a variety of Sophists. Thus scholars generally agree that it is rather difficult to tell in Plato's later works which are his own ideas and which are Socrates'. This points us to one of the central problems that Plato presents in many of his works: how can we 'know' what is true and what is not; what is real and what is merely propositional? This is a problem that most of us have to deal with on a day to day basis, it is a problem that academics and scientists are continually dealing with and it is a problem that is particularly prevalent in emotion studies.

BOX 1.1

And when he had compounded it all, he divided the mixture into a number of souls equal to the number of the stars and assigned each soul a star. He mounted each soul in a carriage, as it were, and showed it the nature of the universe. He described to them the laws that had been foreordained: They would all be assigned one and the same initial birth, so that none would be less well treated by him than any other. Then he would sow each of the souls into that instrument of time suitable to it, where they were to acquire the nature of being the most god-fearing of living things, and, since humans have a twofold nature, the superior kind should be such as would from then on be called 'man.' So, once the souls were of necessity implanted into bodies, and these bodies had things coming to them and leaving them, the first innate capacity they would of necessity come to have would be sense perception, which arises out of forceful disturbances. This they all would have. The second would be love, mingled with pleasure and pain. And they would come to have fear and spiritedness as well, plus whatever goes with having these emotions, as well as all their natural opposites. And if they could master these emotions, their lives would be just, whereas if they were mastered by them, they would be unjust. And if a person lived a good life throughout the due course of his time, he would at the end return to his dwelling place in his companion star, to live a life of happiness that agreed with his character. But if he failed in this, he would be born a second time, now as a woman. And if even then he still could not refrain from wickedness, he would be changed once again, this time into some wild animal that resembled the wicked character he had acquired. And he would have no rest from these toilsome transformations until he had dragged that massive accretion of fire-water-air-earth into conformity with the revolution of the Same and uniform within him, and so subdued that turbulent, irrational mass by means of reason. This would return him to his original condition of excellence. (Tim. 41d–42d)

The views that Plato presents of *pathos* tend to be bound up in cosmology. This is generally attributable to the fact that most accounts of psychology around this period were infused with cosmological ideologies. The above extract essentially points to a distinction between the physical and the eternal *kosmos*. The physical *kosmos* is discussed as being mortal and subject to change and extinction, while the eternal *kosmos* is divine and immortal. Humans, however, were seen as being made up of a mixture of both the divine and the physical. For Plato the immortal principle of the soul is self-motion, in other words the soul is self-initiating motion (autonomous); whereas anything that receives its motion through external forces can be considered as mortal. The soul was seen as prior to and distinct from the body, a prime mover and so, according to Plato, it should be the person's chief concern.

A Dualistic Split

Plato is often portrayed as the archetypal dualist. In setting out his metaphysical and epistemological framework, he depicts the mind (which is synonymous with the soul which in Greek is the *psyche* and in Latin is the *anima*) as a divine substance infused with innate knowledge (*logos*) of the *forms* (sort of blueprints) of which all things on the earth are imperfect copies. The highest of which is the form of 'the Good' (*Agathon*), which is an abstract principle that has some kind of ontological existence of its own in the realm of forms from which our notions of justice and right can be traced. Knowledge of the forms could not derive from sense perception, which only supplies humans with opinion (*doxa*), and thus only allows one to consider relative and shifting truths. For example, in the *Theathetus* he depicts Socrates pitting himself against Hereclitus' notion that 'being is becoming' and against Protagoras' doctrine that 'man is the measure of all things'. Although he agrees that, according to sense perception, this is how the world appears to be, indeed objects of the world are in flux and subject to the definitions of people; but he adds that there are also universal-eternal truths that are stable (in the realm of forms). This type of knowledge, of the transcendental universal forms of everything that exists, only comes about

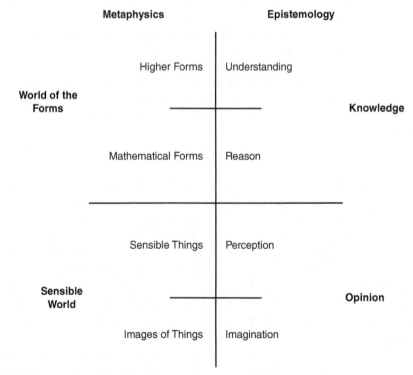

Figure 1.1   Plato's divided line

through rational contemplation and recollection of this innate knowledge that was imparted to our souls in the state of pre material existence. Plato puts forward arguments such as: the knowledge of the objective existence or non-existence of a mirage cannot come about through sense perception, but only through rational reflection. This is true also, he suggests, of mathematics, which provide us with immutable truths which do not come through sense perception but rational contemplation. You can see Plato's hierarchy of knowledge in the above illustration of Plato's 'divided line' in Figure 1.1.

A Tripartite Division

When developing a psychology of the soul Plato's dualistic doctrine becomes much more of a tripartite division, through which he explicitly localises the psyche within the body. In one of his later dialogues, the *Timaeus*, he suggests that since the motion of thought is circular it must be placed in the head, as this is also a spherical object. It also imitates the spherical shape of the *Kosmos* and indeed is positioned as closest to the heavens and is concerned with reason, knowledge and wisdom (known as the rational part of the soul, *logistikon*). While the immortal aspects of the soul are positioned in the head the mortal aspects are placed further down the body so that they do not pollute the rational soul. The neck serves as the boundary to separate the rational from the non-rational. The mortal part of the soul is again divided into two hierarchical spheres. The higher, spirited part (*thumoeides*) is located in the chest, the heart being its principal organ. The spirited part works as an intermediary between the lower and the upper parts. It is concerned with emotions such as self-assurance and self-affirmation (Rep. 4.435a–441c; 9.580d–583a). As this part is closer to the rule of reason, Plato suggests, it will facilitate controlling and restraining the desires which are associated with, for example, food, drink, sexual arousal and the love of money. These base desires or appetitive (*epithumētikon*) parts of the soul are seen to be located in the abdomen below the diaphragm. This tripartite division of the soul was originally detailed in Plato's *Republic* (one of Plato's middle dialogues) and has been hailed as 'the first detailed systematization of emotional phenomena' (Knuuttila, 2004: 5).

   On close inspection of Plato's dialogues, there is a development of thought on the role of emotion. In his earlier dialogues, Plato tended to denigrate emotion as being in total opposition to reason. For example in the *Phaedo* all appetite and emotion were associated with the mortal body and thus constituted the irrational self. As we shall see, this is a line of understanding of emotion that is often portrayed as typifying Plato's theories and indeed characterising ancient and medieval views. Clearly Plato, particularly in the earlier works, did emphasise the need for detachment from the appetites and emotion, as not much good appears to come from them in his writings. Although we do find this line of thought of emotion throughout subsequent philosophies and theories of emotion (particularly through the Stoics, Christian and Islamic theologies of the medieval period) this view fluctuated and certainly should not be tarnished as typifying all subsequent ancient and medieval philosophies of emotion. The more nuanced aspects of his theory are often overlooked in many subsequent commentaries of the history of emotion theories, but there is a more recent trend to look at these early theories in more detail.

An Emerging Blurred Division

In Plato's early dialogues his account of the soul could be considered bipartite, through which appetite (and the accompanying emotions) were generally envisaged as made up of biological, mechanistic, drives and instincts which were quite opposed to the rational faculties. However, in the middle and late dialogues, we see that appetite also involves a cognitive component which evaluates and anticipates pleasure and pain. For example, although the pushes and pulls of appetite are largely concerned with sexual desire, hunger and thirst, it is also concerned with the accumulation of wealth. This latter desire for wealth (money) includes an anticipatory faculty which is commonly related to logic and reason. However, Plato states 'we also call it [=appetite] the money-loving part, because such appetites are most easily satisfied by means of money' (Rep. 9, 580e). Although Plato does not explicitly spell this out, it would seem that rather than appetite having some form of rational or cognitive capacity of its own as Knuuttila suggests, following Plato's line of argument it makes more sense to suggest that the rational faculty is working in the service of the desires of appetite. This understanding embraces the dynamism that Plato speaks of elsewhere in relation to the three faculties. This is most particularly evident when Plato's Socrates discusses the spirited part of the soul as working in relatively close partnership with, or rather in servitude of, the higher reasoning part of the soul through habituation. Plato's logic here draws on the principle of non-contradiction (Rep. 4.436b). All three parts of the soul are envisaged as being separate, although in a dynamic relationship with each other, and therefore have particular desires of their own. He envisages a relatively mechanistic understanding of the lower parts of the soul as being determined through the pushes and pulls of external objects; that is each part of the soul is either attracted or repelled to particular objects but cannot be both simultaneously attracted and repelled by the same object. He illustrates this through a story about Leontius wherein Leontius feels angry at himself (for his desires).

> Leontius, the son of Aglaion, was going up from the Piraeus along the outside of the North Wall when he saw some corpses lying at the executioner's feet. He had an appetite to look at them but at the same time he was disgusted and turned away. For a time he struggled with himself and covered his face, but, finally, overpowered by the appetite, he pushed his eyes wide open and rushed towards the corpses, saying, 'Look for yourselves, you evil wretches, take your fill of the beautiful sight!' (Rep. 4.39e–440a).

The simultaneity of the contrasting affects (desire, disgust and anger) is attributed to the different parts of the soul which are treated as three separate agents, each of which can initiate action. Thus, reason and spirit work in conjunction to invoke disgust at obtaining pleasure from looking at the corpses. However, appetite is much stronger in this instance and cannot be controlled by both reason and spirit. Once the deed has been committed, spirit becomes angry and scolds appetite. This theorisation of the self is thus able to account for the ambiguity (contradictory expression) of affect. Plato's point is that this would not have happened had the rational part been in control of the other parts of the soul. Indeed, if the soul is driven by the rational part, the soul would be just and virtuous which he relates to 'a kind of health, fine condition, and well-being' (Rep. 4.445d–e). In such a condition, spirit can then be habituated through the instructions of reason and appetite calmed. Indeed Knuuttila states: 'In the optimal case, the spirited part is habituated to listening to reason and is activated only by things which the reasoning part regards as worthy of emotional response, and the appetitive part is wholly satisfied with the limited role left to it' (2004: 11).

Plato's Psychosocial Studies of Emotion

Interestingly Plato does develop a form of social psychology of emotion in his attempt to draw out associations between the tripartite soul and the city (*polis*). Plato argued in the *Republic* that the *polis* was made up of three forms of people which reflect the three parts of the soul: the philosopher-guardians (representing rationality), the military class (representing spirit), and the merchant class (representing appetite). Plato's *Republic* has been extremely influential on subsequent utopian visions; indeed it is arguably one of the cornerstones for political theory itself.

In the *Republic*, typically through Socratic dialogue, Plato thinks through what justice is and what its benefits are. He states,

> The investigation we're undertaking is not an easy one but requires keen eyesight. Therefore, since we aren't clever people, we should adopt the method of investigation that we'd use if, lacking keen eyesight, we were told to read small letters from a distance and then noticed that the same letters existed elsewhere in a larger size and on a larger surface. We'd consider it a godsend, I think, to be allowed to read the larger ones first and then examine the smaller ones, to see whether they are really the same.
>
> That's certainly true, said Adeimantus, but how is this case similar to our investigation of justice?
>
> I'll tell you. We say, don't we, that there is the justice of a single man and also the justice of a whole city?

> Certainly.
>
> And a city is larger than a single man?
>
> It is larger.
>
> Perhaps, then, there is more justice in the larger thing, and it will be easier to learn what it is. So, if you're willing, let's first find out what sort of thing justice is in a city and afterwards look for it in the individual, observing the ways in which the smaller is similar to the larger. (Rep. 2.368c–369a)

They enter this mode of investigation by discussing what the ideal city might look like. This includes detailed instructions, for example, as to how the particular parts of the soul would require particular forms of social structures to regulate its inclinations. Plato stresses that spirit and rationality are closer together (if they have not been 'corrupted by a bad upbringing' (Rep. 4.441a)) and indeed need to work together to regulate appetite. Thus spirit and rationality are seen to be nurtured through such things as music, poetry and physical training. Plato writes,

> And these two, having been nurtured in this way, and having truly learned their own roles and been educated in them, will govern the appetitive part, which is the largest part in each person's soul and is by nature most insatiable for money. They'll watch over it to see that it isn't filled with the so-called pleasures of the body and that it doesn't become so big and strong that it no longer does its own work but attempts to enslave and rule over the classes it isn't fitted to rule, thereby overturning everyone's whole life. (Rep. 4.442a)

Justice is then accorded when the city and soul are governed by rationality and,

> each of the three natural classes within it did its own work, and it was thought to be moderate courageous, and wise ... Then, if an individual has these same three parts in his soul, we will expect him to be correctly called by the same names as the city if he has the same conditions in them. (Rep. 4.435b)

Plato then goes on to argue that there are 'as many types of soul as there are specific types of political constitution' (Rep. 4.445c) and he names five: aristocracy, timocracy, oligarchy, democracy and tyranny. As described above, Plato's ideal (healthy) state is envisaged as an aristocracy run by the philosopher kings representing rationality and wisdom. In contrast to what we see today as an aristocracy, in Plato's state the ruling class (philosopher kings) are forbidden to own property. Throughout books eight and nine of the

Republic, Plato discusses the four remaining forms of political constitution. To put the point across that there is an association between forms of human character and the political constitutions, he states:

> do you think that constitutions are born 'from oak or rock' and not from the characters of the people who live in the cities and governed them, which tip the scales, so people speak, and drag the rest along with them? (Rep. 8.544d–e).

Plato here explicitly suggests that a society's characteristics mirror those of the most powerful of its inhabitants. He then goes on to detail these by looking at how each form of society may descend into its lower form, from the aristocracy down to the tyrannical, and emotion plays a central part in these characterisations.

The timocracy's ruling class is primarily made up of the military class. The ruling class is characterised by the spirited souls who are driven by aggression. Although courageous and so somewhat virtuous, these souls would not have been appropriately cultivated and so will eventually (in old age) be focused on accumulating wealth (Rep. 8.549a). This generally comes about because the sons of the aristocratic class can be driven by what they are led to believe (mainly by their mothers) of the perceived father's failings. They are, for example, avoiding honours, have a lack of concern about money, are not meddling in other peoples affairs (which often bring honour), and are indifferent to insults and revenge. The son is thus urged 'to be more of a man than his father' (Rep. 8.549.e). Because the boy's rational soul has been nurtured by the influence of others (including his father) the spirited and appetitive soul pulls in opposite directions; 'he settles in the middle and surrenders the rule over himself to the middle part – the victory-loving and spirited part – and he becomes a proud and honour-loving man' (Rep. 8.550b).

Eventually the victory and honour loving men turn to 'lovers of making money' (Rep. 8.551a) and thus the city descends into an oligarchy wherein the ruling class are driven by the accumulation of wealth and property. Being characterised by the appetitive soul, the pleasure derived from this accumulation is valued over virtue, '[H]e makes the rational and spirited parts sit on the ground beneath appetite, one on either side, reducing them to slaves' (Rep. 8.553c). This form of state thus develops a large income inequality gap coming from the exploitation of the lower classes. The oligarchy is seen to degenerate into a democracy as the lower classes grow and grossly outnumber the ruling class. The democracy is described as a similar state to anarchy where people can almost do as they please. Laws are broken and the people are consumed with unnecessary desires as they are overrun by the unruly appetite. For the democratic man '[T]here's neither order nor necessity in his life, but he calls it pleasant, free, and blessedly happy, and he follows it for as long as he lives' (Rep. 8.561d). Thus tyranny comes about when the soul and society exist in chaos. To overcome the lawlessness power must be seized and the power produces the tyrant. But the lawlessness of the appetite also serves for a downfall, wherein the tyrant lives in fear that he will soon be revenged for his misdeeds.

The faculty of rationality then, throughout Plato's psychosocial theorisation of the political constitutions, is the key to maintaining any form of healthy order in the city and the soul. However, not all desires that arise from appetite lead to chaos and vice, Plato's Socrates draws out a distinction between necessary desires and unnecessary desires (Rep. 8.558d–559d). The former are 'those we can't desist from and those whose satisfaction benefits us rightly', such as the desire for bread. However, if not kept in check by reason, the desires become lawless.

> Those [desires] that are awakened in sleep, when the rest of the soul – the rational, gentle, and ruling part – slumbers. Then the beastly and savage part, full of food and drink, casts off sleep and seeks to find a way to gratify itself. You know that there is nothing it won't dare to do at such a time, free of all control by shame or reason. It doesn't shrink from trying to have sex with a mother, as it supposes, or with anyone else at all, whether man, god, or beast. It will commit any foul murder, and there is no food it refuses to eat. In a word, it omits no act of folly or shamefulness. (Rep. 9.571e–d)

The above extract is quite interesting in that the desires of what psychoanalysts may consider the unconscious are described (which are manifest in dreams!). Plato here puts across the sense that appetite is unleashed when the rational part of the soul slumbers; and he invokes the taboos of incest and murder to illustrate unlawful nature. Thus appetite is generally envisaged through the early and middle dialogues as an under-socialised, if not totally unruly, part of the soul which requires quite a lot of suppression (or perhaps repression) for the soul to move towards virtue. However, the amount and kind of suppression, according to Plato, was very much dependent upon the type of soul that one has (what psychologists might call 'personality', 'disposition' or 'temperament' today) and the form of city that one lives in.

Higher Emotion

In another dialogue of the middle period (*Phaedrus*), the famous charioteer allegory is used which further illustrates the tripartite division. Knuuttila notes that this allegory puts forward the view that it is the immortal soul itself which can be divided into three (2004: 13). To actually describe the soul, Plato's Socrates states that this would be a task not for men but for a god, so to simplify the description he likens 'the soul to the natural union of a team of winged horses and their charioteer' (Phae. 246a). The chariot is made up of two horses and a charioteer, one horse is beautiful and from good stock (representing the spirited part of the soul) while the other horse is from the 'opposite sort of bloodline' (Phae. 246b) (representing the appetitive part). Because one of the horses is unruly, the charioteer (reason) has a difficult task. Here again we see the need for the taming of appetite, the unwieldy horse which is depicted as being driven by mostly erotic desire.

> The heaviness of the bad horse drags its charioteer toward the earth and weighs him down if he has failed to train it well, and this causes the most extreme toil and struggle that a soul will face. (Phae. 247b)

Nussbaum (1986: 221–2) argues that Plato develops a bit of a shift in his thinking in relation to appetite here; stating that the unruly horse 'should be well fed and that, properly controlled, it can play a good and a necessary role in motivating the person, even in teaching the person about the beautiful'. Erotic love is related to a special form of madness between two people (in Socrates' account a man and a young boy) who are passionately but philosophically disposed towards each other. This love reminds their souls of true beauty and the vision of the good that they had glimpsed before being mixed with mortality. This form of erotic love unleashes a kind of madness as when it occurs 'they are beside themselves, and their experience is beyond their comprehension because they cannot fully grasp what it is that they are seeing' (Phae. 250a–b).

   In one of Plato's late dialogues, the *Philebus*, Plato discusses the value of pleasure and knowledge. Knuttila (2004: 18) points out that it is within this dialogue that a distinction is drawn out between bodily processes and the derived sense of pleasure or pain. This distinction may be obvious to us today, but is something he argues had not been systematically discussed before. Plato thus insinuates that non-conscious processes affect the body; but perhaps more intriguingly, he also insinuates that there are affects that are remembered and anticipated that do not necessarily have an effect on the body. In the *Philebus*, Plato's Socrates uses two metaphorical figures to describe the processes of memory and perception. Firstly, he states that memory and perception inscribe words on the soul much like a scribe (Phil. 39a). These inscriptions may be either true or false. Secondly, he states that there is a 'painter who follows the scribe and provides illustrations to his words in the soul' (Phil. 39b). Both work in conjunction with the other to help produce anticipatory pains and pleasures. An example is given of a false impression which induces pleasure,

> ...someone often envisages himself in the possession of an enormous amount of gold and a lot of pleasures as a consequence. And in addition, he also sees, in this inner picture of himself, that he is beside himself with delight. (Phil. 40b)

Thus anticipatory and fantasised pains and pleasures that are both pictorially and discursively inscribed into the soul (memory) 'might precede those that go through the body' (Phil. 39d). Price suggests that therefore in this later account of Plato's we find '[W]hat emotions typically lack in rationality, they make up for in a phenomenology that comes of imaginative recall or anticipation' (2010: 130).

What we begin to see through Plato's dialogues are relatively sophisticated understandings of the social psychology of emotion. Although we have the earlier Platonic thought wherein there appears to be a sharp dichotomisation between emotion and reason, the middle and later dialogues envisage emotion as made up of a variety of forms of memory, perception and cognition as well as being influenced by and influencing social practices. And, to paraphrase Pascal, Plato went on to consider how emotion at times has reason of its own that reason knows not. These early theorisations of emotion are perennially discussed by emotion theorists (as we shall see throughout this book) by all manner of contemporary theorists (from sociologists, psychoanalysts to neuroscientists), but it is the earlier Platonic dualistic notions that are often referenced.

We now turn to Plato's most influential student who takes up his theories and develops them in new ways, which have gone on to shape historical and indeed contemporary thought about emotion.

Aristotle

Although Aristotle (384–322 BC) and Plato had much in common, as would be expected because he was Plato's student for many years, their respective philosophies are often characterised as standing to one another in the relation of thesis (Platonism) to antithesis (Aristotelianism). For example, we may think of Plato as the philosopher of 'being' (transcendental forms) and Aristotle as the philosopher of 'becoming' (the natural world in a continual state of unfolding). The truth of this is more complex; it is important therefore not to over-generalise the distinctions between their philosophies. Both Plato and Aristotle had room in their respective philosophies for both forms of ontology to co-exist. Thus before discussing Aristotle's more social (psychological) theories that are relevant to emotion studies, it is worth getting a flavour of some of the detailed metaphysical theories that he devised. An understanding of what Aristotle considered as 'the powers of the soul' in his book *De Anima* is very influential to many subsequent theorisations of emotion.

Aristotle's metaphysics entails the supposition that all matter is in a state of unfolding between potency and act, namely that a phenomenon has the potential to be actualised as something else. For example, the matter of an acorn has inherent within it the blueprint or *potential* to become *actualised* as an oak-tree; an oak-tree in turn has the potential to become actualised as (among many other things) a table. Actualisation, for Aristotle, is tied to the notion of activity, as for something to be actualised it requires acts (or activities) appropriate to its nature, and matter is tied to the notion of potentiality (that which it may become actualised as). Hence *form* is akin to actuality and *matter* to potentiality. To illustrate this, Aristotle discusses the purely hypothetical notion of prime-matter, that which has no form. As this raw matter has no form it is understood as being purely *passive*, it has no potential for actualisation therefore is not active; but, and importantly, it can be acted upon. Pure matter has the potential to be acted upon to become anything, and although other types of matter also have the potential to be acted upon to become something else, these possibilities are necessarily limited. For example, a block of wood may have the potential to be acted upon to become a table; it does not have the potential to become a blanket.

The Powers of *De Anima*

Of importance to Aristotle's comprehension of form and matter are his concep-tualisations of the soul, and it is here that a rudimentary metaphysics of emotion emerges. Aristotle argues that the soul is not a composite of form and matter but rather the soul is form which combines with the body (matter) to make it a living thing (*De Anima*, 413a2): a soul-body composite. In other words the soul pow-ers the potentiality of the body matter and moreover constitutes its essence. In this way the soul-body composite comprises both active (actual) and passive (potential) parts. These early notions of that which is active and passive in rela-tion to the soul and moreover emotion are important markers in developing notions and discourses of the agentic qualities of affective activity that we also saw emerge in Plato's writings on the soul. Perhaps drawing on and adapting Plato's tripartite division of the soul, Aristotle describes three types of soul: the nutritive (found in plants), the sensitive (found in lower animals) and the human, each of which have powers. Aristotle states,

> Plants have the nutritive faculty only; other creatures have both this and the faculty of sense perception. And if that of sense-perception, then that of desire also for desire comprises wanting, passion, and wishing: all animals have at least one of the senses, touch, and for that which has sense-perception there is both pleasure and pain and both the pleasant and the painful: and where there are these, there is also wanting: for this is a desire for that which is pleasant. (*De Anima*, 414b 1–5)

Thus, the nutritive soul has the power to assimilate and reproduce. This type of soul is found in the most basic of organisms such as plants and animals. The sensitive soul has the power of desire, sense perception and local motion. This form of soul is not found in plants. The highest form of soul is the human. It has the power of scientific thought and deliberation, which are not found in lower animals and plants, but of course the human soul which also contains the two lower forms of soul.

Passive Passions

Aristotle describes the powers of each of the souls as entailing active and passive characteristics. Common sense would lead one to think that the lower soul, possessing fewer powers, would be considered as more passive. However, the nutritive power, which is possessed by all three forms of soul, is considered as being active. This is because the powers to nourish and reproduce are the abilities to transform one thing into another. The organism, for example, nourishes by breaking a food down (acting upon it) into components. The food therefore is changed by the nutritive power and assimilated into the matter of the body. Sensation of the sensitive soul in contrast (wherein much of human emotion is seen to be associated), is considered as passive as the senses require stimulation by sensory objects (*De Anima*, 417a6). On this account it is the object that in some way causes the senses to be stimulated; for example, a lion may *cause* one to fear. This is an important point in relation to the history of emotion, as we shall see, emotions are often related to passive powers of the soul (that which is acted upon). This is different to nutrition in that the object sensed is not acted upon, but rather the object acts upon the senses, whereas in the case of nutrition it is the nutritious object which is acted upon. Additionally, and importantly for Aristotle, the sensitive soul also has the power to judge whether the object sensed will bring about pleasure or pain (incorporating thus a form of cognition). Also Aristotle suggests that the objects of desire or aversion produce particular kinds of pains and pleasures and so do not simply exist upon one single dimension. James notes,

> ...the satisfaction of sensory appetite does not produce the bare emotion of pleasure any more than the failure to satisfy it produces unmodified pain. Rather, it results in particular kinds of pleasure such as revenge or love, which are matched by specific kinds of pain such as hatred or pity. (James, 2003: 40)

Here then we see a cognitive component to emotion, although we may be passively moved, the movement also entails judgment which pulls forth a whole pallet of passions. Thus although passions are passive, they also derive from interpretations, evaluations and judgments that we make about objects based upon habituation. This is a vital aspect of Aristotle's theorisations of emotion in relation to the social. Thus passions are not able to emerge unaided but require objects to stimulate them and the physical effects (bodily motions) of particular passions are to some extent out of one's control. For example, Aristotle writes of anger (*orge*) creating heat around the heart, this heat then moves upwards and causes the face to become red.

Two other powers of the soul, perception and imagination are passive and active respectively. Perception, to some extent, consists of unmediated senses of the external world. Imagination, however, is closely related to perception but is not absolutely passive. We can imagine all sorts of things at will. This is an act of the higher faculty of the human soul: the ability to will something would seem to be an active power. Yet, Aristotle argues, some fantasies that imagination brings about are influenced by the passions and if they are influenced by the passions they in turn must be influenced by a sensory object, thus rendering it a passive process. These then take on their own course within imagination and can often wander in their own direction.

The intellectual powers are that which distinguish the human soul from plants and other animals. The power of thought is of course an active power, and because humans can initiate their own thoughts this is the part of the soul that draws them close to the divine (the unmoved mover). Yet thinking partly depends on perception to provide it with information about sensible objects and imagination. The intellect then makes judgments about (acts upon) these perceptions, rather than simply being pushed and pulled by them. Interestingly, Aristotle sees that thought cannot initiate action by itself but requires the facilitation of what he considers as the 'rational appetites' (wishes that move people to rational acts (James, 2003: 44)).

Hopefully from the above it is becoming clear to the reader how complex Aristotle's view of emotion can become. Emotion on this account is in no clear way active or passive, involuntary or voluntary cognitions or affects. To some extent like Plato, Aristotle therefore does put forward a notion of rationality as being of a superior standing to appetite and in some way an unmoved mover of the higher soul. It is a much more complex picture for many reasons. His understandings of the powers of the soul are based upon a matrix of active and passive constituent parts which are dynamic, overlapping and influence each other. For example, his understanding of the appetite concerns both non-rational and rational aspects which may at times be in conflict, in which case, desires related to the non-rational appetites may overrule the wishes of the rational appetites;wishes can also subdue desires.

Importantly Aristotle moves away from Plato in that he does not rely on the forms of cosmologies and mythologies that Plato drew upon to develop his theories. He was keener, it seems, to attach a logic to the sensible world of nature which largely avoided subscribing to a doctrine of transcendental essences. However, it must be noted that although this may appear as a rejection of Platonic dualistic epistemologies and ontologies, Aristotle still maintained the presence of a supersensible principle in humans tied up in his notion of the activity inherent in his entelechy.

> All nature is conceived as a hierarchy of species, in each of which the essence tends towards its full actualisation in a series of phenomena, drawn, in some rather mysterious way, by the ultimate final causality of the supreme Unmoved Mover, which is itself complete actuality, pure immaterial Being or Thought, self-subsistent and self-contained. (Copleston, 1985: 375).

Emotion and Virtue

Aristotle places a lot of importance upon emotion in his theories concerning the moral virtues. For example, he writes about the virtues of character in the *Nicomachean Ethics* in which he explains that these are positioned in the sensitive soul, the primary seat of the passions. Therefore we would expect to find a full account of emotion in his book on the soul (*De Anima*) but unfortunately he does not offer one. It seems that he never got around to developing a full systematic account of emotion. The most complete account we have of emotion in Aristotle's work is in Book 2 of the *Rhetoric*. In this book Aristotle is concerned with how styles of language affect persuasive arguments. He asks such questions as: 'What are the instruments of reasonable persuasions? What linguistic devices actually work?' It is rather like a handbook on how to be a successful rhetorician. Aristotle suggests that it is important that the orator understands the beliefs of the people in order to stir the corresponding emotions. Cooper suggests that Aristotle describes the successful rhetorician as needing to,

> Induce in their audiences appropriately directed states of emotion that will influence their audiences' judgment on the matter under discussion in a way favourable to the orators and their cases... The orator needs to know how to represent himself to the audience as being moved by such emotions as will help to establish him as a good person in general, and well-intentioned toward the audience in particular; and he needs to know how to engender in them the emotions that will cause them to judge the matter as he wishes them to. (Cooper, 1999: 239).

So the passions for Aristotle are not some blind animal force, but may incorporate intelligent and discriminating parts of the soul. As we have seen they are subject to cognitive modification and moreover, as we will see, cultivation. Central to the cultivation of emotion related activity and virtue is Aristotle's account of moderation (the golden mean). In the below illustration we can see Aristotle's list of virtues and vices.

Table 1.1   Table of virtues and vices

TABLE OF VIRTUES AND VICES			
SPHERE OF ACTION OR FEELING	**EXCESS**	**MEAN**	**DEFICIENCY**
Fear and Confidence	Rashness *thrasutis*	Courage *andreia*	Cowardice *deilia*
Pleasure and Pain	Licentiousness *akolasia*	Temperance *sophrosune*	Insensibility *anaisthisia*
Getting and Spending (minor)	Prodigality *asotia*	Liberality *eleutheriotis*	Pettiness *mikroprepeia*

TABLE OF VIRTUES AND VICES

SPHERE OF ACTION OR FEELING	EXCESS	MEAN	DEFICIENCY
Getting and Spending (major)	Vulgarity apeirokalia, banausia	Magnanimity megaloprepeia	Pettiness mikroprepeia
Honour and Dishonour (major)	Vanity chaunotes	Magnanimity megalopsuchia	Pusillanimity mikropsuchia
Honour and Dishonour (minor)	Ambition philotimia	Proper ambition	Unambitiousness aphilotimia
Anger	Irascibility orgilotis	Patience prdotis	Lack of spirit aorgisia
Self-expression	Boastfulness alazoneia	Truthfulness aletheia	Understatement eironeia
Coversation	Buffoonery bomolochia	Wittiness eutrapelia	Boorishness agroikia
Social Conduct	Obsequiousness areskeia Flattery kolakeia	Friendliness Philia(?)	Cantankerousness duskolia (duseris)
Shame	Shyness kataplexis	Modesty aidos	Shamelessness anaischuntia
Indignation	Envy phthonos	Righteous Indignation nemesis	Malicious Enjoyment epichairekakia

Importantly, we see here that it is the midway point (the mean) which corresponds to virtuous activity, in other words that which Aristotle suggests will lead to the good life (*eudaimonia*). If we consider the desire for food and drink, he suggests that both too much suppression and too much indulgence lead one away from virtue. What is required for virtue is a psychological balance of the appetite and this comes about through the appropriate moral education of the child to form the right kinds of habits, thus the child should be instructed in learning to choose the appropriate types of foods and drinks at the right time in the right amounts. With regard to an emotion such as 'fear', its elicitation is not seen as irrational. Indeed if a person is completely without fear this does not strike Aristotle as virtuous. The courageous person will fear, for example, death, but in an appropriate manner as reasoning instructs. Nussbaum states, '[T]he good person, rather than being the fearless person, is one who will have appropriate rather than inappropriate fears and not be deterred by them doing what is required and noble' (1986: 315).

For Aristotle, then, all types of desire (including emotion) are malleable and could become virtuous (subject to good habits) through reasoning and teaching.

In other words, we are taught to emotionally respond to objects, to form beliefs about those objects. On this account an individual's cognitive beliefs, and therefore their character, are central to the evocation of various emotions: if you think x, then you will experience emotion y. If your belief about a certain object changed, your emotional (active) response (feeling) to the object would also change. So Aristotle suggests that in order to develop good decisions or judgmental practices, a person should learn to consult the passions, such as fear and love, and draw on emotional experience to make the decision more not less rational. Hence for Aristotle, cognition and emotion are intimately entwined in a number of ways. However, in order for this consultation with the emotions to lead to virtuous activity, appetite firstly needs to be culturally cultivated.

Aristotle's Psychosocial Studies of Emotion

Thus we see a very strong social element in Aristotle's account of emotion. It is primarily the family who teaches the child the appropriate kinds of emotional responses that are formed through habit. Additionally, Gross adds that this account of emotion is thoroughly psychosocial (Gross, 2006). For example, although there may be physiological consequences of feeling 'shame', for example, blushing, Aristotle draws our attention to the object of one's shame. This is seen to be directly related to a person's social position and social status. For example, there can be no 'shame' where there is no potential reputation to lose, and, indeed, shame is always felt in relation to others. Gross states that there is shame:

> where social institutions are most dense: where one's reputation really matters, where the opinions of others are valued, where social rank is effective, where credit can be given and debts owed, where honour can be realized or lost, where there are fragile bonds of intimacy, and where social prestige can be measured according to one's institutional access to the truth (for example, through formal education, demonstrated credibility). (2006: 42)

Aristotle's understanding of anger (*orge*) similarly illustrates the importance of its psychosocial nature. It is also induced through relationships of inequality. Some people are seen as being perfectly entitled to belittle others without any recourse for retaliation, such as a king. A slave, in contrast, has no social status and does not then have an entitlement to 'pride' which makes one susceptible to anger. Gross adds that Aristotle's understanding of anger presumes 'a contoured world of emotional investment' (2006: 3). A person not only feels shame when he or she has been belittled, but also when that person does not defend parents, children, spouse, or dependants. Indeed, Aristotle defines anger as

> a desire, accompanied by pain, for revenge at what is taken to be an insult to oneself or those close to one, in a situation where insult is not appropriate (Rhetoric. 2.2.1378a30–2, b1–2).

Aristotle goes on to point out that it is often the case that those who are considered 'better than us' draw our emotional attention. Thus social status often defines the social-cultural contours of emotionality; some people have more rights than others to feel and express certain things.

Conclusion

In this chapter we have pointed to a series of aspects of the philosophies of Plato and Aristotle that we argue provide valuable foundations for social psychological understandings of emotion. This is important as in many histories of emotion Ancient Greek writings are not included, and where they are, it is primarily in the form of brief summaries that focus only on the most common interpretations. We have sought to point to the seeds of social theory that are present in both Plato and Aristotle, not only because these often do not feature in coverage of their work, but also because these are important forerunners to the kinds of social theories of emotion we claim are present in more recent times. Here it is important to note that the empirical desires of much psychology of emotion have led to reduced focus on the more nuanced, complex, and often contradictory elements of people's everyday emotional activity and experience. We seek to throw the spotlight more directly on these elements throughout this book. The journey will take us through many centuries, disciplines and geographies, with the next step being tracing emotion through Hellenistic and medieval theologies.

Although these early theorisations offer sometimes rudimentary and other times offer relatively sophisticated answers, they raise a number of questions relating to the social psychology of emotion; for example, does emotion hinder or facilitate the moral development of the individual and society? Although history tends to favour the view that Plato thought that this was not the case and Aristotle suggests that they could, our account attempts to draw out some of the more knotty view that their understandings were not as polarised as this discourse suggests. Clearly, however, Plato tends to draw a much more visible demarcation between the lower appetitive faculties and the higher rational faculties within his earlier theorisations of the soul. But even this bipartite model was revised to a tripartite model through which *thumos* (spirit) plays a relatively ambivalent role. And even the lower appetites, for example the desire for wealth, incorporates some form of cognition. And of course included in the later theories of Plato is the notion that aspects of emotion actually induce a view of the highest forms. Aristotle is considered as much more of a friend of emotion, in that he sees that if acculturated in the right way, emotion can be of moral service to the individual and society and so can include cognitive elements. Yet even Aristotle's theorisation is based in part upon the notion that the passions are involuntarily driven by external forces as they belong to a passive part of the soul, and thus may require the intellect to harness their influence. Hence, questions concerning emotion's autonomy, value, place, significance, and distinguishing features are concerns that are of absolute importance to the social

psychology of emotion. As Plato and Aristotle attest, emotion is not just important to understand in relation to an individual's psychological makeup, but has
a bearing on our micro relations and our macro social structures.

FURTHER READING

Most academics will recommend that it is always important to do some primary source
reading rather than completely relying on secondary commentaries. We reiterate that
mantra and urge readers to take a look at some of Plato's and Aristotle's works. We specifically recommend Plato's book entitled the *Republic*. We have illustrated in this chapter
some of the social psychology that Plato developed that was used in relation to his early
theorisation of emotion contained in the dialogues of the *Republic*. This included his influential tripartite division of the soul and the understanding that the polis is the soul writ
large. Aristotle is a bit more difficult to read in that his writings are a lot dryer and more
technical. Aristotle of course does not use the same dialogical style as Plato. The two
books that Aristotle wrote that we have drawn upon in this chapter were *De Anima* and
the second book of the *Rhetoric*. The latter book is where we see Aristotle discuss various
emotions and this book is understood by scholars as presenting some of the most detailed
and sophisticated descriptions of emotion from classical antiquity.

Konstan, D. (2006). *The Emotions of the Ancient Greeks: Studies in Aristotle and classical
literature*. Toronto: University of Toronto Press.
Taking many of Aristotle's writings from the Rhetoric as its starting point. Konstan details
the ways in which 11 particular emotions (anger, satisfaction, shame, envy and indignation,
fear, gratitude, love, hatred, pity, jealousy, and grief) were theorised and portrayed by the
Ancient Greeks. This book has set a very high standard and is essential reading for the
serious scholar of the history of emotion studies.

Knuuttila, S. (2004). *Emotions in Ancient and Medieval Philosophy*. Oxford: Oxford University
Press.
Knuuttila develops a number of important entries on Plato's and Aristotle's theories of emotion which are relatively complex and progressive. This book offers new insights into these
early texts through a close reading the primary texts and tracing developments in thought.

James, S. (1997). *Passion and Action: The emotions in seventeenth-century philosophy*. Oxford:
Oxford University Press.
James begins her study of passion and action by firstly detailing relevant aspects of Aristotle's
metaphysics. She traces the development of these Aristotelian conceptualisations of emotion
through the centuries to detail how they influenced seventeenth century thought.

Gross, D. (2006). *The Secret History of Emotion: From Aristotle's rhetoric to modern brain
science*. Chicago: The University of Chicago Press.
Gross' book is unique in that it is one of the very few books to consider the history of
emotion thought in relation to psychosocial phenomena. For example, he is interested in
how concepts are shaped by power and politics. Gross offers us refreshing alternative
views of emotion which challenge the dominant Darwinist perspectives.

2

Hellenistic and Medieval Theologies of Emotion

Key Aims

In this chapter we will present Stoic, Islamic and Christian theological contributions to emotion theories. In doing so we will:

- Reflect on how Plato's and later Aristotle's works influenced these theorisations of emotion
- Discuss how emotion was understood to be regulated and could be used to regulate social activity
- Distinguish how voluntary and involuntary aspects of emotion experience were conceptualised through the first and second movements
- Draw attention to distinctions between higher and lower forms of emotion

Introduction

The theories of emotion that we looked at in the previous chapter were often concerned with morality and ethics; for example, how to live 'the good life'. This was also a predominant theme throughout the medieval period (and beyond). Western philosophy, from the fall of the Roman Empire in the fifth century up until the dawn of the Renaissance period of the fifteenth century, was carried mainly by the Christian Church. The term 'emotion' is relatively recent; the closest we get to the term etymologically is the Latin term *motus* which literally means 'movement'. Theologians throughout the medieval period tended to split what we now call emotion into 'movements' of different functions of the soul. For example, it was demarcated by the lower 'passions' (love, hate, hope, fear and anger) and 'appetites' (hunger, thirst, and sexual desire), both of which were considered to be movements of the lower animal soul and generally decreased virtue. The higher part of the soul was allied to the 'affections' (love, sympathy, and joy); these were seen as wilful acts or movements of the higher rational soul which increased virtue.

After the medieval period the term 'emotion' came into popular use particularly through David Hume's philosophical psychology, although he tended to use the term 'passion'. It is not until the introduction of psychology as a separate discipline in the nineteenth century that we begin to see the term 'emotion' replacing the term 'passion'. During the medieval period, emotion took on many meanings and terms, such as 'passions', 'affections', and 'appetites' among many other terms that are often translated from Latin and Greek as synonyms. Fortunately, some exemplary contemporary historians of emotion (for example, Dixon, 2003; Knuuttila, 2004; Sorabji, 2002), to whom we owe a debt of gratitude, have paved the way to more precise analysis by discussing these distinctions and translations in some detail. In doing so they have dismantled popular beliefs that early periods advocated views of emotion as always leading away from the good life and in opposition to reason (for an example see Solomon, 1976). We follow some of the texts of these early theorists of emotion and conclude, alongside the aforementioned contemporary historians of emotion, that this is a misunderstanding of these early texts, which actually have much more complex and nuanced understandings of the relationships between reason, the passions and the affections.

This chapter runs chronologically through some of the thoughts of prominent theories and philosophies of emotion, up to and including Aquinas. We will begin with Stoicism and include a smaller section on Epicureanism. These were both influenced by Plato and Aristotle; however, there is a significant difference as contrary to Plato and Aristotle, the Stoics tended to believe that one could live without emotion. Thus the Stoics are particularly important to the development of thought on emotion as they offered some relatively sophisticated theorisations of emotion to combat what they saw as its destructive effect upon the soul. Their accounts include the important distinction between the aspects of emotion that were thought to be within one's control and those outside of it. The Stoics offer methods and practices aimed at socialising, moderating and indeed eradicating emotion. The methods that they advocated may be allied to an early form of what we may recognise today as cognitive therapy; namely learning to change one's beliefs in order to eradicate or modify an associated emotion based response. We then turn to look at a particular early Christian theology that included a concern with emotion. Saint Augustine was very much influenced by Platonism and threaded this through his understanding of emotion and its relationship to original sin; he was influenced by Stoic theorisations which he adapted to fit into his own systematic account. More particularly we see here how notions of the involuntary and voluntary aspects of emotion theorised by the Stoics were instrumental in the development of Augustine's influential understanding of the human will.

The medieval epoch of history is often referred to as being 'the dark ages', a term which usually denotes it as an era of little significant writing. In contrast to this was what has come to be known as 'the golden age of Islam'; a broad spectrum of theories and philosophies that had not yet been cemented in, particularly, Christian theologies. For example, while the West had lost touch with the work of Aristotle and focused on Plato, the former had been translated into Arabic and was being widely used in Islamic traditions. In this section we focus on the writings of Ibn Sina and Ibn Rushd. What is of particular interest to us here is how poetry was theorised and used as a tool for socially regulating moral virtue through eliciting emotion. There is no doubt that the many works that were produced through this fruitful era went on to influence Western thought and most notably Aquinas. The last section of this chapter looks at some of Aquinas' extensive understanding of the passions of the soul. Although many of the ideas that Aquinas puts forward are not necessarily original, his works are unique in that they bring together much of the thought that had preceded him and infused his theology with Aristotelian thought. Aquinas' theory of the passions institutes a depth of complexity and detail that was to inform enlightenment thinkers to include detailed discussion of the passions in their works; for example Descartes, Spinoza, Hobbes and Hume (whom we look at in the following chapter). Although Aquinas' account is relatively asocial, it is nonetheless important to the preceding social psychological thought on emotion as traces of the social can be found in relation to the passions and the virtues.

The Hellenistic Period

The Hellenistic period followed the conquests of Alexander the Great (Aristotle's student), which imposed a Greek cultural influence over much of Asia and Europe. Throughout the Hellenistic period and beyond Stoicism flourished for over five centuries. Stoicism is often portrayed by scholars as being represented by three periods: Early Stoa: Zeno of Citium, Cleanthes, and Chrysippus; Middle Stoa: Panaetius, and Posidonius; and Late Stoa: Seneca, Musonius Rufus, Epictetus, Hierocles, and Marcus Aurelius.

Early Stoa

There are a number of interpretations of the early Stoic doctrines that fail to give a full account of their foundations. We only have fragments of their early writings and so have to rely on later Roman Stoic accounts, such as the commentaries of Cicero and Sextus Empiricus. Zeno of Citium (334–262 BC) is seen to be the founder of Stoicism who lectured in Athens upon the famous Painted Porch (*Stoa Poikile*, from where Stoicism gets its name). His teachings incorporated the metaphysics of Heraclitus of Ephesus who theorised the *kosmos* as being subject to eternal change (being as becoming) and that nothing exists higher than the world of nature (*logos*), which individuals are subject to. Socrates was very influential upon Stoic doctrine, his life and death were emblems of rational self-control; as were the Cynics who considered true virtue (such as abstaining from wealth, power and fame) as forming the basis for autonomy (*autarkeia*). Reason was likened to a creative fire (*pneuma*) which resided both in the individual and the *kosmos*. Chrysippus envisaged the soul as being totally entwined with the body and therefore a special type of corporeal spirit (*pneuma*) but essentially a physical substance. The interaction between the soul and the body was simply the interaction between different kinds of matter.

Table 2.1   Emotional processing stages

First	Impression *Phantasia*
Second	Assent *Sunkathesis*
Third	Impulse *Horme*
Fourth	Reason *Logos*

As can be seen from the above table, Knuuttila (2004: 49) describes the various psychological faculties or stages in processing emotional phenomena. The governing faculty 'is the seat of appearance or impression' (*phantasia*), which allows for the receiving of information through the senses. Assent (*sunkatathesis*) is the accepting of the sensory information as true. Impulse (*horme*) moves the assent into some form of action, and reason (*logos*), of course, initiates understanding.

According to most Stoic doctrine there are four main types of emotion: pleasure (*hedone*) and distress (*lupe*), which relate to the present, and appetite (*epithumia*) and fear (*phobus*), which relate to the future (Knuuttila, 2004: 51). Under these primary types of emotion a number of more specific types are put forward. These emotions were typically seen as irrational, a reaching out for a future or present object valued as either good or bad. Thus Early Stoa (for example Chrysippus) regarded the emotions as having a propositional or cognitive aspect to them. They are beliefs about a present or future – good or bad – which is assented to, but are irrational and tend to disturb the soul. So although emotion has a cognitive element to it in terms of beliefs, these cognitions themselves were seen to be irrational. This is because moral beliefs which are swayed by affective judgments are understood as being deaf to the voice of right reason.

The Stoics were monists who believed that humanity should try to live according to the rational laws of nature. As nature was seen as being ruled by rational principles, there are reasons why everything is as it is, and consequently one should accept one's own mortality, or perhaps, personal tragedy. One was to live according to the benevolence and orderliness of the *kosmos*. Essentially Stoic philosophy promoted the authority of reason to enhance inward tranquillity and reflect the orderliness of the *kosmos* and conform to social duty (Edwards, 1967). If attained, one would reach the high state of *apatheia* which is akin to spiritual peace and well-being, or what for example Aristotle discussed as *eudaimonia*. Indeed, similar to Aristotle's philosophy, one needs to live a virtuous life to reach this high state, and essential to this was the moderating of the passions, but as we shall see there are key differences.

The moderating of the passions may appear to go against the Stoics' key principle, to live according to the law of nature. If the passions are natural human inclinations, surely one should live by them? The Stoics agreed to this sentiment to some degree, but they also thought that we can be misled by them. Stoics believed that humans are naturally drawn to objects or actions which benefit them. At times, however, we are drawn to objects by the passions which are disobedient to reason. Similar to Aristotle's understanding, for the Stoics, passion is something which we undergo (a passivity) rather than something that we do (an activity). For example, *apatheia* is not equivalent to the English translation of apathy, or to be apathetic, the view that you should not care about something. Instead, it meant that you should not be psychologically subject to anything or be externally determined and manipulated. They were more concerned with self-sufficiency, the ability to be active, to initiate action rather than being subject to the world. So for example, if we give way to 'happiness' or 'fear' the result of the state of the soul will be 'pleasure' or 'distress', respectively. This state lowers one's ability to act upon the world, but leaves one subject to it through the excitations it produces. So the Stoics believed that we could and should tame our passions; in other words, we need to develop the right type of cognitive beliefs so that we are not unduly moved by emotion. It must be emphasised that this is quite a different view of apathy that we understand today; *apatheia* is concerned with a wilful turning away from that which is considered as being bad for the soul, rather than a state of being passively disinterested.

Middle Stoa

Middle Stoa, particularly Posidonius, came to offer a more complicated and perhaps radical picture of the psychology of emotion. He stressed that the cognitive belief (or judgment) is not sufficient or even necessary for emotional arousal (Knuuttila, 2004: 63; Sorabji, 2000: 109–10). Arousal can occur for example by music, tears can be induced without any attached judgment and young children and animals can be aroused without the attached cognitive judgments. In this way feelings were seen to precede emotions. This was a very significant step to take in the history of emotion, as it was the basis for the Late Stoa doctrine of first movements (*primus motus*) also known as pre-emotions (*propatheia*) which as we will see was quite an influential theory in many subsequent theorisations of emotion.

Late Stoa

Seneca details these first movements in his writings *On Anger* through which he describes the first movements as not being emotions in the full sense but rather involuntary activity: it is simply the preparation of an emotion. He describes the first movements as the presenting of a proposition to the mind. Voluntary assent to the proposition is still required; or what is considered as the second movement, or what we might term the cognitive judgment. The first movements were considered by Seneca as *natural affects* which could not be overcome by reason. These cannot be eradicated by the sage, but emotions in the full sense, with the accompanying assent of the second movement, could be.

Thus the late Stoics advocated a form of cognitive therapy to eradicate unwanted emotional excitation. As emotions *per se* were seen as voluntary secondary movements, one could learn how to manipulate and eradicate them by changing the associated cognitions, beliefs and judgments. Epictetus discusses the possibilities of deconstructing an object's emotional associations and interpretations in order to develop the Stoic disposition of *apethia*. Thus the Stoic is to learn to anticipate oncoming emotion and develop controlled responses. Sorabji argues that the Stoic doctrine 'can be very helpful in dealing with counter-productive emotion' (2000: 2), a view which is quite a way from contemporary everyday notions of Stoicism which tend to understand the doctrine as advocating the gritting of one's teeth and suppressing of emotion in times of adversity.

Epicureanism

Although we will not focus on Epicureanism in great detail, it is worth a mention because of the Epicureans' interesting take on emotion, which influenced several contemporary thinkers. Epicureanism starts with the philosophy of Epicurus (341–270BC). Emotion was central to his view of the goal of human life: 'happiness', which resulted from the absence of physical pain and mental disturbance. Epicurus was also a monist, but his philosophy was more radical than the Stoics in that he believed there was a need to rid ourselves of any beliefs in transcendent entities (such as Plato's Forms), the survival of the soul after death, and importantly any concept of punishment in the afterlife (as there is no afterlife). For him, one of the chief causes of anxiety throughout *life* is the fear of *death*. This fear he saw as often unacknowledged and in turn caused extreme and irrational desires, such as secondary desires including 'self-hatred, greed, and craving for honour' (Gill, 2010: 156). Once freed from these irrational fears and desires one would be open to pursue a life of pleasure without guilt.

Like Aristotle and the Stoics, the Epicureans, such as Hermarchus and Lucretius, believed that there was a cognitive element to emotion, in that beliefs generate emotions such as anger, grief, or erotic passion. The beliefs concerned with the emotions are either 'natural' (appropriate) or 'empty' (erroneous)

(Gill, 2010). The natural beliefs were good beliefs which led to pleasure, which is better described as a freedom from pain, while the empty beliefs led to pain. The Epicureans also advocated a kind of therapy to help revise people's belief-sets with a view of changing their patterns of emotion (Gill, 2010).

One may be critical of the lack of social responsibility in the Epicureans' ethics. They seem to be concerned with a sort of selfishly led concern about pleasure (or lack of pain). However, the Epicureans placed a very high value on friendship (*philia*). It was seen as a source of positive emotions such as joy and therefore objects of intense concern (Gill, 2010: 159). Epicurean communities advocated a high level of criticism and encouragement between each other to facilitate a 'consciousness-raising' towards the Epicurean way of life. Importantly, Epicurus believed that the wise person will always have a tight knit supply of mental pleasures which will counterbalance physical pains. Additionally, friendship can produce a kind of joy that counteracts any fear of death and physical pain.

Augustine

Saint Augustine of Hippo (354–430 AD), a North African Christian theologian, developed a marriage between Plato's philosophy and Christian theology. He was not a believer in Christianity until he was 32 years old; throughout the earlier period of his life he was influenced by Manichaeism and later neo-Platonism. His breadth of writing is extraordinary as he managed to complete some 120 treatises and many sermons and letters. Two of his more famous works, *The Confessions* and *The City of God*, are where we find much of his writing on emotion (or what tended to be termed the passions and affections). The *Confessions* is often cited as one of the earliest autobiographies through which we find a rich tapestry of illustrations pertaining to his struggles with the passions. It is *The City of God* where we find an account of his teachings on the passions and affections. Augustine's philosophy of emotion permeated Western philosophy, particularly throughout the medieval period, and to some extent, it is still visible in contemporary Christian theology. As we shall see, Augustine went on to influence the writings of St Thomas Aquinas in relation to his understanding of the passions and affections, although the latter was distinctly Aristotelian.

Augustine believed that through the original sin of Adam the soul had been divided and disordered and we subsequently live in a state of sickness. In this state divine truth is only represented to us dimly (as St Paul had suggested 'through a glass darkly') but it was the job of the virtuous person to seek this dim inner light. Following Plato (and indeed Aristotle), Augustine distinguished different aspects of the soul. There was the higher 'rational' and 'moral' part that was the seat of reason; and the lower animal or nutritive part of the soul which incorporated the appetites and sense perception. Although he used Aristotelian terminology, the philosophy of the soul was much more inclined to a neo-Platonic duality wherein aspects of the body were distinguished from aspects of the divine soul. Similarly he advocated a neo-Platonic hierarchical epistemology outlining levels of knowledge. The lowest level of which is 'sensation' (common to humans and animals), the highest level is the 'contemplation of eternal things' (peculiar to humans). The former he equated with knowledge while the latter was equated with wisdom. In-between these two was a 'rational' level through which individuals can judge objects of the world according to eternal standards. For example, a circle can be judged to be more or less circular. Following Plato, he suggests that we judge the perfection of a circle in accordance with our idea of the form of perfect circularity. These immutable truths, for Augustine, were infused into the mind of humans by God and then could be beheld through contemplation. It is then the contemplative life through the aid of scripture that enables one to learn how to act virtuously in relation to the desires of the body.

Passion, Affection and the Will

Augustine distinguished what he saw as the lower 'passions' from the higher 'affections'. The passions were for the most part understood as unwieldy and required wilful attention by reason to stop them from negatively influencing a person towards vice. The affections, in contrast, were mostly seen as virtuous (emotional) movements of the will. But not all affections were good and all passions bad for Augustine. It depended on the disposition of the will. A good will produces good affections just as a bad one produces bad affections, and the passions do not necessarily lead to sin if they were under the influence of reason.

In book XIV of *The City of God*, Augustine discusses the central place of the 'will' of the individual in relation to passion and affection. He states,

> But the character of the human will is of moment; because, if it is wrong, these motions of the soul will be wrong, but if it is right, they will be not merely blameless, but even praiseworthy. For the will is in them all; yea, none of them is anything else than will. For what are desire and joy but a volition of consent to the things we wish? And what are fear and sadness but a volition of aversion from the things which we do not wish? But when consent takes the form of seeking to possess the things we wish, this is called desire; and when consent takes the form of enjoying the things we wish, this is called joy. In like manner, when we turn with aversion from that which we do not wish to happen, this volition is termed fear; and when we turn away from that which has happened against our will, this act of will is called sorrow. And generally in respect of all that we seek or shun, as a man's will is attracted or repelled, so it is changed and turned into these different affections. (*City of God*, 14.6)

The above extract illustrates some of the complexity of Augustine's understanding of emotion. As we saw previously, through Aristotle and the Stoics and to some degree in Plato, a distinction is made between the embodied, what Augustine often refers to as, 'motions of the soul', and cognition or perception and the following judgment. Sorabji (2002), following Seneca, calls the former 'first movements' and distinguishes them from emotion proper, which includes the judgment of the first movement. Although Augustine's notion of the 'motions of the soul' seem to suggest a similar thing to what Seneca calls first movements, Augustine's understanding is arguably more complex and tricky. He argues that the will is of central significance, which seems to be pointing to two main things in the extract. Firstly, it concerns the judgment that is placed upon the first movement which is to some extent synonymous to the affection. And to this end, it is the judgment of the first movement which can be distinguished as either good or bad affection, as this is an act of will. But secondly, and perhaps more interestingly, it seems that the disposition of the will can also affect the first movement. As in, for example, desire, it is the will which directs the desire. Augustine almost seems to be suggesting that the will then disposes one in various ways so that stimuli affect the first movements in accordance with the will. In other words, if our will is directed towards good desire, in Augustine's terms, towards the things of God rather than the self, then we *will* be perturbed accordingly. In effect, in one sense, they are no longer first movements at all but are indeed affected by the will. The will, therefore, essentially actively constructs either more negative or more positive meanings that are adopted for both the first movements and the cognitions that follow. Accordingly, the will can be understood as being embedded in both the deep physiology of the body and in conscious processing, forming feedback loops between the two and thus influencing particular kinds of subjectivity.

Sorabji's (2002) analysis suggests that Augustine did not take into account the Stoic distinction between the involuntary first movements and the secondary cognitions and judgments. Knuuttila (2004) disagrees with Sorabji's view; he suggests that not only did Augustine employ the distinction but added that first movements are not always wholly innocent. However, the not wholly innocent first movement that Knuuttila alludes to here is not a psychological understanding of the will that we have illustrated above, but is in reference to Augustine's theological notions of the how original sin affects the will and the first movements. Dixon (2003) explains this via a discussion of Augustine's understanding of Adam before the fall in relation to lust. In the *Confessions* Augustine portrays a self at pains to control sexual desires; Dixon suggests that 'sex was Augustine's own demon' (2003: 51). Augustine tends to portray sexual urges as particularly unperturbed by the good will. Adam, he conjectured, prior to the fall, would have been in full voluntary control of sexual urges. Thus for Augustine it is the sin of the original fall that now permeates humanity and influences first movements that are against a good will. Indeed the root of all human wrong-doing is seen as arising from these first movements, particularly those that are associated with sex and violence. But what of this notion above that Augustine seems to allude to of the will affecting the motions of the soul? In another section of the *City of God* he states,

> It [scripture] subjects the mind itself to God, that He may rule and aid it, and the passions, again, to the mind, to moderate and bridle them, and turn them to righteous uses. (*City of God*, 9.5)

Similar, to some degree, to the Stoic therapy that we looked at previously, Augustine seems to imply here that it is through the reading of scripture that one 'learns' to overcome the bad motions of the soul. But this is not a direct act of God *per se*, it occurs through the mind. So God, through scripture, tames the mind, the mind in turn tames the passions and affections. Thus we are led to believe that the taming of the first movements of the passions, which are involuntarily aroused, can only occur through a lengthy process through which the body learns to react in ways that are in accord with the will, something similar to Aristotle's notion of habit. Knuuttila (2004: 159) states that they can be educated, but also remain a source of spontaneous reactions. Unfortunately Augustine does not appear to treat this aspect of his doctrine of the will in much depth. Of interest here is that Augustine does not recognise the affections as all bad, something which he is often parodied as advocating. Like Plato and the Stoics, Augustine insists that they have the capacity to lead one away from virtue, but unlike the Stoics he did not advocate *apatheia* (the ideal of freedom from emotion that we looked at earlier). He irrefutably states, if the will is rightly disposed, 'the motions of the soul can become praiseworthy' (*City of God*, 14.6).

Thus there are three important issues in this discussion of Augustine vis-à-vis the history of the social psychology of emotion. Firstly, he incorporates the ancient Greek (late platonic) notions of emotion's higher and lower forms, which in turn inclines one towards or repels one from the virtuous life. Secondly, Augustine incorporates Stoic notions of the first and second movements of emotion. Thirdly, and most importantly, Augustine seems to be the first to theorise how first movements can be manipulated and so are not wholly innate or so called 'natural' reactions. Augustine includes the notion of the will which can predispose one towards incoming information, which in turn, in Aristotelian terms, can be habituated. Aristotle did not seem to have a notion of first movements but does include the notion of habit. Aristotle, however, refers this development of habit to one's social environment (e.g. the family), whereas Augustine sees the goodwill only coming about through the reading of scripture.

Although we do see some Aristotelianism within Augustine's works, it is mostly influenced by Plato. Indeed throughout this period and for the next 800 or so years, the philosophies of Aristotle were virtually absent in the development of Western thought but flourished in the Arabic world. Although the West underwent the 'dark ages' after the fall of the Western Roman Empire, much of this period is often referred to as a *Golden age of Islam*.

The Golden Age of Islam

Around the third century of the Muslim calendar (which was the ninth century AD), a vast translation movement evolved in Baghdad. This entailed translating many texts that had been adopted by the Syrian tradition (a tradition dating back to the first century AD represented predominantly by Christians in the Middle East and in Kerala, India) into Arabic; for example scientific, medical and philosophical works from ancient Greece. Christian, Jewish and Muslim philosophers wrote in Arabic to develop the philosophical debates at that time at the Caliphal Court of Baghdad. Not only were translations produced but reinterpretations and commentaries by most notably Ibn Sina (Avicenna) (980–1037 AD) and Ibn Rushd (Averroës) (1126–1198 AD).

Above it can be seen that each of the two scholars have two names. The names in parenthesis, are their Latin names, by which they are usually referred to within the subsequent tradition of Western scholarship. The rediscovery of Aristotle through the Arab world was extremely important for the West, allowing many of the theorists to reconnect with what was almost a lost tradition. For the Arabs, Aristotle was regarded as a foreign influence on already well-established scholarly activity. It is clear that scholars throughout this so called golden age wrote extensively on issues related to the psychology of emotion. For example Ibn Sina, who is mostly recognised today for his contribution to medicine, wrote his own version of the four humours and temperaments that related various emotional states to the physical body and the physical world. Indeed his writings on emotion were to become very influential to Western theorisations throughout the thirteenth century discussions on philosophical psychology. His theoretical understandings of emotion entail Aristotelian and neo-Platonist elements. Through using Aristotelian terminology, he understood emotion as stemming from the powers of the sensitive soul, preceded by various cognitive activities, bodily affects and behavioural changes. He was also interested in the subjective feeling states infused with emotion (occurrent emotions). Much of his conceptual work was reproduced and adapted in Aquinas' theories which are discussed below.

Poetic Evocations

What is of particular interest to the social psychology of emotion is how poetry was understood to socially regulate moral virtue through its power to elicit emotion. Scholars around this era drew on the concept of *takhyil*, which can be understood as a mimetic imaginative creation. In other words, as Hogan states, it 'functions to capture the audience so that they forget reality and accept the creation', a kind of 'imaginative consent' (2000: 31). Ibn Sina wrote that 'the imaginative is the speech to which the soul yields, accepting and rejecting matters without pondering, reasoning or choice' (cited in Kemal, 2003: 87).

Ludescher (1996) suggests that the poet was understood as not simply representing reality but rather had the power to imaginatively transform it. Thus the poet
was as a *seer*, one who perceives reality in ways that others cannot. Poetry was
very important in pre-Islamic society. The poet (*sha'ir*) had many roles. He or
she was essentially a historian, soothsayer and propagandist responsible for
encouraging the virtuous action of the audience. This was quite different from
other forms of rhetoric which tend to persuade through the intellect. Ludescher
(1996) suggests that certain feelings in the audience can be aroused by poetry
which are conducive to moral action, particularly through mercy and piety. In
this way it is argued by Ludescher that the poem works involuntarily on the will
of the reader as a form of subtle training of sensibilities and results in facilitating
or indeed determining good moral decision making processes in later life.

However, Habib (2005) argues something a bit different. He suggests that Ibn
Rushd presumes that virtuous activity should be based on free choice and knowledge, not (as Aristotle had suggested) through mere habit. Ibn Rushd seems to
suggest that this works better when the poet portrays universal emotions: that
which is common to all. Hence Ibn Rushd 'seems to recognize an internal connection between poetic representation and human emotion, based implicitly on a
correspondence between the "external" world of objects and the "internal" world
of human perception' (Habib, 2005: 199). Indeed he was very much an empiricist
and a phenomenologist in this respect; he went as far to suggest that poetry is
most truthful when it is based on the direct experience of the poet. Ibn Rushd
thus urged that the poet should represent virtuous acts which have universal
application rather than individual instances of virtue as these would be easier to
relate to. The virtuous acts have universal applicability when elicitly represented
in poetry, for example, pity and fear through stimulating the imagination. A tragedy, for instance, should not attempt to imitate people as they appear individually,
but rather should represent their character and moral attitudes recognizable to
all. In this way poetry should not merely evoke the pleasure of mere admiration,
but rather should seek to elicit a level of pleasure that incites people to be moved
to virtue through imagination. Ibn Rushd states that 'This is the pleasure proper
to tragedy' (Habib, 2005: 197). Indeed Aristotle had suggested that writings concerned with tragedy should be serious and thus discuss significant moral action.
Habib explains that Ibn Rushd also urges that emotions such as fear and suffering
should be aroused not by the small and unimportant but the difficult and harsh
experiences that are universally experienced. Thus poetry stood for Ibn Rushd as
holding a logic of its own, one which was often dismissed by scholastic thinkers
as being an insignificant branch of logical discourse.

Aquinas

Ibn Rushd was associated with a school of thought by the name of the Mu'tazili
(in the cities of Basra and Baghdad) and was particularly interested in Aristotle's

Organon (Aristotle's writings on logic). This school was frowned upon by Sunni Muslim groups as the Mu'tazili had suggested that one could use reason and logic to interpret some of the writings of the Qur'an. Ibn Rushd was an advocate for the marriage of revelation (through scripture) with interpretation (through reason). He was of the view that there should not be a conflict between religion and philosophy. However, this is an aspect of his work that was not taken up in the Arabic (Islamic) tradition, but one which was certainly taken up by later Christian thinkers, particularly Aquinas. Saint Thomas Aquinas' (1225–1274) understanding of emotion can be thought of as the culmination of thirteenth-century developments. Many of the Latin theories on emotion throughout the twelfth and thirteenth centuries arose from the theological and spiritual treatise of the monastic tradition, such as the *primus motus* theory, inquiries into the subjective feelings of emotion, and the logic of will. There were also a number of medical works that had been translated into Latin in the early twelfth century that influenced emotion theorisation. For example, the *Articella*, the medical encyclopaedia of Ali ibn al-Abbas al-Majusi theorised connections between somatic activity, the soul and various emotions. Thus despite the supposed context of the dark ages, there had been a lot of enlightening theorisation produced in relation to emotion. Indeed Aquinas' influences are multiple in this respect but are of particular interest because he managed to thread many of these theories together.

Although influenced by Ibn Rushd, Aquinas was also critical of him. More recently it has been suggested that Aquinas misinterpreted a central aspect of Ibn Rushd's understanding of the relation of philosophy to religion. Aquinas accused Ibn Rushd of advocating irreconcilability between faith and reason. However, Ibn Rushd actually states something subtly different to this; he suggested that religion cannot be developed upon the principles of pure reason but rather through the philosophical and rational understandings of truths revealed by religion. What is clear, however, is that Aquinas used Ibn Rushd's 'Grand Commentary' as his model; a model of scholasticism that Aquinas was one of the first in the West to emulate. Indeed, following Ibn Rushd, the questionable relationship between faith (religion) and reason (philosophy) was of central importance to Aquinas' writings, and this relationship was further theorised through the handing on of the Arabic predecessor's translations and commentaries on the works of most particularly Aristotle. Hence hereafter, Aristotelianism is an extremely important element of Western philosophy and theology.

The Passions of the Soul

Aquinas developed a very comprehensive, detailed, and complicated account of emotion or what he termed the *passions of the soul*; these were seen to be experienced by both humans and animals and can be described as acts, movements and effects that are caused by external objects. James states that 'Aquinas's analysis of the passions is far more thorough and meticulous than those of his predecessors, and is worked out with a fervent attention to detail to which none of them aspired' (1997: 60). Aquinas' writings on the passions are detailed in the so-called 'Treatise on the Passions' which is found in Questions 22-48 1a2ae of his most famous work, the *Summa Theologica*. Aquinas differentiates his understanding of the passions from the Stoics view of emotion in an important way. He views the passions as having a share in the life of reason and not necessarily afflicting the soul when expressed. They can be moderated through reason and can induce both morally good and evil social activity. They are not voluntary or involuntary in any straightforward way; his complex theory disallows any easy categorisation in this respect.

Aquinas generally followed Aristotle in many ways in relation to his understanding of the passions. For example, he incorporated Aristotle's virtue ethics in relation to the passions; he suggested that there is virtue in moderating the passions so that they are not excessive in any particular direction. A certain amount of sorrow in particular contexts was conceived of as positive; feeling sorrowful for sinful behaviour can lead to the avoidance of sin. The passions, then, can at times lead to positive moral behaviour and at times to negative moral behaviour, but generally were relegated to the more passive aspects of human activity. In relation to this Aquinas also followed Aristotle's metaphysics in that things are made up of form and matter; thus accordingly form was understood as essentially active and matter essentially passive. Additionally, the passions were conceived in Aristotelian terms 'as effects, as instances of being acted on, as powers that may or may not be exercised, and as rooted in matter' (James, 1997: 63). They are generally rooted in the sensitive soul but are distinct from the essence of the soul which is its form and thus active. Being rooted in the powers of the sensitive soul the passions have the potential to be moved by external objects. Again, following Aristotle, he nominates three forms of soul. The sensitive was higher than the vegetative soul and lower than the intellectual soul. The passive powers of the sensitive soul (i.e. the passions) are its capacities to be changed and in typical Aristotelian teleology, change is understood as either helping or hindering a thing to achieve its end. Aquinas tends to discuss passions as occurring in sequences; for example they will either begin with love or hatred, move then through to desire to either attraction or aversion, this may then transform through a number of passions – for example anger or hope – and eventually come to rest in either joy or sadness (depending upon whether the desire was satisfied or not).

Overall, Aquinas identifies eleven basic passions. These are divided by two appetites: six from the *concupiscible* appetite and five *irascible* appetite. Appetite, for Aquinas, is the power of an organism capable of sensation. A feature of sensation of the sensitive soul is the capacity for desiring. The elicitation of the desiring of the appetite follows apprehension. A thing then is apprehended in the external world and either attracts or repels the appetite. Both apprehension and appetite are considered as passive powers. James makes the point that Aquinas saw appetite as being more of a passive power than apprehension. The logic behind this is that we are more passive when we are being drawn towards or repelled from a thing (through the appetitive powers) than when we are simply affected by it (through the apprehensive powers). James claims, 'The image at work here seems to be spatial: if something affects me but fails to move me, I am less passive than I am when it draws or moves me to another place' (1997: 55).

Following Plato, the concupiscible appetite is related to desires which are easy to fulfil, while the irascible appetite is related to desires that are difficult to fulfil. The six passions of the concupiscible appetite are what we feel when our inclinations attend to what we perceive as good and away from evil. The perception of the good originates in the passion of love (*amor*) which in turn induces desire (*desiderium*) and if the good is obtained the passion of joy (*gaudium*) a form of pleasure ensues. Conversely, the perception of something evil originates in the passion of hatred (*odium*), which in turn induces avoidance (*fuga* or *abominatio*) of the evil, and if it is not avoided the passion of sorrow (*tristitia*) a form of pain ensues. These are relatively straightforward as they are appetites for things which are believed to be easily obtainable or avoidable. However, the irascible appetite is essentially concerned with the ability to strive for things that are rather more difficult to obtain or avoid. Here the perception of the good originates in the passion of hope (*spes*); if the good appears impossible to obtain this gives way to despair (*desperatio*). Daring or what some scholars translate as audacity (*audacia*) is an approach to a perceived evil and an aversion to it is fear (*timor*). The resistance of the perceived evil is anger (*ira*) (see James, 1997: 57; and for detailed commentary see Miner, 2009). The distinction between the concupiscible appetite and the irascible appetite also allows Aquinas to develop his understanding of feeling conflicting passions towards an object. For example, it allows a person to criticize his or her inclinations: one may feel like giving up striving for something because it appears difficult to obtain (to the concupiscible appetite); however, the irascible appetite may then overcome the initial desire to give up and strive on in hope to achieve the good. In this way Aquinas, following Aristotle, is able to account for the conflicting passions and the forms of psychological deliberation that they give way to, without recourse to the rational (or intellectual) soul, as these functions generally occur within the sensitive soul.

However, this does not mean that the intellectual soul does not have a part to play in relation to the passions. While the sensitive appetite can desire that which it perceives as either pleasant or useful, it is only the intellectual appetite which can distinguish what things are truly good (*bonum honestum*); these can be desired by the intellect without them actually being pleasant or useful. The passions may actually be modified by the two intellectual powers: the apprehensive power (the intellect) and the appetitive power (the will). These two powers mirror those discussed above of the sensitive soul. The external objects are apprehended by what he calls the *estimative* power. For example, on being presented with a particular object, the object is apprehended and then evaluated by the *estimative* power to be either 'good' or 'bad'. These estimations may also be apprehended in memory (in some animals) and recalled again through this power when required. However, Aquinas suggested that for animals the *estimative* power is mostly instinctual, whereas for humans, one could use reason and experience (memory) to further evaluate the object, and he distinguished this from the estimative power as the *cogitative* power. The cogitative power enables the individual to process information in relation to abstract concepts that are known to the intellect but not directly perceivable through sensation (Miner, 2009: 78). For example, the abstract concept of a particular shade of red can be associated with blood and thus danger. Minor states, 'Attaching the estimation "useful" or "dangerous" to a set of objects sharing particular features seems to be the job of the cogitative power' (2009: 78)). Thus objects may be apprehended as good or bad without any prior experience of the particular species of the object but simply based on its accidents (in other words particular qualities that are abstracted).

Importantly for Aquinas, it is only when the voluntary will of the intellectual soul decides to attend to something that we can then actually call this a moral act. He states,

> We may consider the passions of the soul in two ways: first, in themselves; secondly, as being subject to the command of the reason and will. If then the passions be considered in themselves, to wit, as movements of the irrational appetite, thus there is no moral good or evil in them, since this depends on the reason ... more, therefore, may the passions, in so far as they are voluntary, be called morally good or evil. (ST I-II, Q. 24, Art. 1, ad. 1)

Aquinas' understanding of the human will and morality diverges somewhat from the preceding developing thought related to the *primus motus*. Knuttila describes how many scholars were of the persuasion that even the first movements of the soul could be allied to venial sin, as when passions arise that are understood as inclinations towards evil, one should be actively engaged in pious acts in order to counteract them, in other words one should set the mind on higher things (2004: 179–95).

To complicate matters a little more, Aquinas also incorporated into his doctrine the notion of *syndresis* which he referred to as a 'natural habit' to move towards the good and avoid evil. This is rather like a natural conscience. However, he does not offer a full psychological explanation of *syndresis* but only suggests it may be described as an underlying intuition.

> Wherefore the first practical principles, bestowed on us by nature, do not belong to special power, but to a special natural habit which we call synderesis. Whence 'synderesis' is said to incite the good, and to murmur at evil, inasmuch as through first principles we proceed to discover, and judge of what we have discovered. It is therefore clear that 'synderesis' is not a power, but a natural habit. (ST I, Q. 79, Art. 12, 3)

Aquinas, however, does not spend much time on discussing how the passions may be manipulated, constructed or controlled through interpersonal and social interaction, or indeed where and how the 'natural habit' derives. Yet there are some concepts within his understanding of the passions which, one would have thought, directly relate to these; particularly his understanding of virtue. Similar to Aristotle, Aquinas understands a virtue as like a habit which perfects a power that a certain thing has. As we have discussed, the will and appetites are powers that can be steered towards a variety of ends. In order to dispose these powers towards good ends we need to develop the right kinds of habits in a bid to move towards our ultimate end of genuine happiness. Thus acquiring good habits that move us towards this ultimate end are the virtues.

The Virtues

Aquinas discusses what have come to be known as the *cardinal virtues*: prudence, justice, temperance and courage. Central to the acquisition of these virtues is the role of reason. One requires practical wisdom to make the right choices to help cultivate the right kinds of virtuous habits. For example, these may be cultivated by developing courage by acting bravely in the face of danger, thus conditioning fear responses. Similarly acting temperately in the face of temptations and being just when dealing with people. Additionally, one must not forget that Aquinas was essentially a Christian theologian; following Augustine's platonism he also describes the forms of habits that are infused within us from God. The infused moral virtues differ from the acquired virtues in that the latter do not induce imperfect or deficient forms of happiness. The latter, with God's help, are geared towards a heavenly perfect form of happiness (*bonum honestum*). For Aquinas an essential aspect of human nature is the desire for something supernatural, something which cannot be achieved by one's own power.

Ultimately, however, one may argue that Aquinas' complex theorisation of the passions in relation to developing habits and virtue (which facilitate the manipulation of their expression) was relatively asocial in comparison to Aristotle. Aristotle was quite concerned about how habits are socially produced, whereas Aquinas was much more inclined to stress the central roles of reason (the individual) and God. And yet, as we shall see, his theorisations were to play an important role in the development of more socially aware accounts.

Conclusion

What we have seen throughout this chapter is the influence of platonic thought on the earlier theories discussed (particularly Stoicism and Augustine). Subsequently the golden age of Islam induces a renaissance of Aristotelianism, particularly evident in the work of Aquinas. As we have seen, the philosophy, psychology, and theology of emotion were of considerable concern. There was less emphasis on the more social and relational aspects, although of course this was still evident. It was of value to discuss these developments as they went on to shape subsequent theorisations. Some particular themes that were evident in relation to the socialisation of emotion can be found springing from the important distinction that the Stoics formed between the primary and secondary movements of emotion. This helps to clarify the voluntary and involuntary aspects of emotion. The Stoics considered the primary movements of the soul (*primus motus*) as that which moves the soul involuntarily. For them what was of significance is how one managed the associated feelings and affects. Thus they developed forms of therapy which facilitated the socialisation of the subsequent (cognitive) response. They generally sought to learn how to dispose one in such a way as to rid the self of emotion, encapsulated in the concept of *apatheia*. This is a theme that is very much taken up by some of the enlightenment thinkers in the following chapter, particularly Kant. This view is also a recapitulation, to some degree, of Plato's distinction between embodied emotion and higher rational cognition; a distinction which again permeates most accounts of emotion that follow. Augustine took this a stage further to suggest that even the primary movements of the soul can be habituated through developing the right will. Aquinas was much less straightforward in his account of the passions. He builds upon some of the more complex metaphysics that Aristotle developed to create a much more nuanced understanding of the movements of the soul, will and the passions. There is no one strict dividing line here, as we saw in Plato, but a matrix of interactive faculties that in various ways habituate the virtues.

Overall we have seen increasingly complicated and intricate notions of the regulation of emotion, for example through therapy, reading scripture and the cultivation of good decision-making practices. We additionally discussed an aspect of emotional regulation that was prominent in the Islamic tradition which reflected an early use of mass media: poetry. The sages of this epoch noticed that celebrity culture (the poets of the time) had an important role to play in teaching the people how to be 'good citizens' through being able to tap into 'universal emotions'. Of note here is a subtle distinction between that which may be personal in relation to emotion and that which is fundamental to all. Indeed there was a lot of attention in this period as to how many kinds of emotions (passions and affects) there were (something we have not had time to discuss in this chapter). What we did highlight was the four primary passions described by the Stoics and that Aquinas went on to name eleven. Yet today there is still a lack of consensus in relation to how many (basic) emotions there are and what these might include (see Chapter 6). Indeed there is a question mark over whether we can claim that there are any universal emotions. Nonetheless this period posed some interesting questions and compelling answers in regard to the induction, manipulation and even eradication of emotion through social practices.

What is also of interest to this period of thought in relation to accounts of the passions and theorisation in general, is like the Ancients before them, they were also not tied to the confines of the forms of 'science' that much of present (social) psychology has to adhere to. This allowed for a kind of free thinking rather than having to substantiate every idea with empirical evidence. Of course that is not to say that they were not confined by other, perhaps even more, forms of stratification which they were bound by; they were most particularly subservient to the theologies that their respective religions adhered to for fear of being considered heretical. In the following chapter we move to an era that is often characterised as freeing itself of the shackles of the mythology, religiosity, monastic scholasticism and their consequent metaphysical assumptions.

FURTHER READING

A range of medieval thinkers have been discussed in this chapter and some of their works are difficult to obtain and to read. However, again readers are urged to at least browse through the translated primary sources to get some sense of the scholastic writing style. We thus recommend: Augustine's *The City of God* and *The Confession* and Aquinas' *The Summa Theologica*, particularly section 1a2ae Questions 22–48 (on the passions).

Knuuttila, S. (2004). *Emotions in Ancient and Medieval Philosophy.* Oxford: Oxford University Press.
This book was recommended as further reading for the previous chapter, but it also contains some excellent scholarly writing on Stoicism, Augustine and Aquinas. Additionally it looks at some of the more marginalised medieval writings (for example in the Islamic traditions).

Sorabji, R. (2010). *Emotions and Peace of Mind: From Stoic agitation to Christian temptation.* Oxford: Oxford University Press.
This book is excellent for those (social) psychologists who are interested in the history of emotion and therapy. Sorabji discusses the forms of cognitive therapy that the Stoics developed in detail drawing on a vast range of historical texts. He goes on to show how these early understandings of the Stoics were treated and transformed by early Christianity.

3

Enlightenment Philosophies of Emotion

Key Aims

In this chapter we will present some of the key philosophers of the enlightenment, who made significant contributions to emotion studies. In doing so we will:

- Critically introduce how the so called 'age of reason' was also an 'age of emotion'
- Discuss the important rationalist and empiricist debates on emotion
- Look at conceptualisations of emotion in moral decision making practices
- Introduce some influential psychologies which also included important social elements

Introduction

The enlightenment is often described as 'the age of reason'. It is notoriously associated with rationalist philosophers. The new methods of the age of reason instituted a clear break from scholasticism that dominated the medieval period and the associated metaphysics arising from theologically informed philosophies. Although it is often presumed that there is a clear break between 'the medieval', 'the renaissance', 'the modern' or 'the enlightenment' periods of philosophy there is just as much continuity between them, as Copleston informs us,

> We can of course, become the slaves of words or labels. That is to say, because we divide history into periods, we may tend to lose sight of continuity and of gradual transitions, especially when we are looking at historical events from a great distance in time... change is not creation out of nothing (Copleston, 1985: 3)

For example, three out of four so called 'enlightenment philosophers' we discuss below had some form of faith in the divine: Descartes was a professed Catholic, Spinoza was Jewish and retained some belief in a God (although considered heretical by other members of the Jewish faith) and Kant retained notions of a Christian God. These thinkers were not primarily theologians (in the professional sense) but philosophers, a discipline that was emerging as no longer the handmaiden of theology. Philosophy was also becoming more widely read and attractive to the lay person, as it was no longer necessary to write in Latin but the vernacular was now widely used. One of the main distinguishing features of the Age of Reason was the break from the traditional theological metaphysics and scholastic methods that characterised the medieval period to purer forms of philosophy, particularly in relation to the development and understanding of ethical systems. As we shall see, new understandings of emotion (passion) were central to these endeavours. In this chapter we look at two competing epistemologies that were ferociously debated throughout this period: rationalism and its antithesis empiricism. We will also look at what is commonly considered as the synthesis between these two epistemologies.

A useful distinction between the two traditions is to characterise them as using either inductive or deductive methods. Francis Bacon was at the forefront of the rise of inductivism through embracing and valuing the technological advances that would serve science and culture, such as printing, gunpowder and the magnet. For Bacon this was achieved not through Aristotelian physics but through the advancement of the natural sciences. He advocated a new philosophy with the experimental inductive method at its heart. This method went on to influence the empiricist tradition, particularly in Britain. Empiricism regards sense-perception of prime importance to the development of knowledge. This was true for the empiricist, in relation to developing knowledge in the sciences, and was understood as the way that individuals psychologically develop factual knowledge about the world. However, the empiricists regarded this form of knowing as necessarily limited: it could never bring about certainty, but only varying degrees of probability. Indeed, unlike the rationalists, the empiricists were essentially radically sceptical of the ability of the human to obtain knowledge that could be considered absolutely certain. The rationalists, however, tended to agree that certainty could be obtained through deductive reasoning, such as mathematics and geometry. As we will see through this chapter, the empiricists argued that propositions derived through, for example mathematics, do not give us factual information about the world but are tautological, as Hume put it: they are merely relations between ideas.

We begin with two prominent rationalists of this period, Descartes and Spinoza. In looking at the ideas of these two philosophers we think through some of the enlightenment theorisations of how things exist (ontologically) in relation to the social psychology of emotion. Descartes was a central figure in the development of continental rationalism. In his famous book *Meditations on First Philosophy* he devises a radical form of scepticism by discarding all beliefs that cannot be considered as certain to uncover knowledge that can be claimed as certain and axiomatic. This would lead him, he believed, to 'prove' the existence of God.

Obviously Descartes had pretty high hopes! One of the legacies of this endeavour was a conceptual split between the metaphysics of mind and the matter of body, and it is of central interest to us the role that Descartes envisaged emotion played as an integral node of connection between mind and body. Spinoza, whose telling book title is *Ethics demonstrated in a geometrical manner*, is the second rationalist philosopher that we look at. He was relatively opposed to Descartes' ontological dualism and instead proposed a form of monism that brought him to some extremely interesting theories of the passions, which have only recently begun to have an impact on Western thought about emotion. For instance, Spinoza is a key theoretical resource for post-structural theories of emotion (affect theories) (see Chapter 9). After discussing Descartes and Spinoza, we turn to the moral sentimentalist theories of the empiricists with a focus on the work of Hume who was particularly concerned with how emotion played a central role in moral deliberation. We then move on to Kant who is often characterised as vehemently opposed to Hume's moral sentimentalism and advocated a view of ethics that requires one to do away with emotion (rather like the Stoics) in order to become the 'rational being'.

Therefore this chapter illustrates how the enlightenment enabled the emergence of relatively new forms of philosophy and importantly innovative understandings of the psychological workings of the mind (early psychologies) with some additional emphasis on the social. Descartes emphasised the social development of emotion; Spinoza considered emotion as essentially relational; Hume discussed the fundamental importance of emotion in binding people together in ethical systems and Kant theorised the importance of suppressing emotion for societies to develop morally.

Descartes' Little Gland

Descartes suggested that mind and body are separate substances; but while the body is a material (physical) extended substance the mind is a spiritual (metaphysical) unextended substance. This is now known as Cartesian dualism, which has its roots in the early theologies we looked at, where, for example, the soul is seen as separate to the body. Although Descartes used the French term '*émotion*' to define a specific part of his theory, for the main he was writing on the 'passions', and indeed, most commentators since have associated him with a language of passions rather than emotions (although this is slightly misleading as we will see). Nevertheless, Descartes' writings were a significant source of influence throughout the nineteenth and twentieth centuries, particularly through his framing of the relationship between 'body' and 'soul'.

For Descartes, core to passions are the perceptions through which sensory information passes to the soul. The key distinction between the body and soul is that the latter is not a spatially extended substance as it cannot be located in a particular space, either internal or external to the body. And yet, it is central to the psychological experience of the passions, namely the phenomenologically-oriented feeling(s) that arise from the perceptual movements of the body. This was a significant shift from the dominant Aristotelian theories of the passions that preceded Descartes. Rather than dividing the soul up into parts as Aristotle had done (the nutritive, sensitive and intellectual parts), Descartes argued it is 'thinking' that is essential to the soul and therefore living organisms that do not have this capacity, do not have a soul. Hence the only power of the soul is 'to think', so Descartes is able to do away with the meticulous descriptions of the powers of the soul that his predecessors had laboriously conjectured. Thinking for Descartes did not include such functions involved in for example, nutrition, digestion and other bodily movements, but only processes that explicitly concerned consciousness. We may think about digestion, but this is not necessary to digest. The body then for Descartes is a purely mechanical material substance, while the mind is purely spiritual; the latter has the power of independent volition while the former does not (because it is causally determined). The passions then for Descartes are nominally 'perceptions' of bodily motions. These passionate perceptions agitate and 'disturb' the soul in more powerful ways than other forms of perception that he discusses. However, one can still see the trajectory of thought in relation to conceiving the passions being passive as they are considered as being involuntary perceptions of bodily movements. This notion of course derives from Aristotle and was configured by Aquinas.

The question raised by the mind-body distinction for Descartes was; if they are indeed two distinct substances, how do they interact with each other? Descartes suggested that the two substances met in the pineal gland (an endocrine gland seated near the brain stem). '[T]he ultimate and most proximate cause of the passions of the soul is none other than the agitation with which the spirits move the little gland which is in the middle of the brain' (Gross, 2006: 1). The linking of the body and soul through the pineal gland in the brain allowed Descartes to articulate a causal trajectory for the production of passions, in which bodily perceptions move through the body to the pineal gland, at which point they directly catalyse passionate experience in the soul. This process can be two-way in terms of passions reverberating back into bodily movement and producing physical manifestations of passionate experience (e.g. hairs standing on end when experiencing fear).

The Bio-Social Factors

Descartes' theory of the passions relies heavily on biological and social factors. He believed that certain passions can be innate as they are inherited during pregnancy from one's mother, e.g. preference for a particular food. He also posited that an individual's experience of a passion is dependent on the physical characteristics of their brain as well as the balance of 'bile and other humours in the blood, for instance, which affect its temperature and mobility' (James, 1997: 98). The specific manifestation of passionate experience depends not only on these physical charac-teristics, but also how they interact with the social context in and through which they emerge. For instance, if an individual experiences a traumatic association in childhood (e.g. falling from a playground swing), that activity will form a pattern in the brain of fear, which will be elicited every time the child subsequently sees a playground swing. Whilst for other children playing on the swing will be a pleas-urable experience, for the child who fell, it will remain a negative association, which is manifest in the biochemical configuration of the brain.

Therefore, Descartes' theory of passions involves several biological and social elements, and is also individually specific. Passions develop by repeatedly expe-riencing the same bodily movement, producing increasingly strong patterns in the brain, although they can also emerge through 'recollections of the soul' (James, 1997: 100). Such recollections are not 'memories' in a traditional sense, but are dependent on contents of the soul that were produced by past events 'whose only remaining trace is in the body' (James, 1997: 99). Here we see that for Descartes the passions are intrinsically dependent upon potentially complex and changeable configurations of body and soul, which connect in and through the pineal gland.

Although Descartes' mind-body dualism tends to render the passions as that which traverse the two substances, it is only the mind that should be used to perceive clearly and distinctly, and thus should withdraw from the passions and other bodily motions. Hence Descartes thought that knowledge that comes to the mind through the body is unreliable and only reason (the *a priori*) could bring certainty, so Descartes firmly fits into the rationalist school of philosophy. But, and it is quite an important 'but', emotion (as distinct from passion), takes on a different meaning for Descartes, one which is not often mentioned by subsequent portrayals of Cartesian dualism. Thinking that originates in the mind gives way to what Descartes describes as 'intellectual emotion'. Descartes states that for clear thinking one should ignore that which arises from within body, although intellectual inquiry that begins within the mind is accompanied by intellectual emotion that sustains and encourages the inquiry. Intellectual emotion, in turn, gives rise to certain passions such as wonder, desire for knowledge and joy in philosophising. Intellectual emotion, however, has no bodily expression, as it is the passions that it gives way to that are expressed in the body. James (1997: 207) argues that this division is 'uncomfortably' close to Aristotle's division between the sensitive and the intellectual soul (as discussed in Chapter 1). The split between the emotions of the mind and the passions of the body is one that is taken up by Spinoza, but in a distinctly non-Aristotelian theory of the soul.

Spinoza and *affectus*

Baruch Spinoza (1632–1677) was a Dutch seventeenth-century philosopher who was seventeen when Descartes died. Spinoza was heavily influenced by Descartes' philosophy of the passions, and it catalysed his own writings on emotions (which he called affects and passions). Indeed, the categories of passions Spinoza began with were taken almost entirely from Descartes. Spinoza's primary text, which is often cited as 'The Ethics' but was actually entitled '*Ethics demonstrated in a geometrical manner*', was published posthumously in 1677 (it had been ready in 1675 but Spinoza had delayed publishing it as he feared it would be seen as the work of an atheist (Jarrett, 2007)). The Ethics was a substantive piece of philosophical work on the nature of God, mind, body, emotion and ethics. It was written in the context of Descartes' dualistic theory being the primary source of understanding of the human condition, although, as we will see, Spinoza took a different approach than Descartes.

Conatus

Spinoza believed in three basic affects : desire, joy and sadness. (He used the word affect when discussing what we now term 'emotions'. Several translations of 'The Ethics' incorrectly translate *affectus* as emotion, despite the fact that Spinoza never used the word 'emotion'). Desire is the most general and basic affect. He referred to it as 'conatus', which means a general endeavour to prolong, to survive. Spinoza believed that the primary human force was this desire to prolong one's life, to persist. Here we can see that the notion of power is key. To be able to prolong one's life, one needs the power to do so. Indeed, power is central to the definition of the two other basic affects for Spinoza; joy is an increase in one's power, whilst sadness is a decrease. Power is not understood as something used in a hierarchical sense, used by those with it over those who do not. Spinoza's notion of power was more nuanced, a way to define relations between people and objects. For Spinoza, power was the means through which activity was produced. All social activity is seen as being produced through movements of power that lessen and/or increase bodies' capacities for affective activity. In addition to desire, sadness, and joy a range of more complex affects exist, such as anger and fear, which are made up of differing configurations of the three basic affects. Spinoza argues that affects should not be viewed as some form of frailty of humanity, a defect of the mind/body, but actually be seen as 'natural phenomena' (E. III, p 127). This means they are produced in the same way as any other natural phenomena, in terms of having 'causal laws' (E. III, p 127).

Affects for Spinoza are not subject to some notion of 'free will' because they are subject to the causal laws of the natural world. We should note that Spinoza also used the term 'passions', when drawing out a broad distinction between activity and passivity. Affects, which was the dominant term, referred primarily to the body's capacities to act, and changes in those capacities. Passions on the other hand are what Spinoza thinks of as 'passive affects', which can be thought of as 'inadequate' because it is difficult to have a clear idea of the causal relation through which they are formed. Affects then refer to volition and feelings of control, regardless of whether one's power increases or decreases. Passions on the other hand relate to feelings of a lack of control, whereby any change in the body's power, and associated mindful idea, are experienced as caused by something outside of one's control. Hence passions are seen as passive, and relate to the category of sadness, as to be without control is to be sad.

A Dual-aspect Monism

Spinozist theory has been differentiated from Descartes through defining it as a 'dual aspect monism' (James, 1997: 142). This means that Spinoza did not view mind and body as fundamentally distinct substances, but rather as two attributes of a unified substance. He states 'that mind and body are one and the same thing, conceived first under the attribute of thought, secondly, under the attribute of extension' (E. III, prop 2, note: 131). Consequently, Spinoza saw all activity as being 'two-sided'; one side relating to activity of the body and one side to activity of the mind. Neither side can act as a causal force on the other and therefore a clear distinction could not be made on the grounds of either body or mind holding a total position of power over the other. In this sense, Spinoza's theory of affect sought to move on from the dualism core to Descartes, and to do so through emphasising power relations between 'natural phenomena' (which included human bodies), rather than rely on marking out clear boundaries within individuals (i.e. between body and mind).

Affective Change

Spinoza felt that Descartes' ultimate aim was to articulate a theory in which the mind has complete control over the body, and yet for Spinoza, affective change could only be enacted by external forces. Indeed, Spinoza was not particularly interested in physiological factors related to affect, only insofar as they run alongside the operation of the mind. Part of the reason for this is the onus Spinoza places on the pantheist view of a unity of substance, named God. In The Ethics Spinoza states: '[A]ll modes of thinking have for their cause God, by virtue of his being a thinking thing' (E. III. prop 2: 130). This means that bodies cannot cause changes in thought, only God can, through thinking, not the body. Spinoza's dual aspect monism relies on his underlying philosophy of unity, in which he posits one all encompassing nature, of which everything is a part. This is different from Descartes' dualistic rendering of an active and powerful mind controlling the passive 'extended substance' of the body and objects. Spinoza framed this unifying substance as God, meaning very literally that God is all powerful and dominant as everything is a part of the substance of God.

Spinoza's account of affects is more explicitly social than Descartes' theory of passions. As we have seen, core to Spinoza's ethics is the notion that affect is dependent on the relationships bodies have with external objects (which include other bodies). In addition to this, Spinoza argues that external objects can affect people in a variety of ways. An object does not have a single mode of affect, which is then felt by anyone coming into contact with it. Instead, the experience of affect felt by an individual will always depend upon the specifics of the relationship between their body and the external object it interacts with at the given moment in time. The importance of the relational nature of affect comes from the underlying philosophy of one substance (God/Nature) being the only thing that can act as a causal force. If God/Nature is the only substance, from which all other things are formed, then only God/Nature can be framed as 'free'. Here Spinoza differs from Descartes, for whom the mind can act with active free will, particularly with reference to the passive body. Spinoza's single substance ontology means that mind and body are modes of activity that are formed within the single cause of God/Nature. Moreover, if everything is deemed to emerge as an element of the overall single substance of life then every individuation is by definition relational (no one thing can be characterised as having a distinct essence). An individual's being then becomes dependent on the nature and form of the interactions it has with others. An example would be to think about one's feelings about a past memorable event (e.g. child's birthday) being enacted through the re-engagement with objects associated with that time (e.g. specific present or location) rather than purely as an act of cognitive retrieval from 'inside' one's mind.

This is fundamentally what makes Spinoza's philosophy of affect a social one, and much more so than Descartes' passions. Emotions as we understand and categorise them today (e.g. love, hate, fear, anger) are all relational patterns whose existence is dependent on different configurations of passivity and activity, or in Spinozian terminology, increases or decreases in one's power to act. For instance, we may come to love someone or something that in general increases our powers to act (to affect or be affected). On the other hand, we may come to hate something that in general decreases our powers to act. For Spinoza, the three basic affects, along with all their subsidiaries, can be geometrically understood according to their position on a continuum of increasing to decreasing the power to act.

Hume and Moral Sentimentalism

In opposition to rationalist philosophy were the philosophers who suggested that emotions (or passions and sentiments) facilitate moral decision making processes. We focus here on David Hume (1711–1776) who was an empiricist and so believed that all useful knowledge that individuals have comes about through sensual (empirical) experience. More particularly Hume was a 'sentimentalist'. Sentimentalism is a moral philosophy which proposes that moral truths are essentially derived from the senses, particularly through feelings, passions, affect and emotion. The enlightenment's moral sentimentalism did not start with Hume, but he constructed his understanding from a line of British philosophers: the Third Earl of Shaftesbury, Joseph Butler and Francis Hutcheson. It is a tradition that is now quite well known, but perhaps under-appreciated in relation to the enlightenment, which is more often synonymised with 'the age of reason' and its rationalist associates. The sentimentalism of Butler and Hutcheson concentrated on theological notions of how moral senti-ments were placed within human nature by God so that we could fathom through introspection the divine laws sculpted into our hearts. Indeed ethics began to be understood as the examining of the realities of the psychic inner world; in other words, this was an early 'experimental' psychology. This was achieved through identifying the sentiments or rather the sympathy (or com-passion: see Frazer, 2010: 18) that we have for others. Thus not only was it an early psychology but an early social psychology as sympathy was understood as a bridge between the social and psychological, mental states that are shared between individuals: 'Specifically, sentimentalism offers an empirically grounded sociology and psychology of moral and political reflection that focuses on the key social-psychological faculty of sympathy' (Frazer, 2010: 8).

Hobbes and Fear

Pitted against this form of sentimentalism are those that advocated human nature as not being fundamentally benevolent but rather saw humans as driven by selfishness and fear. A main proponent of this thesis was Thomas Hobbes (1588–1679) who was born in England and lived there throughout the civil war. This was essentially a war between Royalists and Parliamentarians, which saw the execution of King Charles I and the establishment of the first Commonwealth of England, headed by Oliver Cromwell. Throughout this period England was a very chaotic place shaped by numerous competing ideologies; for example, Royalists, Parliamentarians, Catholics and Protestants. Hobbes' psychological and political writings were very much influenced by the chaos of this particular period. His view of humanity was that it was 'solitary, poor, nasty, brutish and short'. He suggested that by nature humans are not social creatures but are in need of a strong sovereign state which needed to govern through fear to keep people in line. This he characterised as the Leviathan (a biblical sea monster), a metaphor of a state ruling over its people with the force of fear. Individuals thus needed to enter into a social contract with the state, through which they would give over their freedoms and be given law and life in return. Without a strong government Hobbes believed that humans would lapse into a state of war of all against all.

Hobbes had a mechanistic and materialist understanding of the world and thus psychic functions. The human mind was understood as machine-like, with mental processes simply consisting of movements of matter inside the skull.

Indeed he was very much the empiricist and so conceived of metaphysical substances, like the mind, as being made up of physical events. Hobbes was particularly interested in movement. He was friends with a lot of influential theorists of the time, including Galileo, who suggested that all physical bodies were in motion, including the earth and everything on the earth. All things would carry on moving in a straight line unless some other force was to act upon them. Hobbes' conceptualisation of psychological motivation was also influenced by this theory. He felt that we were driven by the push and pull of motivation in that we are simply driven by attraction and aversion; for example, liking and disliking, loving and hating, joy and sadness. We are driven (attracted) by the objects of our needs and wants, but moreover we are driven through repulsion and ultimately repulsed through the fear of death.

Much of the writings of the early sentimentalists was spent attempting to refute this form of (selfish) empiricism. However, it turned out to be extremely difficult to prove that human motivation was no more than expressions of self-interest. For example, compassion for another's misfortune could be interpreted as the fear that the same misfortune might happen to oneself. Yet the early sentimentalists insisted that conscience is made up of psychological sensations of the mind which are far more altruistic and benevolent and not selfish in the way Hobbes described. Hutcheson went as far as to suggest that not only do we have the five senses but we also have a 'moral sense'. Just as the eyes can see so can our moral sense determine right from wrong. However, this was the seventh sense, as he also advocated a sixth internal sense for beauty (the aesthetic sense).

Post-scepticism

Hume was completely against theological or metaphysical views of human activity. Norton (1993) states that Hume is often regarded as advancing empiricism to its logical and sceptical conclusions. However, Norton goes on to argue that Hume should be better known as a 'post-sceptical philosopher':

> By this I mean to suggest that Hume supposed (a) that the Cartesians (especially Malebranche) and Locke and Berkeley had in fact already taken traditional metaphysics and epistemology to its sceptical conclusions; (b) that these sceptical conclusions had been soundly and validly established; and (c) that the most important remaining task of philosophy, given these well-established and obvious conclusions, was to show how we are going to get on with our lives, particularly our intellectual lives. (Norton, 1993: 5)

The sceptics' philosophical suppositions brought about the notion of no certainty whatsoever. This presents the question, what of morality and civility? For Hume philosophy had failed and he set about attempting to develop a science of human nature upon which all other sciences would rest. Although Hume sided with the empiricism of sentimentalism, he was sceptical of the notion of an inner divine moral sense, and went on to distinguish the theological connotations of Hutcheson's 'moral sense' through the concept of 'moral sentiments'.

Hume's Psychology

Hume began his philosophical endeavour in his two most notable books ('*The Enquiries: Concerning the human understanding and concerning the principles of morals*' and '*The Treatise of Human Nature*') by describing the workings of the 'mental world'; in other words he begins with psychology. In arguing for the importance of starting with psychology, in the *Enquiries* Hume states,

> It becomes, therefore, no inconsiderable part of science barely to know the different operations of the mind, to separate them from each other, to class them under their proper heads, and to correct all that seeming disorder, in which they lie involved, when made the object of reflexion and enquiry. This talk of ordering and distinguishing, which has no merit, when performed with regard to external bodies, the objects of our senses, rises in its value, when directed towards the operations of the mind, in proportion to the difficulty and labour, which we meet with in performing it. And if we can go no further than this mental geography, or delineation of the distinct parts of the power of the mind, it is at least a satisfaction to go so far; and the more obvious science may appear (and it is by no means obvious) the more contemptible still must the ignorance of it be esteemed, in all pretenders to learning and philosophy (EHU. 1. 8)

Thus Hume develops his moral sentimental philosophy by firstly thinking about perception; '[A]ll the perceptions of the human mind resolve themselves into two different kinds, which I shall call the Impressions and Ideas' (T 1.1.1). The differences between these two forms of perception are understood through their liveliness or vivacity. Impressions are usually formed through direct sensual experience while ideas are the recollections of these initial impressions. This, Hume states, does not require much explanation as they are self-evidently (through internal observation) the difference between feeling and thinking, the former being more lively and vivacious than the latter. In this way Hume develops a kind of phenomenological perspective regarding external 'reality' and perceptions. His view is that we cannot know the external world but only our perceptions (sensations and ideas) which are in some way related to external objects but may not completely represent them. His endeavour then was to attempt to explain how we come to 'believe' that our perceptions represent the external world. Norton suggests that Hume, in this way, was attempting to rescue philosophy from scepticism.

Hume goes on to distinguish between simple and complex impressions and ideas. The former are made up of rudimentary senses, for example the greenness of an apple, while the latter (complex) would unite the many attributes of the apple (for example, colour, taste, shape etc.). Thus complex impressions and ideas are made up of the simple. Hume's first proposition in the *Treatise* states: '[T]hat all our simple ideas in their first appearance are deriv'd from simple impressions which are correspondent to them, and which they exactly represent' (T 1.1.1). This proposition is the foundation through which Hume develops his empiricism. Thus there is nothing in the mind (ideas) that has not come about firstly through the impressions (senses).

The Association of Ideas

Hume argued that these ideas in the mind are *causally bound together* through the principles of association, in other words he advocated what we today in psychology call *associationism*. The causal connections (associations) between the ideas were: resemblance, contiguity, and cause and effect. The principle of resemblance can be thought of as a trigger for relating one thing to another. For example, you may meet a woman that *resembles* in some way your mother, thus the associated idea of your mother will be brought to mind. The principle of contiguity suggests that when one idea is followed by another idea, these two ideas are then often bound together and will follow each other associatively on future occasions. So, for example, if one often has cheese with crackers the idea of crackers is likely to bring forth the idea of cheese. The principle of cause and effect suggests that we often look for causes of events. For example, if someone has died we often want to know the cause of death which in turn leads to thoughts about causes of deaths in general.

Reason Enslaved to Passion

Hume's famous dictum was that '[R]eason is, and ought only to be the slave of the passions, and can never pretend to any other office than to serve and obey them' (T 2.3.3). This saying was of course quite controversial at the time, as Hume himself points out, and as we have to some degree (albeit critically) attested to in the previous sections of the book that,

> Nothing is more usual in philosophy, and even in common life, than to talk of the combat of passion and reason, to give the preference to reason, and to assert that men are only so far virtuous as they conform themselves to its dictates. Every rational creature, 'tis said, is oblig'd to regulate his actions by reason; and if any other motive or principal challenge the direction of his conduct, he ought to oppose it, 'till it be entirely

subdu'd, or at least brought to a conformity with the superior principle. On this method of thinking the greatest part of moral philosophy, ancient and modern, seems to be founded; nor is there an ampler field, as well for metaphysical arguments, as popular declamations, than this suppos'd pre-eminence of reason above passion. (T 2.3.3)

Hume's full account of the passions can be found in his second book in the *Treatise*. He understands them as 'secondary or reflective impressions', that is they are not 'sensory impressions' but arise from them. In other words, he states that they arise from 'all the impressions of the senses, and all bodily pains and pleasures' (T 2.1.1) which essentially emanate from the body. The associationism that we had just discussed was concerned with the association of ideas (rather than impressions). Hume suggests that changeableness is essential to human nature and 'Tis difficult for the mind, when actuated by any passion, to confine itself to that passion alone, without any change or variation' (T 2.1.4). For example '[G]rief and disappointment give rise to anger, anger to envy, envy to malice to grief again...' (T 2.1.4). Unlike ideas that are associated by resemblance, contiguity and causation, impressions are only associated through resemblance. Hume also divided the secondary impressions between those that are calm or violent. As the distinction suggests, the violent passion will be stronger in its felt intensity than the calm passion. This is different to its strength, which is the degree to which it can influence decision making. Strong passions may be calm but have the ability to overcome a violent passion. Importantly Hume stresses that it is not reason which curtails a passion, but it can only be quashed by another passion: 'Nothing can oppose or retard the impulse of passion, but a contrary impulse' (T 2.3.3). Here we particularly see how Hume argues against the rationalist conjectures that reason has pre-eminence over passion. Although he concedes that reason can discover why we might feel the pleasure or pain that comes from an impression, it 'alone can never produce any action, or give rise to volition, I infer, that the same faculty is as incapable of preventing volition, or of disputing the preference with any passion or emotion' (T 2.3.3). Hume additionally argues that passions are not in and of themselves irrational (he uses the term 'unreasonable'). He employs quite a convoluted argument here to stress the point that reason draws on ideas, and passion is induced by secondary impressions; and so impressions, unlike ideas, do not have a 'representative quality' of other objects.

A passion is an original existence, or, if you will, modification of existence, and contains not any representative quality, which renders it a copy of any other existence or modification. When I am angry, I am actually possest with the passion, and in that emotion have no more a reference to any other object, than when I am thirsty, or sick, or more than five foot high. 'Tis impossible, therefore, that this passion can be oppos'd by, or be contradictory to truth and reason; since this contradiction consists in the disagreement of ideas, consider'd as copies, with those objects, which they represent. (T 2.3.3)

For Hume then, passions cannot be unreasonable, or associated to reason as they are of a completely different order. For a passion to be considered unreasonable Hume argues, it must be accompanied by a false judgment, and in which case it is the judgment that is unreasonable and not the passion. One of the examples he uses to illustrate this is '[T]is not contrary to reason to prefer the destruction of the whole world to the scratching of my finger' (T 2.3.3). Strength of mind then, is not the ability to reason, but 'implies the prevalence of the calm passions above the violent' (T 2.3.3).

Sympathy and the Psychosocial

It is through Hume's understanding of sympathy and its relation to the self and others that we begin to see a genuinely 'social' aspect to his philosophy. Hume remarks that,

> No quality of human nature is more remarkable, both in itself and in its consequences, than that propensity we have to sympathize with others, and to receive by communication their inclinations and sentiments, however different from, or even contrary to our own. (T 2.1.11)

Indeed sympathy is so remarkable to Hume that he understands it as conferring to individuals a sense of self that importantly comes from shared societal passions.

> A good-natur'd man finds himself in an instant of the same humour with his company; and even the proudest and most surly take a tincture from their countrymen and acquaintance. A cheerful countenance infuses a sensible complacency and serenity into my mind; as an angry or sorrowful one throws a sudden damp upon me. Hatred, resentment, esteem, love, courage, mirth and melancholy; all these passions I feel more from communication than from my own natured temper and disposition. (T 2.1.11)

Hume suggests that in everyday activity we witness various signs in the conversations, countenance and behaviour of others which give us an idea of the possible related passions. When infused with sympathy the idea becomes so lively and vivacious that it actualises as an impression and hence 'the very passion itself, and produce an equal emotion, as any original affection' (317). This form of sympathy is bound up with what Hume declares are impressions of ourselves that are always in some way present in consciousness. Therefore the more closely we are related to the other the more vigorous the sympathetic impression will be.

> The stronger the relation is betwixt ourselves and any object, the more easily does the imagination make the transition, and convey to the related idea the vivacity of conception, with which we always form the idea of our own person. (T 2.1.11)

Thus, sympathy for Hume, is a sort of *emotional contagion* that we catch from others, a kind of resonance of our experienced self with theirs.

> As in strings equally wound up, the motion of one communicates itself to the rest; so all the affections readily pass from one person to another, and beget correspondent movements in every human creature (T 3.3.1).

Hume argues that because of our human likeness to each other, the idea of the passion of another leads us to think about ourselves. A recollection occurs of a memory of when we experienced such a passion and/or we remember our own vulnerability to it. This is in some ways similar to the argument for selfish passions that Hobbes put forward. However, unlike Hobbes' Leviathan form of social contract, for Hume it is sympathy or fellow feeling, which binds society together and generates social cohesion. However, although sympathy is aroused for friends and strangers, the stronger the relationship and likeness to the other, the more it is likely to resonate with the self. This tends to be understood in terms of blood ties and kinship, but he also discusses how people of similar temperament will be drawn together: 'that people of gay tempers naturally love the gay; as the serious bear an affection to the serious' (T 2.2.4). People of likeness then are drawn together in this way and can create factions which Hume remarks are some of 'the most visible, though less laudable effects of this social sympathy in human nature' (EPM. 5.2.35). Penelhum remarks on how Hume's 'deep hostility' towards the rationalist tradition of his time, 'is the result of its [rationalism] being a theoretical force that can only encourage self-distancing from the sources of emotional nourishment that make us what we are' (1993: 143).

Kant's Synthetic *a priori*

The German philosopher Immanuel Kant (1724–1804) was a pivotal figure of the enlightenment. He is often quoted as stating that Hume woke him up from his 'dogmatic slumber' (PFM 4: 260) and is registered in the annals of philosophy for bringing together the two opposing epistemologies of rationalism and empiricism, which is often termed his Copernican revolution. We saw that Descartes and Spinoza argued for the importance of *a priori* knowledge (knowledge that is independent of experience, intrinsic to the human mind), such as mathematics or Plato's 'innate forms', as being the only reliable (true) knowledge that can be known. Reacting against this stream of self-contained rationalism were the empiricists who were predominantly from the British Isles. While the rationalists had downgraded the role of the senses in obtaining true knowledge, the empiricists, such as Locke, Hume and Berkeley were more sceptical of the reliance on *a priori* knowledge such as mathematics. Mathematical formulations were argued by the empiricists as merely tautological: one plus one is simply a definition of two. In this way they argued that mathematics (the *a priori*) do not tell us anything about the world. Dixon notes that it was John Stuart Mill in 1859 who named the two schools of thought the *a priori* and the *a posteriori* schools (2003: 99). Logicians understand the difference between the two forms of knowing as the distinction between deductive (the *a priori*) and inductive reasoning (the *a posteriori*), and of course we have seen some of these philosophical debates mirrored in differences between Plato (the rationalist) and Aristotle (much more the empiricist).

Kant supposed that both the rationalist and the empiricist traditions overlook the fact that humans have fundamentally limited capacities in regard to what they can know with their minds and senses. Humans are constrained by a number of what Kant described as categories through which the mind works: substance, quantity, quality, relation, place, time, position, possession, action and passivity. Human knowing is understood by Kant to be fundamentally limited by these categories, all that it presents of the world is a mere 'flawed representation' of a particular thing, which disallows one from apprehending the thing itself. What we can know about the world that comes through the senses then is what he called the *phenomenal* world and the way things are (in themselves) is what Kant called the *noumenal* world, that world is 'transcendental' and cannot be registered in human experience, it is beyond the grasp of the experiencing self, despite the efforts of the rationalists. The *noumenal* consists of metaphysical things such as universal law and free-will, which are not determinable by the physical world.

Kant had very particular beliefs about free will and the ability of humans to rise above the *phenomenal* world of nature and enter into the *noumenal* world through acts of free will; he believed it to be self-evident that we sometimes have free choices. If we didn't believe that we had free choices then we would never be able to apply praise and blame to others. It is through this free will that moral choices are made. This is where Kant provides a key link between the *noumenal* and *phenomenal* worlds in what he terms the synthetic a priori. If morality is real, Kant argues, then human freedom must also be real. In this sense humans are not only subject to the laws of the *phenomenal* but can also share in the *noumenal* world. So Kant argued that the 'human will' is subjected to two influences. Firstly, human beings have desires, inclinations and emotions which are related to their physical nature; for example, these may be desires to be happy. Secondly, as rational beings, humans have the ability to recognise the laws of freedom despite their desires, inclinations and emotions.

The Rational Being

To illustrate this ability, Kant developed an ethical system concerned with rational decision-making practices that are devoid of emotion. Kant suggested in order to make good moral judgments our reasoning ought to be free from emotion.

Emotional responses were seen to represent the lower side of human nature and would simply hinder moral judgments; these judgments he proposed, would be far better if they were made through a state of pure reason. In order to act in this way one must become what Kant famously denoted as a 'rational being'. Rational beings will be, according to Kant, subject to an absolute moral law, this distinguishes them from other material things in the world which are subject to the laws of nature. Kant distinguishes physics, which is concerned with objects that are subject to the 'laws of nature' (the *phenomenal*) and ethics, which is concerned with objects that are subject to the 'laws of freedom' (the *noumenal*).

Kant suggested therefore that all rational beings who follow the laws of freedom will recognise the universal law of morality which he called the 'categorical imperative' in accordance with how they *ought* to act. Thus the imperative is a command to constrain the inclinations and emotions, to act objectively from reason. Kant's law of the categorical imperative stated that one should '*Act only in accordance with that maxim through which you can at the same time will that it becomes a universal law*' (MM, 4: 421). A maxim is a general principle according to which an individual acts; for example a maxim could be, 'I will steal items from my neighbour'. But one should only have a maxim if the person desires it to become a universal law; so, if you adopted the above maxim you would be willing to allow your neighbour to steal items from you. However, Kant's second formulation of the categorical imperative included the maxim that no one should be treated simply as a *means* but as an *end* in themselves, in other words, the rights of others must be respected.

For Kant, human beings are only truly free if they are able to recognise the categorical imperative out of rational duty, rather than sentimental *inclination*. Moral worth can only be applied if acts are conducted through duty, by restraining the desire and emotion. For example, Frazer (2010) explains that Kant draws attention to two different kinds of philanthropists: one who is motivated by sympathetic inclinations, the other by duty. The former may act from benevolent feelings and perform what is considered to be a good deed. Kant suggests that such a person 'deserves praise and encouragement but not esteem, for the maxim lacks moral content, namely that of doing such actions not from inclination but *from duty*' (G 4:398). Kant supposes a person who may be shrouded in grief who lacks inclination to perform such moral actions and a person who may be born with very little capacity to be sympathetic towards others. People in these kinds of states who morally act purely from duty rather than sentimental emotion are of high moral worth.

Sympathy's Infection

However, Frazer argues that the story that is typically told of Kant's understanding of emotion (as described above) fails to consider the influence that the sentimentalists before him had on his theories of ethics. It is only in the later period of his life that he came to reject sentimentalism, before this he was very much camped within this tradition. Indeed Frazer argues that the above is often understood as Kant 'making a normative case against the sympathetic sentiments here or urging us to extirpate such soft feelings from our psyche' (2010: 115). But this is apparently not the case, Kant was concerned with free will, and he presumed desires and emotions, even if benevolent, are not under wilful control and so activity arising from them is not of moral worth. In other words, emotion and the like are reactions that are caused by a chain of events in the *phenomenal* world, while duty comes from the laws of freedom arising from the *noumenal*. Indeed Kant stated that 'evil consists in our will not to resist the inclinations when they invite transgressions' (RBR: 6:59, footnote). But that is not to say that Kant totally condemned moral acts that derived from the sentiments, indeed they can be instrumental in developing the good will, if the inclinations are towards morally right activity; but these cannot be the grounds of morality as they are unreliable. The morally determined will, however, should cultivate the inclinations (this notion is similar to Augustine's that we looked at in the previous chapter). This can occur through pitting contrary inclinations against each other, in this way the inclination against the moral law can be weakened.

Contemporary scholars are somewhat puzzled by this aspect of Kant's work as it seems to run against his categorical imperative to morally act through duty. Sherman (1990) and Frazer (2010) suggest that Kant uses inclination (or more specifically, sympathy) here as a kind of fall-back motivation for moral acts when the motive for duty fails, just so long as it is not necessary to do one's duty. Yet it is still quite difficult to square this, as if the motive for duty has failed then surely it does become necessary? Kant answers this through stating that it is the wisdom on nature's part to provide humans with sympathetic inclinations so that they 'could handle the reins provisionally, until reason has achieved the necessary strength' (APV 7:253). And yet he also states that although sympathy may alert one to, for example, help 'a man sitting in distress', but if a person can be of no practical help to the person in distress, Kant suggests that it is better to be like the Stoic, stating '[W]hat is it to me? My wishes cannot help him' (LE 27: 421). Sympathy in such a case, Kant stresses, would be useless, so it is better to be indifferent. He goes as far as to suggest that sympathy in such a case can actually be harmful, one then allows the self to be open to sympathy's infection: 'I let myself be infected by his pain (through my imagination) then two of us suffer, though the trouble really (in nature) affects only one' (MM 6: 457). Kant even goes as far as to suggest that sympathetic feelings, for others who claim to be in need, can be manipulated easily, particularly for those who are considered subject to overpowering sympathetic feelings. Again Kant uses the notion of the form of causation one can be subject to in the *phenomenal* world, to imply that the beneficiary then acts on pathological impulses rather than appealing to reason (Frazer, 2010: 127).

Affects and Passions

Frazer suggests that it is important to distinguish between the two terms of 'affects' and 'passions' in Kant's psychological writings.

> Neither of these Kantian terms of art bears much of a relation to what we commonly call 'affects' or 'passions' in the English of the twenty first century, in the German of the eighteenth, or in any Western language before or since. To the contrary ... the turbulent experiences of sudden emotions that he calls 'affects' are more commonly termed passions in the Latin Christian traditions, while the calm and reflective phenomenon that Kant calls 'passion' is more commonly termed *affectus* or 'affection.' Perhaps this is why a distinction so central to Kant's rejection of reflective sentimentalism has been so widely misunderstood. (2010: 128)

Of course the distinction that Frazer describes here would appear to be odd in the light of the discussed differences between *passion* and *affectus* of this and the previous chapter: *affectus* being of a higher order than passions according to the theological texts of the medieval period. Affects in Kant's sense then are those feelings that tend to determine people to act in ways that disallow reflection. Kant suggests that skilled orators may elicit the affects of their audience 'to move people like machines' (CJ 5:328, footnote). In this way affects are rather like diseases which infect people and incapacitate them. It is rather difficult to see, however, how Kant supposes that one can avoid being affected by *affectus*; although he quotes Stoic *apatheia* as being 'a sublime moral principle' (APV 7:253). While the affects work in small but strong bursts, it seems that the passions, according to Kant, occur over a longer period. In this way passions allow for more reflection. For example, an affect may give way to a fit of anger, while the associated passion would give way to brooding, vindictiveness and hatred. Not only then do they differ to affects in relation to duration but also to the involvement of reason. This is where Frazer argues against the likes of Nussbaum who characterise Kant as portraying emotion (or in this case passion) as wholly impulsive, animalistic and non-cognitive. A passion for Kant 'takes its time and reflects no matter how intense, to reach its end' (APV 7:252).

Social Passions

Importantly Frazer adds that passions do not arise only through the natural causal order but are social. Although there are 'natural' (innate) passions which Kant states are 'the inclinations for freedom and sex', he calls these 'burning passions (*passiones ardentes*)'. There are also a second order of passions which are socially constructed, which he calls 'cold passions (*passiones frigidae*)'; these are 'ambition, lust of power, and avarice, qualities which are not linked with vehement affectus but with the persistence of a maxim meant for a certain purpose' (APV 7:267–8). Of course Kant here is suggesting that the social passions are linked to reason (a maxim) and not affect (vehement affectus) while the natural passions are only linked to affectus. However, it is worth noting that Kant suggests that they only *appear* or 'seem' to be tied to reason and are in fact 'inclinations of delusion':

> Since passions are inclinations concerned merely with the possession of means, and since all inclinations have to be satisfied that concern this purpose directly, passions seem to manifest characteristics of reason. Particularly, passion appears to imitate the idea of a faculty which is closely linked with freedom, by which alone those purposes can be attained. Possessing the means to any desired ends, however, reaches much farther than the inclination directed at a single inclination and its satisfactions. Therefore they may also be called inclinations of delusion. The delusion consists in equalizing the mere opinion of someone regarding the value of a thing with the actual value of the thing. (APV 7:270)

Conclusion

What we have attempted to draw out in this chapter are some of the nuanced ways that emotion and reason are theorised by the protagonists represented here. They are often presented in texts as developing theories as either fixed within the rationalists' traditions, wherein reason is of primary epistemological importance, or in the case of the sentimentalists, as advocating the opposite. Of course this is the case, but only to a degree. The psychologies that each of these theorists develop allow for both forms of deliberation to play a part. For example, in both Descartes' and Spinoza's philosophies they advocate the primacy of reason but additionally stress the important role of 'intellectual emotion' and '*affectus*' respectively. Even Kant, albeit ambivalently, discusses how some passions incorporate a rational element and indeed that sympathy could at times be used in moral reasoning. Additionally Hume's account of associationism could be considered a form of reasoning, one which is integral to his psychological understanding of emotion.

These micro-psychology oriented conceptualisations of emotion also feed into their more socially aware macro views of structuration. We see Descartes concerned with the dynamic relation of developing the right forms of intelligent emotions that required social habituation. Similarly *conatus* for Spinoza requires forms of socialisation in what can only be described as a form of behaviourism, wherein society should reward and punish socially acceptable and unacceptable desires. Hume of course saw emotion as 'the' central node in the structuring of human relations that make up society while Kant saw, to a large degree, nothing good coming out of a society that was ruled by emotion.

Many of the discourses that have come out of these philosophies are still prevalent today. That is not to say that they started in this era. Hopefully the reader will be able to see how these have been prevalent throughout the history of emotion studies but take on nuanced forms. For example, the ascent of mind over emotion is not something that started with Descartes nor did he completely advocate this. These forms of simplistic dichotomisations tend to get caught in discourse (language) and go on to inform subsequent thinking, conceptualisations, policies and everyday practices.

Many of the contemporary ethical systems that have developed are based within the Kantian tradition. The main governing bodies in psychology (e.g. APA, APS and BPS) either explicitly or implicitly adopt a Kantian perspective on ethics. These are rule-based systems otherwise known as deontological ethical systems. Yet there are contrary opinions that can be seen as stemming from sentimentalism. Of particular note are feminist critiques which put forward a *context-respectful approach*. Held states that rather than judging action through abstract rules, there should be more of a focus on 'caring, empathy, feeling for others, being sensitive to each other's feelings'. She adds that all these 'may be better guides to what morality requires in actual contexts rather than abstract rules of reason, or rational calculation' (1993: 223).

FURTHER READING

Reading the primary sources of this epoch is a lot easier as the authors tended to write in the vernacular. As he was a native English speaker, Hume's books, such as *A Treatise of Human Nature* and the *Enquiries Concerning Human Understanding*, are extremely accessible and a joy to read. Although of course Descartes' *Philosophical Works* have been translated into English as has Spinoza's *Ethics* and Kant's *Critique of Pure Reason* (among his other works). To be more specific we would recommend the reading of either of Hume's works (mentioned above), Descartes' *Discourse on the Method* and Spinoza's *Ethics*. Kant's writings are perhaps a bit more inaccessible. It is also worth noting here that some of the English translations of these works often lack precision. For example, we had some challenges attempting to distinguish what some translations were referring to when reading Spinoza'a Ethics. Translations sometimes use the term 'emotion' when Spinoza denotes the more nuanced terms of 'affectus' and 'passion'. These have very important differences as can be seen in Kant's rather controversial use of these terms.

Frazer, L.M. (2010) *The Enlightenment of Sympathy: Justice and the moral sentiments in the eighteenth century and today*. Oxford: Oxford University Press.
As the title suggests, Frazer discusses in detail the development of sentimentalism. His analysis converges on Hume but looks at precursors and later developments. We have drawn in this chapter on some of his unique insights into Kant and his lesser known sentimentalist background. Frazer additionally looks at how sentimentalism has influenced the contemporary social sciences and political practice.

Prinz, J.J. (2007) *The Emotional Construction of Morals*. Oxford: Oxford University Press.
This is another good read that addresses arguments that flourished throughout the enlightenment period concerning moral decision making processes and emotion. Prinz offers some very good commentary on Hume's and Kant's ethics and offers some interesting insights of his own.

4

The Role of Emotion in the Development of Social Psychology as a Discipline

Key Aims

In this chapter we will critically discuss the emergence of early social psychological understandings of emotion. In doing so we will:

- Develop an emerging trajectory of social psychological thinking regarding emotion from late nineteenth to mid-twentieth century psychology
- Detail the importance of emotion in the work of key social psychological theorists (McDougall and Lewin)
- Identify the emerging relations between early social psychological theories of emotion and group psychological thinking

Introduction

The previous chapters have discussed a range of theories and philosophies of emotion that speak to social psychological approaches to emotion. In this chapter we seek to focus on the emergence of psychology as a distinct discipline and explore the role that emotion played in this. We will see that some of the foundational thinkers of psychology at the time were very interested in emotion, with some well known figures (e.g. William James, Walter Cannon) featuring heavily in psychological histories of emotion. We will discuss these, before moving on to cover the more specific emergence of social psychology itself as a distinct sub-discipline. Here the work of McDougall is important. The chapter ends by emphasising the importance of Kurt Lewin as a social psychological thinker of emotion, a point not commonly made in other histories.

The topic of emotion has been a core concern for psychology since its emergence as a discipline in its own right in the mid to late nineteenth century. The context from which psychology emerged revolved around mental and moral philosophy, in which concepts of mind, bodies and mental function were core concerns. As we saw in Chapter 3, theories of the passions had long been theologically-oriented. With the advent of the Scientific Revolution a focus on secular theories emerged, with Scottish philosophers as key early developers. During the period (1800–1900) two significant writers in the history of emotion published theories that were to be very influential on psychological accounts of emotion in the discipline's formative years. The first of these was Thomas Brown (1778–1820), who is credited with introducing the term 'emotion' to mainstream theories of the human condition in his 'Lectures on the Philosophy of Mind' (1820). As noted, the first significant aspect of his theory was adopting the term emotion in place of the previously commonly used 'passions' and 'affections'. It is not clear why Brown felt this was important, although it may well have been useful for distinguishing his (secular) theory from the theologically-oriented accounts of passions and affections.

The 'Peculiar Vividness of Feeling'

Brown was an admirer of the growing success of the physical sciences as knowledge-producing disciplines, and sought such success himself in developing theories of mental activity. He believed that he could develop a theory of emotion that adhered to the scientific criteria advocated by the predominant scientific theories of the time, namely Newtonian physics and Bacon's 'Novum Organium' (Dixon, 2003). This meant categorising emotion as multi-faceted, breaking it down into component parts, categorising them, and then attempting to map their interactions. Brown's main system of the mind involved the categories of sensations, intellectual states/thoughts and emotions. The latter two he believed were 'internal affections', with sensations seen as 'external affections'. This model presented emotion as one of three primary facets of the human mind. With his model Brown sought to expand previous theories that had relied on a notion of 'active powers' to define passions and affections. For Brown emotions were, 'by definition, a category of passive (rather than active), non-intellectual feelings or states (rather than actions of a power or faculty)' (Dixon, 2003: 124). Brown's position was that emotions are not wilful reasoned acts, as they do not emerge from a position of total freedom of choice. Instead 'will' refers to the prevailing of a particular emotion, sensation or passion. This is not dependent on a form of morality, which would mean that a wilful decision is by definition a morally 'right' one.

It is important to note that even though Brown produced a comprehensive classificatory system of emotion it still lacked a clear definition of the term. He stated that '[T]he exact meaning of the term emotion is difficult to state in any form of words' (Dixon, 2003: 125). It is perhaps through the influence of Brown on the second key emotion thinker of the time, Thomas Chalmers (1780–1847), that the closest to a definition of emotion can be found. In discussing emotions Chalmers stated: '[T]hey are distinguishable both from the appetites and the external affections, in that they are mental and not bodily – though in common with these, they are characterised by a peculiar vividness of feeling which distinguishes them from the intellectual states of mind' (Chalmers, 1853: 346). This rather interesting phrase 'a peculiar vividness of feeling' is perhaps as close to 'putting emotions into words' as was possible at the time. It captures the significance of emotion as a mental activity through framing it as 'vivid' whilst also positioning it in a discourse of 'feeling'. Chalmers shared with Brown the idea that emotional activity was not the result of wilful reasoned voluntary action, believing instead that it emerges through involuntary processes outside of the intellectual mind that come to be understood retrospectively. Chalmers exemplifies this point through a comparison between visual perception and emotion. We involuntarily perceive a colour as red, it is not a wilful act. Similarly, emotional reactions (e.g. fear) are felt involuntarily. However, in some ways these 'psychology' inspired developments would have done well to consider some of the ancient and medieval theorisations that we looked at concerning the first and second movements. These were more sophisticated in that they distinguished between the involuntary nature of the feeling but they considered the actual emotional response and to some extent expression, could be cultivated through the will and the intellect. But there was likely a motivation not to refer to these sorts of theologically informed texts.

Brown and Chalmers are now seen as important figures in the history of emotion, and were heavily influential on the development of early psychological theories of emotion.

Evolutionary Psychology

The second half of the nineteenth century saw the establishment of a scientific psychology of the mind, in which emotion was a core category. Theories drew variously on physiological and evolutionary accounts of the mind, although they shared a concern to not rely on theological doctrine. Key figures at the time were Herbert Spencer (1820–1903), Alexander Bain (1818–1903) and Charles Darwin (1809–1882), and despite it being Darwin who became the most well known of the three by some margin, it was at the time Spencer and Bain whose ideas on emotion and mind were more influential. Spencer, Bain and Darwin all shared a vision of a scientific psychology based on physiological and/or evolutionary principles. The influence of Brown, as well as Chalmers, was clear, with Spencer, Bain and Darwin all drawing on a terminology of emotions made significant by Brown and Chalmers. At the time the concepts associated with the mind tended to be well established categories such as will, sensations and intellect. These have long been used in theological and moral philosophy, and in that sense the new psychological accounts were very much working on the classificatory territory of Christian thought. The introduction and spread of classifications of emotion allowed psychologically-oriented theories to carve out a new space, with clear links to the more traditional categories.

Bain, Spencer and Darwin were committed to an agnostic account of the mind, one built upon the theoretical and methodological principles of existing sciences, e.g. evolutionary biology and neurophysiology. Methodological influences from the sciences included utilising observation, induction and classification. This is not to say that Bain, Spencer and Darwin developed identical projects. Indeed, Bain was more focused on a theory of mind in relation to the nervous system. Darwin, as is well known, was an evolutionary theorist, whilst Spencer took theoretical resources from both. They were all committed to an 'agnostic monism' that did not rely at all on theological writings or theory. Furthermore, there was no desire to rely on a dualistic account of mind-body, in which the material body was seen as some kind of tool or instrument of the mind (Dixon, 2003). Instead, the influence of Spinoza could be seen in the underlying use of a 'dual-aspect monism' in which mind (subjectivity) was seen as one side of an event, the other side of which was the physical or 'objective' side (this ontology has been influential on recent theories of affect covered in Chapter 9). So it was not the case that subject and object were framed as distinct entities with their own inherent properties, but rather as the two constituent elements of events.

Despite the adherence to a dual-aspect ontology Bain, Spencer and Darwin tended to focus disproportionately on the physical side in their writings. This may well have been due to the force of their desire to portray their theories as scientific. Emotions were viewed as the subjective 'side' of objective processes taking place in the nervous system. In doing so analysis would primarily focus on changes in the nervous system as key to emotional activity. One of the issues with this imbalance towards the 'objective' side is that it opens up the possibility that they were suggesting an epiphenomenalistic account of the mind, in which mental activity is seen as a 'by-product' of the physical activity of the body. The danger with this is that instead of the body being seen as a tool for the mind as in a dualistic account, the mind is seen as a secondary layer of bodily processes, akin to a subsidiary. This was not something Bain, Spencer and Darwin were accused of at the time of their writing.

During this period Spencer offered the first major evolutionary theory of emotion, in which traditional associationist ideas that emotional activity could be reduced entirely to an individual's specific mental experience, as we saw in the previous chapter Hume advocated, were disregarded. In their place were the evolutionary principles of heritability, which framed emotion as formed from the collective evolutionary past. This meant that free will was not possible for Spencer, as no individual could act with a complete freedom due to being bound to a certain extent by collective heritability. Spencer did not believe that emotions were either entirely cognitive or sensational. Instead, he offered an aggregate model that held emotions to be 'added elements' of relations between multiple sensory processes. The more sensations connected the stronger the emotional feel, which could also occur through increased longevity of evolutionary past.

Despite sharing the same dual-aspect ontology as Spencer, Bain did not advocate an evolutionary account of emotion. Instead, he recognised only physiology and phrenology as scientific approaches to psychology. Bain's adherence to physiology and phrenology meant he developed a scientific psychology in which emotions could only be classified according to observable objective bodily activity. The embodied 'side' of the emotion had to be witnessed for it to be categorised. Moreover, rather than base his theory on a set of emotions (e.g. love, hate, fear, shame etc.) Bain included thirteen topics of emotion, including 'emotions of harmony and conflict, emotions of relativity, emotion of terror, tender emotions, emotions of self, emotion of power, irascible emotion, emotions of action/pursuit, emotions of intellect, emotions of sympathy and imitation, ideal emotion, the aesthetic emotions, the ethical emotions' (Dixon, 2003: 157). The manifestation of any of these 'topics' would occur through the activity of multiple sensations happening simultaneously. In this sense, Bain's theory of emotions was also an aggregate model. No single emotion was deemed to have a unique set of inherent properties. Bain was key to making emotion a core psychological category, in addition to will and intellect. Emotion was not seen as a subsidiary of either of the previous two, which had previously been thought of as the two main categories of the mind.

We have intentionally not talked about Darwin in detail here as he features in Chapter 6. Having laid out the early foundations of emotion in psychology, we now turn to the development of psychology of emotion through the first half of the twentieth century, beginning with one of the biggest names, William James.

William James' Emotional 'mind stuff'

William James (1842–1910) has commonly been cited as one of the first early twentieth century thinkers to develop a scientific theory of emotion. James (1890) advocated an *epiphenomenalist* approach to psychology, in which mental events are seen as side effects of physical processes of the body, e.g. the nervous system. For James, the relationship is a one way causal one; body states affect the mind, but the mind in turn does not affect the body. In the logic of physics, this notion made sense, in that only a physical event can cause another physical event. Consequently, James understood feelings as arising causally through physiological and neurological changes that came about through the perception of something stirring. In other words the feeling of these bodily changes that occurred due to the perception is what James referred to as the emotion. The example that James used to illustrate this emotional process, an illustration often used by emotion theorists, is the perception of a charging bear. James (1884) asked the question: do we run from the bear because we are afraid or are we afraid because we run? The common sense answer would be that on perceiving a charging bear, the perception induces physiological changes equated with fear and then the person runs. However, James suggested that the perception causes the person to run and the feeling of the bodily movements induced through the running activity is the emotion: fear in this case. So it is not the case that the emotion (fear) causes us to run, but rather that we fear because we are running – emotion is directly related to bodily activity. In this way the mental state or feeling is the outcome of the physiological response but the mental state or feeling does not in turn affect the body. Critics at the time argued James misplaced emotions by placing them *after* bodily action, suggesting instead that a person runs *because* they fear the bear. James though preferred to think of bodies as having 'pre-programmed' responses (that developed through evolutionary processes) to aid survival. Such processes were not emotional as they required nothing from the 'mind' to make them happen. Instead, emotions were seen as the *perception* of the bodily movement, which can only come *after* the fact. Therefore, for James, emotions are the perceptual aspect of bodily movement. Before him the traditional (common sense) view of emotion had been that emotions are motives for action. Motives, in this respect, are conceived of as the thoughts, cognitions and perceptions which move one to act.

James sums this up when stating:

> I now proceed to urge the vital point of my whole theory, which is this. If we fancy some strong emotion, and then try to abstract from our consciousness of it all the feelings of its characteristic bodily symptoms, we find we have nothing left behind, no 'mind-stuff' out of which the emotion can be constituted, and that a cold and neutral state of intellectual perception is all that remains (1884: 193)

Emotion then is not to be located 'in' the mind for James. Without bodily 'affectations' there can be no emotion, only cognitive perceptual and intellectual work. This is not to say that we cannot have an 'idea' of emotion that is not embodied, but this would not be an actual emotion for James. The necessity that emotions were grounded in physical manifestations meant that certain affections were no longer seen as emotions. For example, anything that could not be seen, due to being rendered purely mindful was categorised as cognitive or intellectual, rather than emotional. In this sense, the passive emotions seen in the earlier writings of Descartes and Spinoza (e.g. shame, grief) were not so immediately emotional for James. This supports the claim that James' theory was ephiphenomenal, if you consider his argument that emotions can only be categorised if a physical expression occurs as meaning that emotions are consequently a 'by-product' of physiology. However, a counter claim could emerge that suggests that James' view of the physical manifestation of emotions was stronger than suggested when classifying them as 'by-products'. For James it seems that emotions are not merely by-products but are the actual behavioural activity.

What is clear is that James' theory (which became known as the James-Lange theory[1] as it was very closely associated with a similar model proposed by Carl Lange) was the subject of significant criticism at the time (and since) in that it was reductionist and potentially materialist in nature. James attempted to counter such accusations by stating his belief in subjective 'aspects' of emotion, and yet was unremitting in his argument that emotions were manifest in physiological activity. Dixon (2003: 214–5) provides a neat summary of the central criticisms levelled at James' (1884) *What is Emotion?* paper. We will not repeat them all in detail here, but to summarise they included: James' theory did not allow emotions to be distinguished from non-emotions in that they did not account for conscious awareness of bodily changes that are non-emotional (e.g. digestion); James did not map different patterns of bodily change to specific emotions; and the notion of 'bodily changes' is far too generic. Nevertheless James' theory was hugely successful and despite a raft of published criticisms, often in journals James published in (including *Mind*), it was not until Walter Cannon's refutation in the 1920s that James' theory lost its place as the primary scientific theory of emotion.

In any other era James' theory of emotions may not have been as successful. The context in which he was writing can be argued to have played a significant part in his success. Psychology was emerging as a professional academic discipline that took influence intellectually from the earlier Scottish and English mental and moral philosophy, which theoretically underpinned experimental work emerging in a range of new psychological laboratories, initially in Germany (e.g. Willhelm Wundt) and then in greater number in America. James was working at the centre of this new experimental discipline, and as such, his theory became one of the first 'products' of the new experimental psychology. His success was also aided by the sheer simplicity of his theory, which fited so well with the *raison d'être* of laboratory science; emotions are manifest in physical bodily activity – this can be observed and 'tested' in experimental psychology laboratories.

Walter Cannon's Emotional Thalamus

Walter Cannon was critical of James' theory because he felt its physiological focus lacked detail and rigour. Whilst Cannon was fully committed to physiological understandings of emotion, he felt that the physiological basis of emotion was neurological, and specifically involved the thalamus. Cannon argued that the body's predisposition for post-stimulus activity was generally the same across all emotions, and therefore further detail was needed of the emotional process and how it differentiated across different categories of feeling. Emotions needed to be more than just the perception of these predisposed general motor responses. Given the speed with which information is passed through the body Cannon argued that emotions occur almost simultaneously with bodily changes.

Cannon's theory fitted well with the developing scientific criteria by which psychology was being judged, externally and internally. The link to specific parts of the brain gave Cannon's theory strong currency in psychology. He was able to present experimental findings that he claimed demonstrated that James' theory misrepresented the relationship between stimulation and emotion. Cannon's work led him to argue that emotions do not *follow* bodily movements, but that brain processes are independent of associated physiological activity. This meant that there does not need to be somatic stimulation prior to emotional response. Cannon's criticisms of James formed part of a larger body of alternative approaches, of which his was held to be one of the main alternatives to the dominant theory of James.

The Classification of Emotion

It should be noted that although we are highlighting the prominence of the work of James and Cannon, their work was emerging within a context of broader psychological thinking on emotion (for a useful review see Ruckmick, 1936). For instance, Willhem Wundt was working on a model that saw emotion as the accumulation of a set of single feelings into a collective feeling with higher intensity than the single feelings themselves (Ruckmick, 1936). This was a time when a number of attempts were made to develop a workable classificatory system of emotion. Wundt proposed a broadly tridimensional system based on '(1) the quality of the feelings which make the emotion, (2) the relative intensity of these feelings, and (3) the temporal pattern of their occurrence and their temporal changes' (Ruckmick, 1936: 116). Here a distinction is made between feeling and emotion, with the latter seen as a collection of the former. A weighting towards so-called 'unpleasant' emotions existed for Wundt, which can be potentially explained by the relative ease with which such feelings draw attention. Wundt's system is also notable due to the lack of biological referents it incorporated. Instead emotions were categorised according to the dimensions of intensity, quality and durability. This is because Wundt generally used introspection as a method for measuring psychological phenomena.

Alongside the system of Wundt came Mary Calkins' (1863–1930) classification of emotions based on her model of a 'psychology of the self'. Calkins kept the notion of a conscious individual at the heart of her thinking on emotion. Calkins based her classificatory system on a relational model in which emotions emerge through the connections the conscious self has with others, humans and objects. In this sense, her model of emotions acts as an important precursor to later social psychologies of emotion. Indeed, Calkins' system demarcates social and non-social emotions, with the former a broader category. For Calkins the bulk of emotional activity occurs through the 'self' engaging in relations with others. Although Calkins very much retained the notion of an individual conscious self as the centre of her model of emotion, its focus on relations, and explicit use of the term 'social emotions', means it was an important influence on psychological thinking that during the early parts of the twentieth century led to the emergence of a demarcated 'social psychology', in which emotion was a core topic of theoretical and empirical analysis.

William McDougall's Introduction to Social Psychology

During its early years psychology quickly broadened with key areas of research emerging, one of which was social psychology. Given the prominence of debates regarding emotion at the time, it unsurprisingly formed a central topic of interest for early social psychologists. Indeed, one of the earliest social psychology books, William McDougall's (1908/1960) *An Introduction to Social Psychology* focused on emotion and closely related material in over half of the book. Whilst the prominent theories of James/Lange and Cannon sought to articulate the physiological aspects of emotion, and increasingly looked to the brain to do so, McDougall developed an approach that was more attuned to the external aspects of emotional activity.

The relevance of social forces to emotional experience is strong. A vast swathe of emotional activity relates to clearly social factors (Manstead, 2012). For instance, fear when public speaking, falling in love, jealousy of a sibling, hatred for a political group etc. The reality of people's emotional experiences is in the main intrinsically linked to social context. Despite this, early psychological theories sought to frame emotions as primarily physiological, and that such processes should be the analytic and theoretical focus for psychology. McDougall (1908/1960) did agree to an extent that biological activity is important for emotional experience. For instance, he believed that emotions were instincts, based on a physiological predisposition for certain actions. In this sense emotions for McDougall were automated biological reactions. He also categorised 'primary' and 'complex' emotions, and classified the biological responses accordingly. Primary emotions were ones that were non-human specific. McDougall identified seven primary emotions: fear, disgust, wonder, anger, subjection and elation (also referred to as positive and negative self-feeling), and tender emotion. For McDougall all affective states that were understood as emotions derived from aggregates of the primary emotions, along with feelings of pleasure and pain. Complex emotions were defined as occurring when 'one or more of the primary emotions, developed within a system of a strong sentiment, plays an essential part' (1908/1960: 130).

Pseudo-instincts

In addition to the above, McDougall named a number of 'pseudo-instincts' that he argued were important to social life, including sympathy, imitation and suggestion.

These pseudo-instincts differed from the primary and complex emotions due to the non-specificity of their outcome. For McDougall primary emotions would always have a 'specific quality and a native impulse towards some specific end' (McDougall, 1908/1960: 77). They were assumed to be innate and therefore their activity could be defined according to a set of inherent properties. The pseudo-instincts were not classified as innate, and therefore the outcomes of their excitation were variable and diverse. When discussing imitation McDougall wrote 'the modes of action in which this tendency expresses itself and the accompanying subjective states are as various as the things or actions that can be imitated' (1908/1960: 77). The social credentials of McDougall's theory start to strengthen when discussing the pseudo-instincts, with their excitation dependent on interaction between at least two people. Clear sociological influences can be seen, particularly when McDougall drew out Gabriel Tarde's writing on suggestion and sympathy, and used it as a foundation for his work on imitation. McDougall spends considerable time in his *Introduction to Social Psychology* articulating his theory of primary emotions, and yet at the beginning of Chapter 5 states '[W]e seldom experience the primary emotions discussed ... in the pure or unmixed forms in which they are commonly manifested by the animals' (1908/1960: 104). This is an important stage in McDougall's theory. The importance and influence of evolutionary theory on his writing is clear, with nearly all his categories of emotion discussed in relation to instincts, along with their cross-species relevance. However, McDougall does go on to make a clear distinction between animal and human emotional activity in relation to primary and complex emotions. In essence he claims that humans do not experience emotions in pure form, only in aggregated form. McDougall initially frames this distinction in terms of neural underpinnings of emotional, and sentimental, organisation. Drawing on the work of A. F. Shand, McDougall argues that there is a subtle yet important distinction to be made between primary emotions and sentiments, with particular reference to the way such terms are used in common speech.

Common terminology related to emotions played an important part in the development of social psychological theories. Words such as love and hate were often thought of amongst the public as emotional forms. McDougall shifted this focus somewhat as he felt that things became too complex and unwieldy when trying to understand how love and hate, for instance, were formed from primary emotions. Instead of thinking of them as complex emotions McDougall felt that Shard's notion of sentiment was of greater value. In doing so, McDougall could develop a map of emotional activity that incorporated primary emotions, sentiments, along with their neural dispositions (1908/1960: 108).

The aim was to develop a structural account of emotional activity that was based on neural activity, and yet accounted for social experience (e.g. expressions of love and hate). The social aspects of emotional experience are key to the presence and operation of sentiments. According to McDougall sentiments are developed through habitual association with objects that excite a particular emotion. Repetition increases the strength of associations with objects, which over time develop into sentiments, such as love and hate. The reason McDougall sought to call such habitual feelings sentiments rather than emotions was because not all instances of sentiment result in a change in physiology. The importance of the biological underpinnings of emotion theories of the time meant that McDougall grounded his primary and complex emotions in physio-logical excitation. Consequently, the ability that a sentiment has to be felt without direct physiological change (e.g. to have a constant love for someone), meant it could not be classified purely as an emotion.

The insistence that emotions are non-species specific meant McDougall's early social psychological theory of emotions owed a lot to the earlier evolutionary orientation of Darwin. McDougall was less bound to the proposed biological underpinnings of emotion though. Indeed he was explicit in arguing that emo-tion could not be reduced to mental activity in entirety, and therefore was not a cognitive entity. McDougall's view was more socially relevant in positing that emotions are 'a mode or quality of experience' (McDougall, 1920: 315). In this sense, emotions were not inherently different from other forms of psychological activity, e.g. memories. McDougall drew on Spinoza's idea of *conatus*, the striv-ing towards an end, and suggested all psychological activity followed this pattern. The social stance of his work was further strengthened through placing significant importance on context. McDougall argued that emotional experience depended on the situation in which it was produced. So, two people facing the same stimulus can have different emotional experiences.

When McDougall published *The Group Mind* in 1920 (which is discussed in the following chapter) the initial concern was to address the relationship(s) between individual and social activity, as he was clear that 'we cannot foretell the behaviour of the group from our knowledge of the individuals alone' (1920: 21). The concept of emotion was central to his writings on 'group mind', as he had observed how emotional responses to stimuli can spread very quickly through crowds. Existing concepts were present, such as the notion of a 'cultural con-sciousness', used to define the phenomenon of shared emotional experience. McDougall felt that for a viable 'collective psychology' to emerge the notion of a collective consciousness had to be addressed. In discussing the notion of a col-lective consciousness McDougall drew on Comte, Spencer and Schaeffle and their attempts to define society as an organism. Thus we can see that the early social psychological attempts to think beyond the individual were shaped by the existing biological framing of individuals, and a desire to apply these beyond the individual to society as a whole. Spencer was wary of pushing the theory of organism too far away from the individual due to the danger it may pose in terms of the ethics of individual responsibility. Comte and Shaeffle were more convinced by the perceived benefits of a detailed theory of society as organism.

McDougall's analysis of the theory of collective consciousness initially rested on the question as to the impact of 'the complete subjection of the individual to the State' (1920: 36). The idea of a collective consciousness at the time was based on a model in which individuals in society are defined as the individual cells that constitute the organism of society. McDougall had a number of issues with the theory as it stood at the time. Firstly, it required consciousness to operate at two levels, the individual and society. This did not apply to individual organisms as cells were not deemed to be 'conscious', and yet with a societal model in which individuals are defined as cells, it would need to apply. Secondly, McDougall could not fathom what and where the parameters of a cultural consciousness would be. Were they country specific, continent specific or more localised? These questions had not been adequately addressed in existing theories of the time. These issues led McDougall to consider that 'at the present time no such evidence of a "collective consciousness" had been brought forward, and that there is no possibility of any such evidence being obtained before the principles of social psychology have been applied far more thoroughly than has yet been done to the explanation of the course of history' (1920: 39).

McDougall did not completely rule out the idea that at a future point evidence of a collective consciousness may emerge, but that at the time it was too ambiguous and insufficiently detailed to be useful. He instead focused on the more theoretically localised notion of 'the emotional characteristics of simple crowds'.

McDougall's crowd psychology was premised on the notion that emotions can spread readily through crowds, although the potential for this was dependent on the kind of emotional activity at work. The simpler emotions (e.g. anger, fear) were seen to spread more easily than more complex subtle forms (e.g. jealousy, shame). Furthermore, certain kinds of emotion lend themselves to flowing through crowds, specially when elicited by stimuli that have relevance to the crowd as a whole. For instance, national pride at a significant achievement (e.g. success of national sports team). Consequently McDougall did not believe that all emotional responses possible for individuals could transition to groups. Indeed, he did not believe that all possible manifestations of emotion in crowds could be experienced by individuals themselves. Despite not advocating a theory of collective consciousness, McDougall did believe that a notion of 'collective mind' could be of value, '[I]n the absence of any "collective consciousness" we may still speak of collective minds; for we have defined a mind as an organised system of interacting mental and psychical forces' (1920: 47). Such a definition could be applied to organised and structured groups (e.g. nation states), although not to what McDougall termed 'simple crowds'. Collective minds in common crowds were thought of as featuring a set of common characteristics, namely a diminished sense of responsibility, increased suggestibility, rashness of thought and action and fickleness (McDougall, 1920). These features of crowd behaviour were said to be specific to the crowd, with individuals not exhibiting them once they had left the group.

As *The Group Mind* develops, McDougall works to set out the conditions for group and collective development, whereby the organisation and management of collective emotion become more sophisticated, and as such, the group's ability to be emotionally active increases. Five conditions are said to be necessary to improve the emotional intelligence of the crowd; group longevity, awareness of group purpose, interaction with other groups (e.g. rivalry), shared values of members, and finally a clearly defined set of roles for members (McDougall, 1920). McDougall looks to established institutional groups to work through his theories, with particular reference to the organisation and the function of armies as highly organised groups. Key to McDougall's writing on collective emotions in and through different types of group is the distinction between the will of all and general will. Taking his definition from Rousseau, McDougall referred to the former as constituting the will of all individuals, and the latter as a shared corpus of wilful intention, that by definition cannot incorporate the entirety of all individuals' volition. The relationship between individual and collective will McDougall marks out as important in terms of the degree of emotional significance a group can achieve.

McDougall was not convinced by the concept of a cultural consciousness, however, as he felt it relied too much on the idea of conscious awareness of others' responses, and consequently not enough on the potential instinctive nature of emotional activity moving through individuals and groups.

As this section has demonstrated McDougall's social psychology of emotion was predominantly an evolutionary-influenced instinct based model. In *The Group Mind* McDougall develops his theory and its potential social utility through extensive discussion of organised forms of group and collectives in society, and how they shape the emotional disposition of nation states. McDougall's work can be seen to have had a significant impact on emotion research in social psychology (as evidenced by the fact that his *Introduction to Social Psychology* is still in print). We pick up on group psychology, the crowd and the notion of the group mind in the following chapter. However, it was not the only 'scientific' approach to emotion and social psychology emerging in social psychology's formative years; there was also a movement born in Germany, and influenced by theoretical physics and developed through Gestalt psychology.

Lewin

During the 1920s, an alternative approach to that of evolutionary and instinct based theories of the mind and emotion emerged in Germany. It was known as Gestalt psychology, and shared with the evolutionary approaches the desire to develop a scientific psychology that utilised existing scientific theory in classifying and defining psychological phenomena. It could be distinguished from evolutionary and instinct based theories though by its use of theories and assumptions from physics, rather than biology. A key part of this was the concept of the 'field', in which a phenomenon is defined not by a set of individual properties, but by the organisation and interaction of constituent parts of a defined 'field'. Put simply, field theory is based on the notion of needing to analyse at the level of the whole, rather than the individual parts of that whole. It was the focus on the 'whole' that led to Gestalt theory being seen as particularly relevant to social psychology. Indeed its main theorist at the time, Kurt Lewin (1890–1947), has often been referred to as the 'father of social psychology'.

Despite the differences in their scientific influences, Lewin's Gestalt theory shared with McDougall's instinct approach an advocation of the experiment. Lewin believed that a scientific psychology needed to begin with a sophisticated and rigorous theory, which could then be tested through experiments. Lewin also shared a desire to engage with the key psychological theories and concerns of the time, namely personality, emotion, will, and action. These needed to be studied from a clear and structured theoretical start point, with a specific empirical prob- lem in focus. Lewin was clear about the need for rigorous theory, but did not advocate abstract theory-only approaches. The empirical focus of his approach can be seen in one of the first overviews of Gestalt psychology, which states:

> the experimentalist must prove the correctness of his (sic) hypothesis by an appeal to a psychic event occurring in a perfectly concrete situation and at a definite moment of time within a certain individual and a pre- scribed environment. (Hartman, 1935: 203)

In this sense, Lewin was concerned to develop a scientific approach to psychol- ogy, rooted in the logic of physics, which was grounded in studies of people's everyday lives:

> But an experimental investigation of needs, of action, or of emotions cannot be carried out without taking into account the characteristics of the person, his momentary state, and his psychological environment. (Lewin, 1936: 5)

Lewin saw emotions as a core psychological category, along with perception, sensation, action, will and thought processes (1936), to be studied according to the principles of 'field theory' and through experiment. Lewin developed the notion of the 'psychological life space', which incorporates the situation of the person and their environment:

> [I]t is not thought then that the environment of the individual serves merely to facilitate or inhibit tendencies which are established once and for all in the nature of the person. One can hope to understand the forces that govern behaviour only if one includes in the representation the whole psychological situation. (1936: 12)

For Lewin emotional activity experienced by an individual is always the product of the relationships between the individual and environment in a particular life situation, in which emotion is not dependent on a dualistic model of either person or environment, but on the specific relationship(s) between the two at the given time. Here the influence of field theory from physics can be seen clearly, in terms of the psychological life space understood as greater than the sum of the individual constituent parts. The key principle is that the field needs to be analysed as a whole, rather than by its individual elements. This was a difference from the preceding instinct theories that were based on the biological evolutionary principles that defined emotional activity in terms of individual bodies, with little consideration of the environment. Lewin states: '[E]very psychological event depends upon the state of the person and at the same time the state of the environment' (1936: 12). Here we can see how social Lewin's Gestalt-influenced theory was. He moved away from the individualistic basis of evolutionary instinct based theories such as McDougall's towards a theory that was premised on the idea that all psychological activity was socially situated, and analysis had to account for the environmental pattern of experience. He even developed an equation for this, namely $B = f(PE)$ where B is behaviour, P is the person, and E environment. Therefore behaviour is always the function of the interaction(s) between individual and environment, and needs to be analysed in its relational form, not reduced down to a set of prefigured constituent parts.

Lewin sought to analyse the intricacies of everyday life spatially, and he believed this could be done through segmenting behavioural activity into analysable chunks, which he called 'units of action' (Lewin and Gold, 1999). Any given temporal situation can be broken up into its respective units of action, which, crucially for Lewin, can be studied experimentally. Lewin gave the example of the behaviour 'entertaining guests' being broken up into the units of action; 'calling for friends, riding in the car to the picnic place, ordering lunch, eating lunch, taking a walk, etc.' (Lewin and Gold, 1999: 199). Alongside units of action can reside 'emotional units', which can be ordered differently and follow related yet distinct flows. For instance, one emotional unit may encapsulate several units of action, e.g. with the entertaining guests example the emotional units of 'strangeness and formality' and subsequently 'easiness and familiarity' may exist across several of the units of action. For Lewin emotion runs through activity and behaviour, as a core relational concept, even in situations that may not traditionally be seen as particularly 'emotional'. Furthermore, behaviour is not defined as emotional in entirety, but rather as multi-layered, with emotion being one of the layers. For Lewin, its prominence is entirely dependent on the specific context under focus.

Lewin then offered us a thoroughly social account of emotion, one which has not featured very often in psychological histories of emotion. It provided an alternative scientific model of psychology to the instinct-based theories dominating in the United States and United Kingdom at the time. One of the reasons that did not help Lewin's theory become more prominent in psychology was that circumstances resulted in Lewin's research being severely disrupted, namely the rise of Nazism and the Second World War. The budding Gestalt psychological laboratories in Germany were disbanded as Lewin and his colleagues sought refuge in the United States. There they were firmly in the territory of evolutionary psychology, and consequently the possibility of Gestalt psychology becoming mainstream subsided. Nevertheless we think that Lewin's account of emotion is a valuable part of the history of emotion theory in social psychology. We argue that it can be seen to mark out a distinct social psychology of emotion that does not rely on evolutionary or biological theory, which distinguishes it from the work of McDougall, whose founding social psychology has featured more prominently in histories of the discipline. Instead of thinking about possible underlying evolutionary and/or biological processes at work in the manifestation of emotional experience and activity, Lewin was more focused on the organisation of emotional work, in which distinctions between individual and collective become less important and obvious. This work can then be seen as an important antecedent to psychologies of the group, and the role of emotion therein.

Conclusion

In this chapter we have identified the role that emotion played in the theoretical work through which social psychology developed from the mid nineteenth century. The aim was to demonstrate that emotion acted as a catalyst for psychological thinking, the study of which was shaped significantly by the desires at the time to produce psychological theories that would be seen as scientific. Hence we saw that the psychological accounts of emotion were biased towards the physiological (e.g. Spencer, Chalmers, Brown). The interest in emotions continued throughout the establishment of psychology as a distinct discipline, and through the later emergence of social psychology as a demarcated sub-discipline. In this chapter we have sought to draw out the importance of emotion in the development of social psychology as a recognisable subdiscipline of psychology. Histories of social psychology tend to focus on what are now commonly seen as the core concepts, e.g. attitudes, inter-group processes etc. Emotion was commonly not seen as having 'social' characteristics, and therefore does not feature in many social psychology texts. Through the study of the work of McDougall and Lewin we have argued that in fact, emotion was a core concept for formative social psychological theories, even if it does not feature in the headline coverage of such work.

Extending emotion into a core phenomenon through which social psychological elements of human experience are understood, rather than only being a physiological characteristic, is an important part of developing our social psychology account of emotion. In discussing this we have pointed to the ways that focusing on emotion in the history of social psychology can lead us productively towards other collectivist accounts of psychology. In the next chapter we develop this in terms of group psychology and how emotion featured in thinking about the organisation and management of group activity.

Note

1 For Ruckmick (1936) it was the James-Lange-Sergi theory, as he included the Italian psychologist Sergi, whose existence has been largely written out of history of emotion since, with the term James-Lange used most commonly.

FURTHER READING

Lewin, K. (1936). *Principles of Topological Psychology*. New York: McGraw Hill.
As we have discussed in this chapter, although emotion does not feature throughout Lewin's principles of topological psychology, we argue that it has a considerable amount to offer social psychological understandings. Particularly in relation to placing a primacy on relationality and the connections we have with others when defining and analysing emotional experience and activity.

McDougall, W. (1908). *An Introduction to Social Psychology*. [33rd edition 1960] London: Morrison and Gibb.
McDougall's seminal introduction to social psychology is still in print over 100 years since its first edition. This provides a very useful insight into the embryonic social psychological thinking regarding emotion, particularly in relation to the socialisation of earlier evolutionary instinct based theories of emotion. This is well worth a read.

5

Group Psychology and Emotion

Key Aims

In this chapter we will critically discuss theorisations of emotion and the group. In doing so we will:

- Illustrate the development of the emotional contagion thesis and the crowd
- Discuss social identity theories of crowd activity
- Review some of the contemporary and post-Freudian theories of group processes and emotion

Introduction

In this chapter we pick up on some of the group-mind theories of the previous chapter and look at how a variety of theorists have used and critiqued them. We see familiar discourses of emotion emerge in various guises that have run through the book; most particularly its relation to the irrational and the uncontrollable. Emotional contagion is of particular significance to this discourse, wherein emotion almost becomes disease-like, something that infects the mind and determines subsequent behaviour. A critique of the contagion thesis of group behaviour that we offer in this chapter is concerned with social identity. We start with a very brief overview of relevant aspects of Freud's psychoanalysis to situate his particular understanding of emotion. Here we see Freud draw on the influential crowd psychology of Gustav Le Bon, as well as McDougall whom we looked at in the previous chapter. Then, after discussing some of the social identity theories and their critique of the instinct conceptualisations of crowd psychology, we look at some contemporary views of emotional contagion. The chapter concludes with the post-Freudian group psychologies of Bion and Foulkes.

Freud's Drive Theory

Freud does not dedicate particular sections of his works to specifically discussing what emotion is, but it plays a central role in his theories of the psyche. He rarely uses the term 'emotion', preferring the German psychological term *'Affekt'* (affect). Hillman points to several ideas which are significant in relation to psychoanalysis and Freud's conceptualisations of *Affect*. Freud notes the significance of the idea (representation) in relation to emotion; he looks at emotion as a kind of physiological quantum; he notes a double function of emotion – that it be felt in consciousness and that it internally alter the body (Hillman, 1992: 57). Hillman suggests that it is no easy task to summarise Freud's view of emotion. Indeed as we may know, Freud's concepts concerning psychoanalysis go through a vast number of adaptations as does his understanding of affect. In this section we will draw out some of the important aspects of Freud's concepts in relation to affect (although we will not have time to discuss them all in detail).

Let us just remind ourselves of some of the central associated concepts that were put forward by Freud. Freud firstly developed a topographic model of mind in his notorious book 'The interpretation of dreams' (Freud, 1900) which consisted of the three systems: conscious, preconscious, and unconscious. These systems can be related to two general psychic processes. Firstly the unconscious system was related to 'primary processes' which are determined through the 'pleasure principle'. These are non-verbal mental processes which attempt to avoid unpleasure (*Unlust*) and gratify wishes. The preconscious and the conscious systems were related to 'secondary processes' which are mental processes related to delaying gratification, which are determined by the 'reality principle'. Each of these processes is concerned with the distribution of 'mental energy' which arises in the body. Conflict emerges between these two systems as one system operates to discharge the mental energy and the other to delay the discharge. Freud's theorisations of mental energy drew on a constancy principle. This principle stresses that the psychic apparatus work to keep stimulation to a minimum, as close to zero as possible. Thus quiescence (a low level of psychic activity) is pleasant and excitation (a high level of psychic activity) is unpleasant. The neural system was therefore conceived of as seeking to rid (discharge) itself of mental energy that causes tension.

Freud found that the topographic model did not sufficiently account for his clinical observations and other theoretical considerations (for example, the development of a social conscience), which led him to develop the structural model of mind. The id, ego, and superego divisions of the mind, represented in the structural model, were generally both determined by the mental energy of the body and external reality. It also harboured a more complex understanding of the drives (sometimes referred to as *instinct* or *trieb*, a discussion that we will not enter upon here (see Bettelheim, 1982) which now incorporated both life and death drives associated with love and aggression respectively. Each drive is seen by Freud to 'express itself in terms of affect and in terms of ideas' (Laplanche and Pontalis, 1988). The affect is seen as the qualitative expression of the quantity of the drive's mental energy. Positive affects (associated with pleasure) accompany the gratification of the drives and negative affects (associated with unpleasure) accompany the inhibition of the drives. However, it is not that simple, as of course Freud adds that when we act in accordance with the superego, by effectively channelling the id impulses in socially acceptable ways, we may also experience positive emotions and pleasure. When we violate social norms and act on the id impulse which was initially for pleasure, we then feel pain from the guilt and shame which may come directly from moral forces in the external world or from the internalisation of these moral forces in the superego.

Affect and Idea

Above we mentioned a distinction between ideas and affect. Ideas for Freud are rather like memory traces that are attached to affect. Key to the notion of repression is that there is some form of separation between the idea and the affect. It is the job of psychoanalytic therapy to align the affect with the memory-trace (idea). Freud obviously was more concerned with early childhood experiences (mainly those of a traumatic nature) which were repressed. However, we often use such mechanisms of suppression and repression in everyday life. For example, we may find ourselves sexually attracted to somebody that we know we shouldn't be (a friend's partner for example). Because of the taboo associated with this affection, we are likely to feel anxious; this Freud called 'signal anxiety'. These anxiety signals are used by the ego as a signal to initiate defensive activity. For example, they facilitate the repression or suppression of the unwanted ideas and affects. However, we may find ourselves acting rather strangely around that person; this can be either more or less conscious. The signal anxiety also elicits the help of particular defence mechanisms, such as 'reaction formation'; that is, we may act-out opposite forms of behaviour. In the case of being sexually attracted to someone we ought not to be, using the reaction formation defence mechanism, expressions of dislike towards this person can manifest, for example by avoiding them in conversation etc. Over a period of time these defence mechanisms which try to manage the affects associated with unacceptable impulses can build up in intensity and feedback to further distort the individual's perception of reality.

Displacement and projection are also important processes in relation to repressed mental energy. The repressed mental energy continues to circulate in the mind. It often then finds a safe outlet through projecting this onto another person. For example, if one has repressed anger in relation to one's mother, this anger then could be projected onto another individual female who is neither the mother nor the self. One therefore sees the repressed anger in the character or behaviour of the other and one does not associate this with the self. Sublimation is also another means through which one can re-channel mental energy of an unacceptable impulse in creative ways. In Freud's models therefore the affects (emotions) that are usually repressed are predominantly anxiety and guilt;

however, these can be transmuted into different affective feelings and expressions through the ego defence mechanisms.

Freud's Group Psychology

One particular area that Freud wrote about that is of interest to social psychology scholars of emotion, was his understanding of 'emotional contagion' detailed in his influential book entitled 'Group Psychology and the Analysis of the Ego'. Freud suggests in this book that the individual when in a group (or according to a footnote the term 'group' is used for the more complex German term *Masse* and Le Bon's term *foule* which translates more correctly to crowd (1919: 1, footnote 1)) he or she feels, thinks and acts in a manner which is quite different when in isolation, in other words they acquire the characteristic of 'a psychological group' (1919: 6). Freud asks three fundamental questions that he attempts to answer in this paper:

> What is a 'group'? How does it acquire the capacity for exercising such a decisive influence over the mental life of the individual? And what is the nature of the mental change which it forces upon the individual? (1919: 6)

Freud begins this by looking at Gustav Le Bon's seminal work on what is termed 'the group mind'. Le Bon suggests that the psychological group is formed of heterogeneous elements which when combined create a new being with different characteristics: 'exactly as the cells which constitute a living body form by their reunion a new being which displays characteristics very different from those possessed by each cell singly' (Le Bon cited in Freud, 1919: 6). However, Freud notes that Le Bon does not go on to explain what it is that unites the people together. What Le Bon does suggest is that it is the *unconscious mind* which emerges as a motivating force of the individual in the group. However, the unconscious that Le Bon refers to is quite different to Freud's. Le Bon assumes that the characteristics of the unconscious mind are mainly inherited 'from generation to generation, which constitute the genius of race' (Le Bon cited in Freud, 1919: 6). Thus a form of racial unconscious emerges. However, more in step with Freud, he states that through the group mind the individual acquires 'a sentiment of invincible power' (Le Bon cited in Freud, 1919: 9) by yielding to instincts that would otherwise be kept under control. Because of the anonymity of the individual within the group, the sentiment of responsibility disappears. For Freud this process provides the conditions through which repressions are allowed to be thrown off, paving the way for the unconscious instincts to emerge; in other words, the superego (conscience) no longer constrains the id. Freud then turns to look at Le Bon's understanding of the enhanced *suggestibility* of individuals within the group that occur through *contagion*. Le Bon states that it is difficult to explain but easy to identify: '[I]t must be classed among those phenomena of a hypnotic order' (Le Bon cited in Freud, 1919: 9). For example, in this state the individual is no longer in control of his or her own acts but is under the influence of suggestion, as someone who is hypnotised. Additionally the feelings of the group are 'very simple and very exaggerated' and give way to extremes; for example suspicion becomes certainty and antipathy to furious hatred (Le Bon cited in Freud, 1919: 9). Although Le Bon stresses that the individual within the group will succumb to 'cruel, brutal and destructive instincts', and the individual under the influence of suggestion is capable of high achievements, such as selflessness and devotion to an ideal. The group, like 'children', 'neurotics', and 'primitive people' is subject to the magical powers that are ascribed to names and words and give way to illusion over truth. Indeed, the picture that Freud paints of the group through the work of Le Bon, very much mirrors his own psychoanalytic account of the unconscious. Freud then looks elsewhere in the early twentieth century group psychology literature to substantiate his group psychology thesis. For example he extensively discusses McDougall's view of the group,

> its [the group's] behaviour is like that of an unruly child or an untutored passionate savage in a strange situation, rather than like that of its average member: and in the worst cases it is like that of a wild beast, rather than like that of human beings. (McDougall, 1920: 45)

Emotional contagion is envisaged as occurring through the perception of the signs of an emotional state (1920: 45) which induces automatic processes essentially giving rise to the same emotion in the perceiver. In an earlier book of McDougall's (1908/1960), wherein his primary thoughts on emotion and the group mind can be found (*An Introduction to Social Psychology*, which we looked at in the previous chapter), he describes what later is understood as 'emotional contagion'. It was not called emotional contagion at this point, but defined as a form of human sympathy, similar to the form of sympathy that we looked at when discussing Hume and the sentimentalists (Chapter 3). McDougall states,

> A merry face makes us feel brighter; a melancholy face may cast a gloom over a cheerful company; when we witness the painful emotion of others, we experience sympathetic pain. (1908/1960: 81)

McDougall then, in a footnote, gives an interesting example of sympathetic pain. He states:

> Shortly after writing these lines I was holding a child in my arms, looking out of the window on a dark night. There came a blinding flash of lightning and, after some seconds, a crash of thunder. The child was pleased by the lightning, but at the first crack of thunder she screamed in terror; immediately upon hearing the scream, I experienced, during a

fraction of a second, a pang of fear that could not have been more hor-
rible had I been threatened with all the terrors of hell. I am not at all
disturbed by thunder when alone. This incident illustrates very well two
points – first the sympathetic induction of emotion by immediate
instinctive reaction to the expression of emotion of another; secondly,
the specific character of loud noises as excitants of fear. Regarded as
merely a sensory stimulus, the flash of lightning was far more violent
than the thunder; yet it proved no fear in the child. (McDougall,
1908/1960: 81, f1)

Importantly, however, Freud makes the additional point: 'The most remarkable
and also the most important result of the formation of a group is the "exaltation
or intensification of emotion" produced in every member of it' (Freud, 1919: 24).
Freud particularly notes McDougall's point that there is an unreserved surrender-
ing to the passions which is experienced by the individual as pleasurable.

This [crowd formation] is for most men an intensely pleasurable experience; they are, as they say, carried out of themselves, they feel themselves
caught up in a great wave of emotion, and cease to be aware of their
individuality and all its limitations; that isolation of the individual,
which oppresses every one of us, though it may not be explicitly formulated in his consciousness, is for the time being abolished. (McDougall,
1920: 24)

Indeed, the greater the amount of people perceived to be experiencing the emotion, the stronger the automatic process of contagion. This mutual interaction is
understood as forming a sort of feedback loop which intensifies the emotion of
the group. However, why this is the case is not answered for Freud in both Le Bon
and McDougall's accounts. Freud thus goes on to ask the particular question of
why do individuals imitate emotional activity in the group? Suggestibility in and
of itself is not a good enough answer for Freud.

Libidinal Ties

Freud then institutes one of his chief psychoanalytic concepts, the libido, as the
driver of emotional contagion. 'The libido,' he states 'is an expression taken from
the theory of the emotions' and of particular significance is that it constitutes
'love' and moreover 'sexual love with sexual union as its aim' as the essence of
the group mind (Freud, 1919: 90). Thus the individual is understood as being
particularly impressionable within the group as the person 'feels the need to be
in harmony with them rather than in opposition' (Freud, 1919: 92).
    To illustrate his theory Freud uses two case examples: the Catholic Church and
an army. Here Freud emphasis another point: the central place of the leader. For the

Catholic Church this is Christ and in the army it is the Commander-in-Chief. The two heads are understood by Freud as creating the illusion that they love the individuals of the group equally; which again, binds the group with libidinal ties. Additionally the love that is shown to them by the leader, they are to show for eachother; so they become both brothers (sisters) in Christ and an army of comrades. The psychoanalytic concept of 'identification' is key to Freud in the developing of libidinal ties of group members. Identification is the process whereby one person wishes to be like another person; for example, a young boy wishes to be like his father. This occurs through 'introjection': the person introjects the wished for person into his or her ego. Thus the common tie of the group is 'introjective identification'. Every member wishes to be like the leader; for example, members of the Catholic Church wish to be Christ-like and identify with what is perceived as the good aspects of Christ and thus develop an 'ego ideal' model of Christ to guide behaviour.

The Pathologisation of the Crowd

Steve Reicher is one of the most prominent contemporary social psychologists writing extensively on crowd psychology. A lot of Reicher's work has focused on understanding crowd behaviour in particularly heated situations; such as the St Pauls 'riot' (1984) which occurred in Bristol in the South-west of the UK in 1980 and more recently the riots that occurred across England in the summer of 2011 (Reicher and Stott, 2011). In a chapter entitled *The Psychology of Crowd Dynamics*, Reicher (2001) works up an interesting critical review of former crowd theories and develops what he calls 'an elaborated social identity model of crowds'.

To begin with Reicher elaborates on Moscovici's understanding that the former theorisations of the crowd and the group mind (that we have discussed above) served not only as early social psychologisations, but went on to influence 'mass politics of the 20th century' (Reicher, 2001: 186). They (although Reicher focuses specifically on Le Bon) 'influenced a plethora of dictators and demagogues, most notoriously, Goebbels, Hitler, and Mussolini' (2001: 186). Reicher argues that since the nineteenth century the rise of industrialisation had brought about the destabilisation of traditional social hierarchies of village life and gave birth to 'mass society', the question of social control was of paramount importance to those in power. The perceived lack of order and rootlessness that mass society was supposed to give way to would culminate in anarchy as the crowd would thus be susceptible to unscrupulous agitators. Reicher argues that much of the early engagement with 'crowd psychology' was in relation to controlling (repressing) the working class and less about understanding the crowd. Additionally there was a fascination with the crowd, particularly of the energy that it brings about. For example, what power it would bring if one could harness this energy, which is exactly how Le Bon sold his psychology. Indeed Reicher states that,

> The majority of his [Le Bon's] crowd text is, in fact, essentially a primer on how to take advantage of the crowd mentality, how to manipulate crowds, and how to recruit their enthusiasms to one's own end. (Reicher, 2001: 186)

However the power of the crowd was an aspect of Le Bon's theory that was hardly taken up by subsequent theorists. But the emphasis that came to influence social psychologies of the crowd were concerns with submergence and its derivative: deindividuation.

Deindividuation

One of Reicher's main concerns with Le Bon's crowd psychology is that he does not take (social and cultural) context into consideration. For example, no sense of the grievances and the social conflicts are discussed in Le Bon's analysis of the angry demonstrations of working-class crowds of late nineteenth century France (Reicher, 2001: 186). Reicher argues that such events do not occur in isolation; Le Bon shows no concern for the social injustices that may lead to crowd activity. Le Bon, as discussed above, uses the term 'submergence' to denote the loss of self-consciousness (or conscience) within the crowd or what later scholars denote as deindividuation. For example, Le Bon suggested that under the conditions of deindividuation, antisocial behaviour is more likely. A number of other studies went on to develop the deindividuation hypotheses within social psychology, all relatively confirming the initial work of Le Bon, McDougall and Freud and the psychopathologisation of individuals' emotional activity within groups (Reicher, 2001).

Social Norm Theory

The body of work that Reicher draws on to facilitate the development of his model of crowd dynamics is essentially to counter the pathologisation propositions. Firstly he draws on social norm theory – a theory deriving from symbolic interactionism in conjunction with psychological research – in order to identify the social coherence of collective action (Turner and Killian, 1987). The gist of the theory is that rather than tying crowd action to irrational, submersive and thus pathological behaviour, various norms emerge guiding collective behaviour. These arise not through a particular leader but through what is recognised as a primary stage of 'milling' (hanging around) before social action takes place. Individuals at this stage engage with others sharing accounts and listen to others. Various 'keynote' individuals propose action and resolve ambivalence within the crowd to facilitate unanimity. Reicher argues that this theory makes a welcomed break from earlier crowd psychologies, particularly as it stresses the 'sociality of crowd action' (Reicher, 2001: 193). However, Reicher points out that emergent norm theory moves from the elite individual level of crowd shaping to an elite inter-individual level. In other words, it still relies on certain members of the group to shape the crowd activity and thus does not include 'larger-scale social factors' (2001: 194).

Social Identity Theory

The social identity theory of crowd action concerns the distinction between what is personal to me – as identity – and what I share with others. The latter could be, for example, a religion, a football team I support, or the profession I work in. These are shared identities that may distinguish one group from another. By defining ourselves into a particular category, we partake in a form of self-stereotyping. In the crowd situation rather than look to specific members of the group to follow and lose one's personal identity (for example as submergence theory would have it), individuals shift to the relevant social identity and act according to the norms of that identity and those who are recognised as being part of the particular category in this context (creating prototypical group norms). Reicher argues that this theory does well to explain the linking of 'society to identity and identity to action' (2001: 197) in relation to crowd events. It also speaks for the energy and power of the crowd to undertake actions normally impossible for the individual. What it is less able to explain is how crowd action (in Reicher's opinion, which is supported in field research) leads to a transformatory potential through which individuals feel different after being part of the action of a crowd (particularly in relation to significant events such as riots) in other words, aspects of identity change.

Reicher suggests that field work has found that when individuals come together to form a crowd (particularly crowd events such as football matches, demonstrations and protests) a common dynamic is evident. Although the moderate element of the crowd will define themselves as law abiding and responsible citizens, those outside of the crowd distinguish the crowd as a danger to social order (particularly the police). The crowd's action is likely to be impeded and thus the moderate members come to see the impeders as an illegitimate opposition. This opposition further extends the ingroup category, solidarity and a willingness to challenge; thus a movement in identity occurs from moderate to oppositional.

Reicher notes the limitations of his elaborated social identity model of crowds by stating that it may not fit all configurations of crowds as some crowd events may be particularly routinised. Additionally it may not always lead to forms of radicalisation and empowerment. Moreover, and of interest to us, is that Reicher's account perhaps overplays the cognitive aspects of crowd phenomena and does not specifically analyse emotion activity. He readily suggests that research should look at such phenomena but, perhaps importantly, we should not make the classic mistake of counterposing intellect and emotion and seeing the latter as usurping the former. He suggests that progress in crowd psychology depends on investigating how emotion relates to the self-understanding of crowd members. For example, there may be joy in being part of a crowd, in being fully recognised as a group member, and being able fully to express one's identity; there may be anger at outgroup attempts to impede such expression (Reicher, 2001: 203).

The dynamics of emotional contagion, however, it seems for Reicher, is at most a spin-off of the more important function of the dynamics of social identity. The contagion hypothesis seems too bound up in the submergence and deindividuation hypothesis to include. Indeed Reicher states that the theory of contagion (as Le Bon would have it) implies that individuals 'are unable to resist any passing idea or, more particularly and because the intellect is all but obliterated, any passing emotion' (2001: 186). Although, in a more recent book concerned with the 2011 English riots, Reicher and Stott (2011) concede that crowd members are likely to be influenced by others' facial expressions. Yet this point is only made as a way of counteracting the 'milling' hypothesis of the social norm theory. Ultimately, however, which should be of interest to the social psychology of emotion, Reicher makes a good case to counteract the early models of emotional contagion looked at above – although they bring the centrality of emotion activity within crowd (group) dynamics to the forefront, they tend to conjure-up dualistic and negative notions of emotion which we have extensively discussed throughout this book. Reicher instead emphasises how existing cultures and societies are central in shaping crowd activity (and, we might add, emotion activity) rather than the previous focus on the individual within the group as a unit of analysis without considering the wider context.

Primitive Emotional Contagion

Hatfield, Cacioppo and Rapson are quite possibly the only authors to explicitly dedicate a book to the subject of emotional contagion[1]. Rather than focus on the forms of highly charged gatherings that are mainly discussed above, they tend to focus on commonly occurring forms of emotional contagion; for example, through simply being exposed to another person's emotional activity. Their theory on 'primitive emotional contagion' discusses the ways that emotional mimicry and synchrony occur through facial, vocal and postural feedback. They claim that emotional contagion 'is best conceptualized as a multiply determined family of psychophysiological, behavioural, and social phenomena' (1994: 4). Although they do well in discussing some of the micro interactional activity that plausibly induces this thing called 'emotional contagion' and thus include social (interpersonal) dimensions, they are less concerned with Reicher's focus on socio-cultural contextual factors and macro structural features.

Emotion, they suggest, can be 'caught' in a number of ways; which they specify as: cognitive conscious processes, conditioned and unconditioned emotional responses, and mimicry/feedback. Emotional contagion through cognitive conscious processes is understood to occur through thinking about what others feel, through, for example, imagining and analysing what appears to be their feelings and thoughts. This is rather like a cognitive version of Hume's sympathy that we looked at in Chapter 3. Conditioned and unconditioned emotional responses are considered as reflecting emotional contagion processes; this is a bit more puzzling because they suggest that the emotions caught do not have to be of the same kind. So far, the emotional contagion theories we have looked at tend to suggest that the form of emotion that is caught is the same kind of emotion that was in some way perceived; for example, the anger of one person causes anger for another, happiness causes happiness and so forth. Yet Hatfield et al. state that conditioned (learnt) responses – for example being conditioned at a young age to fear or become anxious in response to a father's habitual anger – can in turn become a conditioned response to anger in other situations (even when, for instance, anger was not the primary emotion to be caught). Perhaps the concept of emotional contagion becomes a bit blurred here as it seems to concern any emotion that one may feel in response to another's emotion. However, there does not seem to be a precise definition of emotional contagion in relation to whether the form of emotion that one contracts is indeed of the same form that the other experiences.

Primitive Emotion

Although Hatfield et al. do not explicitly explain why they use the term 'primitive' in their concept of emotional contagion (i.e. 'primitive emotional contagion'), it seems that it relates to their focus on how mimicry and synchronisation are understood as central determinants. Primitive emotional contagion is understood by them as

> The tendency to automatically mimic and synchronize facial expressions, vocalizations, postures, and movements with those of another person's and, consequently, to converge emotionally. (Hatfield et al., 1994: 5)

It seems that they equate 'primitive' functions to those that are 'automatic' and perhaps non-conscious. In a later paper Hatfield, Rapson and Le (2009) discuss a variety of empirical research to substantiate their views on mimicry. For example, according to Lundqvist's (1995) EMG response pattern research on facial mimicry (mimicking the facial expressions of others) is seen as swift and subtle, producing no observable change in facial expressions. When participants were shown various emotional facial expressions, the observers evoked different

EMG responses which are seen to be associated with each particular facial expression. For instance, when shown happy facial expressions there was increased muscular activity over the cheek region (the zygomaticus muscular region). Then they discuss research concerning interspeaker influence as evidence for vocal mimicry as an aspect of primitive emotional contagion. Interspeaker influence, as it suggests, concerns the speaker influencing the speech rates, utterance durations and latencies of responses. Lastly they look at postural mimicry which suggests that people mimic and synchronise the postures and movement of others unconsciously. Subsequently the mimicking of facial expressions, vocal expressions, posture and movement behaviours are understood to create in the mimicker feelings that are a pale reflection of others' emotions that result in people tending to catch one another's emotions (Hatfield et al., 2009).

Asocial Theory

As mentioned, although Hatfield et al.'s work does well to emphasise the micro-interactional elements of this thing called 'emotional contagion' there is a dearth of field work and much of the evidence cited comes from laboratory forms of experimental psychology and neuroscience. These forms of studies are often understood by some social psychologists (for example Reicher) as particularly problematic when looking at this type of interactivity as it tends to play down the importance of context and lacks ecological validity. Consequently the important role that social factors may play are not sufficiently accounted for. In an edited book on emotional expression and group dynamics, Hess and Philippot (2010) emphasise the way that social phenomena, such as gender, ethnicity and status influence emotional expression and their interpretation in relation to social rules and norms. Although they concede that the neo-Darwinian framework of emotional facial expressions – that is, the innate signals that have evolved phylogenetically – has paved the way for the understanding of their important role in social coordination (which Hatfield et al.'s 'primitive emotional contagion' emphasises), they also suggest that there is evidence that these innate signals can be modulated by social conventions. Of course the neo-Darwinian perspective has dominated psychology over the last few decades, whereas sociologists have developed understandings of emotional social communication which are rarely drawn upon by (social) psychologists; Hess, Philippot and colleagues are an exception. Additionally, and importantly for contemporary social psychology, Hatfield et al. conclude their book by stating,

> With the expansion and increased power of new communications, should we attend more carefully to the way this phenomenon functions? What is the effect on social bonds and relations of technologies (i.e., personal computers, electronic mail) that facilitate the transmission but diminish the parallel transmission of emotional communication? (Hatfield et al., 1994: 205)

Virality and Contagion

We look at some of the contemporary responses to these questions in the final chapter. But to somewhat answer this question in the 'contagion' context, we turn to a publication entitled *Virality: Contagion Theory in the Age of Networks*, through which Sampson develops a theory of 'how discourse is intimately interwoven with a prediscursive flow of contagious affect, feelings and emotions' (2012: 3). Sampson is particularly concerned to respond to a growing fear that there is 'too much connectivity' in today's rapidly developing systems of digital networks. For example, these connectivities are often understood to bring about 'increased chances of infection from wide-ranging social, cultural, political and economic contagions' (2012: 1). Thus the term *virality*, which denotes the spread of a biological disease, and of course we now use the term not simply as a metaphor but to connote the spread of, for example, computer viruses. 'Going viral' today, like the spread of a biological virus, means the rapid spread of a piece of internet content. He contends that digital networks can be used to enable a discursive mobilisation of negative emotions through fear, panic, terror and fright and also positive affects are transmitted through the 'intoxication of hope, belief, joy, and even love' (2012: 5). However, there is another sense of virality that Sampson draws attention to, a rather more accidental one. Indeed he looks at how at times small events which are unpredictable can spin out, or are 'nudged' into becoming 'big, monstrous contagions without a guiding hand' (2012: 6).

Tarde

Underlying many of Sampson's notions of contagious virality is the work of Gabriel Tarde, a French social theorist who produced a number of influential papers around the turn of the twentieth century. Tarde went on to influence such figures as Bruno Latour (particularly actor network theory) and Gilles Deleuze (whom we will be looking at in Chapter 9). However, it is only relatively recently that his unique philosophical theories on society have started to gain favour with social theorists. Unlike Tarde's contemporaries (and particularly Emile Durkheim), his social theory was interested, not so much in the individual person or collective representation, but rather in the networks or *relational flows* that spin out in at times unpredictable ways and form multiple connections with other networks and flows. Without getting into the complex detail of Tarde's process philosophy, we will mention an aspect of the Tardean approach which will be more familiar to readers at this point. Tarde was particularly interested in the ways that desires determine human interactivity. Like a number of the early theorists of emotion that we looked at in the historical sections of this book, Tarde understood the soul to possess powers. Two of these powers were belief and desire which importantly were dynamically interconnected. However, unlike LeBon, McDougall and Freud he did not see them as arising simply through biological processes, and unlike Durkheim, he did not see them as arising simply through societal processes. Instead, Sampson suggests, Tarde theorises a process 'whereby the first [biology] becomes translated into the second [society], which can, when encountered and copied, take on a vital and contaminating role of its own' (2012: 12). Thus the first kind of desires are akin to the needs of organic life; such as the desire to drink, eat and protect the body from harm. The second kind of desires are social and are of a special kind. They seek 'satisfaction, new sensations, ambitious or amorous fevers, intoxications, and ecstatic joy' among other things. These desires are periodically satisfied and are again reborn in an indefinite cycle of repetition. The distinctive trait of the second form, however, is that they are not simply everyday desires but begin as fantasies, only to later be consolidated into habits. Thus Sampson states that these processes are helpful in understanding one of the central mechanisms of capitalism: 'the reproduction of desire' (2012: 12).

Somnambulism

Tarde, much like many of his contemporaries that we discussed above, suggests that contagion occurs through imitation and suggestibility which happens mostly unconsciously. Thus the individual for Tarde was what he called a som-nambulist. That is individuals almost sleep-walk through everyday life being hypnotically absorbed by the contagions of others and 'mesmerized and con-taminated by the fascinations of their social environment' (Sampson, 2012: 13). Sampson argues that although the concept of 'an agentless, half-awake subjectiv-ity, nudged along by the force of relational encounter with contaminating events, is unsettling' he suggests there is contemporary evidence for this. For example, he cites the theories of the automatic processes that people engage in due to so called 'mirror neurons' (which we will look at in the following chapter). Sampson states that the somnambulist theory of Tarde is particularly relevant 'in an age when subjectivity is increasingly embedded in technological network relations' and prefigures 'an increasingly inseparable and exploitable intersection between what is experienced biologically and what is encountered socially and culturally in a network' (2012: 13).

Sampson's book is complex and one cannot do justice to it here, it really is worth a read. Of relevance in the context of this chapter is that Sampson, through the theorisation of Tarde, is able to demonstrate some of the ways con-tagion may occur in not just groups or crowds but through wider global networks. Moreover, he attempts to develop this theory by looking at the dynamic interplay between biologies, societies and cultures. Yet, and Sampson admits this, one is left feeling a bit uneasy with the somnambulist theory of human subjectivity. We are left again, as Reicher might argue, with another dein-dividuation theory and perhaps another pathologisation of emotional contagion. It must be added, however, that Sampson does end with a note of hope. Following

Tarde, it is stated that educating the senses can lead to resisting somnambulism. Educating the senses will enable states of *antipatheia*: 'antifeelings that may fend off the contaminations of unwanted and mostly unconscious epidemics...' (2012: 192). According to Tarde, Sampson argues, this requires a form of 'pure antipathy' through 'nonimitation' which entails a conscious and cognizant 'refusal ... to copy the dress, customs, language, industry and arts which make up the civilization of [this or that] neighborhood' (Tarde cited in Sampson 2012: 190). This is the way through which the truly new emerges and thus inserts itself as a unique type of virus, which of course is caught by others through affective transmissions.

Post-Freudian Groups

As we started this chapter on Freud's drive theory of groups and emotion, it would not be complete without some mention of the development of psychoanalytically informed understandings of emotion and groups. Bion's theory of groups is probably the most widely known psychoanalytic understanding of groups which was developed through both Freud's theories and the later object relations (psychoanalytic) theory. Theorists in the object relations traditions are often critical of some of Freud's concepts as his drive theory draws heavily, in a quite unsubstantiated way, on biological understandings of psychological functioning. Freud's drive theory can be understood at times as an unspecified quasi-physiological quantity. To this end it is suggested that psychoanalysis should not proceed as if it is a biological science but it is rather an interpretive science (Greenberg and Mitchell, 1983). Object-relations theories tend to focus instead on the vicissitudes of the object that one is in relation to. Melanie Klein, for example, 'regarded stimulation of the body as giving rise to the primary mental events which were subjective interpretations of bodily stimuli as provoked by an object' (Hinshelwood, 1991: 326–7). Generally object-relations theory tends to be thought of as doing away with Freud's drive theory concerning the pleasure-seeking nature of individuals, to emphasise what they tend to see as the individual as fundamentally object-seeking. It can be argued that psychoanalytic object relations theories give a more central place to the concepts of emotion compared to Freud's drive theory. This is because the focus is much more on the communicative exchange between the self and the other, particularly in early development between the infant and the primary-carer. There is a focus on the exchange of expressions (especially facial). For example, Klein was interested in what she saw as the extreme nature of the young infant's emotions. In what she termed the 'paranoid-schizoid position', the infant directs love and hate onto partial objects of the primary-carer (this was usually denoted as the mother). The infant essentially splits the mother between good and bad parts. The classic example is that of the breasts of the mother are split between a good breast (that arrives and gives milk when the infant is hungry) and a bad breast (that doesn't arrive when hungry).

This creates a split in the ego of the infant inducing affects such as anxiety, envy, hate and aggression directed towards the bad part-object and love towards the good. Later when the infant achieves the 'depressive-position' (wherein the other is recognised as an integrated whole object), feelings of guilt and grief for the negative feelings of the paranoid schizoid position emerge and thus the capacity for empathy.

Bion's Basic Assumptions

In Bion's (1961) book entitled *Experiences in Groups*, he writes about the affective states that bind individuals together in a group (group dynamics). These dynamic affective states are what Bion called basic assumptions of the group. The basic assumptions of the group tend to characterise the function of the group in unconscious ways and these are threefold: 'a fight or flight group' (BaF), 'a dependent group' (BaD) or 'a pairing group' (BaP). The mechanism of the basic assumptions is characterised by the paranoid-schizoid position evoked through the (pre-Oedipal) internalised primitive fears (phantasies) about the contents of the mother's body. These internalised psychic mechanisms, to a greater or lesser extent, persist throughout the life of an individual, but are especially revealed in the context of the group according to Bion.

> The adult must establish contact with the emotional life of the group in which he lives; this task would appear to be as formidable to the adult as the relationship with the breast appears to the infant, and the failure to meet the demands of this task is revealed in his regression. (Bion, 1961: 142)

This *failure* and subsequent *regression*, following Freud, leads to the loss of individual distinctiveness (Bion, 1961: 142) or what has come to be known as deindividuation.

In BaF, the anxiety within the group leads to a desire to either fight or run away from a perceived external threat. This basic assumption is fuelled by hate; Bion states the release of hate 'finds an outlet either in destructive attacks on a supposed enemy or flight from the hatred of the object' (Bion, 1961: 163). In BaD, the group comes to depend upon a leader and not give the other members a hearing as they will then be seen to be rivals to the leader's position, which is based on guilt and depression (Bion, 1961: 166). And in BaP, there is a pairing within the group which is characterised through *hope* and *expectation*. For example, the hope that the pairing will (of course this is psychoanalytically related to sexual union) produce a 'Messiah' (a Messianic hope: 'be it person, idea or utopia' (Bion, 1961: 152)) which will solve its problems. Thus the leader of this group is as yet unborn. Bion states,

It usually finds expression verbally in ideas that marriage would put an end to neurotic disabilities; the group therapy would revolutionize society when it had spread sufficiently; that the coming season, spring, summer, autumn, or winter, as the case may be, will be more agreeable; that some new kind of community – an improved group – should be developed, and so on. ... The feelings thus associated with the pairing group are at the opposite pole to feelings of hatred, destructiveness, and despair. (Bion, 1961: 151)

These group dynamics therefore do not address the group's problems and tasks and so are considered to be psychopathological, regressive, primitive and thus 'basic'. He states that the affects related to the basic assumptions (described by terms such as anxiety, fear, hate and so forth) may have different qualities in the various basic assumption contexts. For example, he states 'anxiety in the dependent group has a different quality from anxiety evident in the pairing group' (Bion, 1961: 154–5). Importantly, however, unlike his predecessors such as Le Bon, McDougall and Freud, the 'basic assumptions' are not the only mechanisms present within the group. In contention is the 'work group mentality', wherein individuals cooperate together and are able to focus on the given task for which they came together. The work group is always in evidence with one of the basic assumptions and although its function may remain present and unaltered, the basic assumption may change from one to the other over time (Bion, 1961: 154). This dual mechanism enables the group to be understood as apparently stable and organised and yet simultaneously quite 'mad'. Brennan (2004) uses the example of the Heaven's Gate cult as an extreme or a university department that might seem to function well most of the time, but may have additional irrational persecutory tendencies.

Foulkes' Psychosocial Theorisation

Siegfried Heinrich Foulkes (1898–1976), psychoanalyst and group analyst, developed an interesting perspective of groups that was influenced by the psycho-social ideas from the Frankfurt school, Gestalt psychology and the social psychology of Norbert Elias. He was particularly interested in how the individual was determined by their social surroundings; for example the community and the group of which they are a part. However, he attempts to do away with 'the old juxtaposition of an inside and outside world, constitution and environment, individual and society, phantasy and reality, body and mind and so on' (Foulkes, 1948: 10). He is much more concerned with the interconnection of phenomena rather than abstracting out the elements. Although he suggests that the latter may be a useful logical device for commentary, it is important to bear in mind that these abstractions have no real meaning and existence on their own (see Dalal, 1998). Thus Foulkes suggests that the (psycho)analysis of the individual should be concerned not just with the individual but that '[T]he group, the community, is the ultimate primary unit of consideration, and the so-called inner processes in the individual are internalizations of the forces operating in the group to which he belongs' (Foulkes, 1971: 212).

Foulkes' emphasis is not on the instinctual nature of humans as Freud envisaged but on what he determines as the 'social instinct'. His theory of a 'social instinct' is based, Dalal (1998) argues, on the mistaken Freudian notion of 'recapitulation': ontogeny recapitulates phylogeny. In other words, our biological, instinctual inner nature has evolved from genetically inherited behaviours. This of course constitutes what is known as a 'Lamarckian heresy'. Behaviours that are learnt within a life-span are not genetically inherited (to one's progeny) but nature selects genes to inherit. However, Foulkes suggests that groups are more fundamental than individuals because individuality arose from the groups that constituted the primal horde of antiquity (prehistoric human social organisation, theorised in Freud's paper *Totem and Taboo* (1922)). Thus our social nature relates to our primitive past, so accordingly the group is more 'primitive' than the individual. Hence in typical Freudian fashion, Foulkes argues that the social instinct (similar to Freud's instinct theories of them influencing primitive behaviours) seeks to get back to this primitive group-state of being: to rekindle a lost era. Dalal argues that this implies that 'people do not group in present because of contemporary needs and desires, but to fulfil a desire from a lost prehistoric time – the time of ancient tribal feelings' (1998: 42). Thus we are left again with a version of group behaviour as inducing or recapitulating basic and primitive feelings and emotions.

One of the things that is not very clear in Foulkes' writings is how this social instinct is 'inherited', indeed he at times uses the term 'transmitted' instead of 'inherited' here. Dalal argues that although he attempts to move away from dualistic notions as described above, we often find his writings quite contradictory, for example many of his arguments focus on the nature/nurture dichotomisation. In Foulkes' defence, Dalal goes on to suppose that we may apply the Gestalt notion of figure and ground to Foulkes' writings. For example, at times the group is at the forefront of analysis with the individual in the background and at times the individual is at the forefront and the group in the background.

What is perhaps more important about Foulkes' understanding of the group in relation to emotion studies and groups, is that he suggests we fundamentally 'desire' to 'belong' to a group. This implies, Dalal states, that we have an 'emotional need to belong' to a group. Foulkes would have this need as stemming from the social instinct, but he also considers that this comes about through his theory of the 'social unconscious'. The social unconscious differs from the Freudian unconscious in that it has not solely come about by repression, but rather through our ways of being that we have unconsciously adopted, essentially from our primary group – the family – that we are now unaware of.

He states

> ... the way of expressing oneself, of breathing, of sleeping, of waking, of being amused, of speaking, the individual's total behaviour has been decisively shaped by the original family group. The individual is unconscious of this in that he is normally convinced that his way ... is the natural right one. (Foulkes, 1971: 231)

Hence, in some ways, Foulkes manages to turn the direction of analysis of groups and emotion around. Rather than thinking about the individual within a group and the emotions that flow from the experience of being in a group, Foulkes is stating that 'the individual mind' is essentially 'a group mind' and it is in some ways pointless attempting to separate the two within analysis. On this account, emotion, to some extent, is that which is formed through group phenomena and always relates to the group. Nonetheless, this understanding still tends to follow the thesis that emotion is something that is primitive and basic even though wholly social.

Conclusion

With some notable exceptions the group psychologies discussed above tend to draw on the notion that emotion is that which almost drives people mad in groups. When we are within a group emotion is expressed as primitive, basic, infantile, unintelligent and irrational at best and dangerous at worst. It is almost as if emotion within the group setting is dangerously contagious, it is bound in some way to infect us and make us ill and indeed make us lose our own self! Of course this is an extreme characterisation of the general thesis of emotional contagion, but there is no doubt that elements of these extremes exist in the theories discussed above. Again we see the dichotomous discourses prevail in these theories and not just those emanating from the first half of the twentieth century but even the recent research we have looked at subtly uses terms such as 'primitive' in relation to emotion. It is interesting that in Hatfield and her colleagues' work that this term is not discussed or defined, but it is almost given as self-evident as to what it implies. Reicher begins to denote the possibilities of reframing the forms of emotion that may be in evidence in particularly highly charged group gatherings in a more positive light, but only in a passing statement that some field work along these lines may be of use. In an article concerned with the philosopher Ernst Bloch (Ellis and Tucker, 2011), we looked at Bloch's understanding of hope. The article uses the example of the student demonstrations against cuts to higher education and increased student fees that occurred in London in the winter of 2010. Here we focused on the forms of hope that seemed to be an important element of the demonstration and how it dynamically transmuted throughout the day and into the evening. Indeed we related the affects of the event not to irrational processes (although they were likely in some ways to incur forms of transmission) but to the more rational affect that Bloch refers to as 'educated hope'; indeed the demonstration was about the 'hopes for education'. However, the demonstration went on to be portrayed by the media as a sort of 'mad mob' episode by choosing to focus their attention on a small minority of student activists who were pictured and filmed inflicting various forms of criminal damage. These activities and affects were not typical of the demonstration, to the contrary most people appeared to be engaged with conversation, debate, dance, song and music making. In the conversation and debate that we witnessed, people spoke about their hopes and indeed fears for the future of higher education. These perhaps more rational and positive affects appeared to be much more prevalent, even in the face of the anger and frustration that many felt towards the government. Maybe Foulkes does have something to offer here. Perhaps there was some 'desire to belong' at play as well as other desires. The point is, however, that these, as far as we can tell, were not irrational but perhaps as Descartes would have it, they were expressions of the passions that spring from 'intelligent emotion', or what Augustine, Aquinas and Spinoza might call *affectus*.

Note

1 Although Brennan's (2004) book is very much concerned with emotional contagion it is reframed under the title *The Transmission of Affect*.

FURTHER READING

Freud, S. (1922). *Group Psychology and the Analysis of the Ego.*
Hopefully anybody studying the social sciences will at some point read a text written by Freud. As I (Darren Ellis) lecture in Psychosocial Studies, I invite my students to a *'Freud Reading Group'* wherein we read and discuss a text by Freud. Freud's 'Group Psychology' is a very accessible and dare I say entertaining read. It is twelve quite short chapters where many of Freud's pivotal ideas are conveyed, particularly those related to the social psychology of emotion.

Reicher, S. (2001). 'The Psychology of Crowd Dynamics', in M. Hogg and S. Tindale (eds) *Blackwell Handbook of Social Psychology: Group Processes.* Oxford: Blackwell. pp. 182–208.
Steve Reicher is a pivotal figure in the social psychology of crowd psychology, as I have discussed in this chapter, he is more concerned with social identity than he is with emotion. However, Reicher produces some excellent critiques of the emotional contagion thesis and has conducted some very relevant field studies.

Sampson, T. (2012). *Virality: Contagion Theory in the Age of Networks.* Minneapolis: University of Minnesota Press.
This is an excellent book which offers an unusual contemporary theorisation of the transmission of affect through contemporary forms of networking. As discussed in this chapter Sampson draws on the early sociological theory of Tarde (who has been very influential

to Gilles Deleuze) to think about how metaphors and discourses 'go viral' to affect, inflect and infect the social.

Bion, W. (1961). *Experiences in Groups and Other Papers*. New York: Tavistock Publications Limited.
Anyone remotely interested in how emotions work in group settings should at least know of Bion's psychoanalytically formed understanding of the 'basic assumptions' in groups. *Experiences in Groups* is the classic text where Bion writes about his ideas. It isn't the easiest and most compelling of texts, but it has of course been extremely influential.

Foulkes, S. (1948). *Introduction to Group Analytic Psychotherapy*. München: Heinemann.
As hopefully we have made clear, Foulkes, although one needs to read particularly critically, offers some very interesting truly psychosocial thinking to group psychology. Dalal (1998), in his book *Taking the Group Seriously. Towards a Post-Foulkesian Group Analytic Theory*, offers some good critique of some of the more contentious aspects of Foulkes' theory and extends it.

6

Biological Understandings of Emotion

Key Aims

In this chapter we will critically discuss some relevant biological theorisations which are key to emotion studies. In doing so we will:

- Consider Darwin's universality theory of emotions
- Explore theories concerned with brain structure and emotion
- Reflect on affective neuroscience and neuropsychoanalysis
- Discuss Damasio's somatic marker hypothesis

Introduction

Drawing support from Darwin's universality thesis, many contemporary notions of emotion have been territorialised by psychobiological (neuroscientific) conceptualisations. Researchers within the bio-psychology field also tend to regard emotion as rooted in primitive organic systems which have been hard-wired into the matter of the body through evolutionary processes. As we have seen, historical philosophies have tended to frame emotion as irrational, animalistic, involuntary and ultimately facilitating immorality. For example, as we shall see through Darwin's thesis, the notion of emotional expressions as vestigial did very little to dissociate them from the irrational. Although this was not Darwin's intention, the discursive construction concerned with the biologisation of emotion tends to fuel dualistic divides between the rational and the irrational, the social and the individual, the cognitive and the emotional, and more recently instead of the mind-body formulation we find a brain-body dualism in its place (a dualism within a monist tradition!). Psychobiologists throughout the 1980s and 1990s continued to develop rather closed notions of emotion virtually excluding and ignoring the social context. However, as we shall discover in this chapter, a number of much more socially oriented understandings have begun to emerge wherein social scientists and neuroscientists are able to develop much more sophisticated, holistic and integrated theories of emotion.

In this chapter we look at Darwin's theories on emotion, which lead into discussions of some contemporary neo-Darwinian notions of basic emotions. Contemporary biologically-informed accounts of emotion have been concerned with brain structure and its emotion-related zones. Hence we offer an introduction to McLean's triune brain theory before moving on to look at theories that have been concerned with hemispheric distinctions. We then look at some of the more innovative and socially aware biologisations of emotion through a body of work entitled 'affective neuroscience' and Damasio's somatic marker hypothesis.

Darwin's Expressions

Charles Darwin's (1809–1882) theory of natural selection suggested profound biological continuities between humans and animals. Not only are humans biologically close to animals but descended from them, and indeed they are a type of animal. This new theorisation of humans stripped them of any transcendental properties that were previously seen as peculiar to humans. His theory fundamentally changed the way humanity was understood, and in turn, how emotion was understood. Darwin wrote in 1872 arguably one of the most cited books that has been written on emotion; it was entitled *The Expression of the Emotions in Man and Animals* (The Expressions).

Darwin was particularly interested in how emotions were expressed in humans through facial or other bodily movements and is often credited as developing what has come to be known as 'the universality thesis' of facial expressions (see Russell, 1994). Darwin had previously been interested in the work of Charles Bell, a physiologist who had studied human anatomical expressions in paintings. Bell had concluded that the human face had a unique musculature which allowed the facial expression of various emotions which were not present in other species. In this way he argued that they offer some evidence of God's design: God had given humans these facial muscles so that they would be distinctive in expressing emotion. Of course Darwin vehemently objected to this position and went to great lengths to disprove it, but nonetheless was influenced by Bell's interest in the facial expressions of emotion. For example, Darwin stated:

> Consequently, when I read Sir C. Bell's great work, his view, that man had been created with certain muscles specially adapted for the expression of his feelings, struck me as unsatisfactory. It seemed probable that the habit of expressing our feelings by certain movements, though now rendered innate, had been in some manner gradually acquired. (Darwin, 1872/2002 : 20)

Bell was a respected physiologist who had earned a prestigious position in the scientific community in relation to his work on the nervous system; for example, he was the first to form a distinction between the sensory and the motor nerves. However, Russell (1994) argues that despite common assumptions, Bell and Darwin were not the first to write about facial expressions and emotion. Indeed Aristotle wrote 'There are characteristic facial expressions which are observed to accompany anger, fear, erotic excitement, and all the other passions' (Aristotle, cited in Russell and Fernandez-Dols, 1997: 3). Although the universality of facial expression thesis tends to be credited as Darwin's hypothesis (for example, see Ekman's 1980 history), Russell adds that there was great interest in this before Darwin's book appeared in 1872. For example Russell states that Bain (1855), Duchenne de Boulogne (1862), Piderit (1867) and Spencer (1855) all developed theories on this. However, they are hardly mentioned for their work in this area as they generally developed discredited creationist theories. Darwin was unique in that he proposed an evolutionary theory rather than a creationist understanding of the universality of emotional expression. Dixon (2003) persuasively argues that one of Darwin's main objectives in *The Expressions* was to disprove this creationist approach.

Dixon notes that Darwin had an early interest in Herbert Spencer's essay on the physiology of laughter. Spencer theorised that the excessive nervous excitation associated with emotion would have to find some outlet when it reached a certain propensity. This outlet would be found in particular forms of muscular activity. Darwin was struck by Spencer's statement that '[S]trong feeling, mental or physical, being, then, the general cause of laughter, we have to note that the muscular actions consisting it are distinguished from most others by this, that they are purposeless' (Spencer, 1863: 111). Darwin underlined the word 'purposeless' and noted in the margins: 'so for frantic gestures of rage or intense grief' (see Dixon, 2003: 165). Although Darwin suggested that facial expressions and other bodily movements related to emotion were purposeful in various ways, he emphasised that they are often not purposeful to present humans but for our ancestors further down the evolutionary chain. Indeed he suggested that the emotional expressions that we have are rather ill suited to modern humans. Dixon argues that he worked laboriously to prove that emotions were formed in humans from the habits of our evolutionary past and thus they occur in humans whether they are useful or not. He saw them as rather like fossils, 'vestigial' parts of our bodies. For example, the tail-bone (coccyx) is a vestige of our past, a bone that no longer has any use for humans but assisted balance, mobility and forms of communication for our distant ancestors. Indeed Barrett states that 'vestiges can be an even stronger proof of concept for natural selection than are useful adaptations, because they persist despite having no function' (2011: 400). Think about the facial expression of surprise. A distinctive feature of this is that we tend to raise our eyebrows. Darwin suggested that this is related to opening the eyes widely to quickly scan the surroundings on sensing something that we need to quickly be alerted to. Or the way hair tends to stand on end when we are frightened, this probably occurs in animals so that they appear larger and therefore are less likely to be attacked. These no longer serve the same purpose for humans.

The Universality Thesis

Importantly Darwin's theory of evolution brought him to the conclusion that facial expressions of emotion are universal, that is, they are the same across cultures for humans. Not only does this universality help to consolidate his theory that humans have evolved from animals but also that humans have descended from a common progenitor, rather than different races having different progenitors. This should have helped Darwin's theory to facilitate the equality of races, but as history has taught us, this was not to be the case. And yet, he was the first to conduct a systematic cross cultural analysis of facial expressions. He analysed photographs of different emotional expressions from people in a variety of cultures. He was also one of the first researchers to use questionnaires and interviews. He sent out a questionnaire around Britain and the Empire asking, what Dixon paraphrases as, 'missionaries, colonists, zookeepers and asylum directors to observe the expressions of "savages", animals and the insane' (2003: 160). Adding to the 36 respondents, Darwin meticulously observed the expressions of his young son William. Indeed, he developed a number of unique methods to collect data on the various forms of emotional expressions (as can be seen from the below taxonomy) and decided to compile his findings into a book. Initially this was just intended to be chapter in *The Descent of Man*.

Table 6.1 Darwin's taxonomy of emotion

Expression	Bodily System	Emotion Example
Blushing	Blood vessels	Shame, modesty
Body contact	Somatic muscles	Affection
Clenching fists	Somatic muscles	Anger
Crying	Tear ducts	Sadness
Frowning	Facial muscles	Anger, frustration
Laughing	Breathing apparatus	Pleasure
Perspiration	Sweat glands	Pain
Hair standing on end	Dermal apparatus	Fear, anger
Screaming	Vocal apparatus	Pain
Shrugging	Somatic muscles	Resignation
Sneering	Facial muscles	Contempt
Trembling	Somatic muscles	Fear, anxiety

Source: Taken from Oatley, Keltner and Jenkins, 2010, page 6.

Natural Selection, Habits and Instincts

Darwin wrote that emotional expressions have formed in humans through habit and association: 'whenever the same state of mind is induced, however feebly, there is a tendency through the force of habit and association for the same movements to be performed though they may not then be of the least use' (1872/2005: 19). The notion of habits was seen as in contrast to instincts but only in terms of their origins. Habits were understood as stereotypical forms of behaviour that have been acquired throughout a lifespan. For example, this may form through the repetition of a behaviour that an ancestor performed. The inherited expression would later most likely be rendered useless in successive generations as environmental conditions changed. These actions were at first voluntary but when inherited over many generations they become innate involuntary tendencies induced in relation to particular feelings. In this way he sided with Lamarck's theory that some habits could be passed on to one's offspring (as discussed in the previous chapter). Instincts, however, are not acquired via experience but are directly biologically inherited through natural selection. This is noted by Dixon as being quite a different tack from his famous book published just a year previously (*The Descent of Man*) in which he advocated natural (sexual) selection. Dixon argues that this emphasis was in part because Darwin could therefore disprove the creationist's (particularly Bell's) facial expression theory. As the expressions were mostly purposeless they could not have been a product of God's design. Dixon makes the rather controversial point that: '[D]arwin's thinking about the expressions of emotions is that he did not think that they were "expressions" at all' (2003: 165). That is, their primary function is not to communicate a creature's inward state, if this did occur it was just a fortunate addition. Dixon states that Darwin's book *The Expression of the Emotions in Man and Animals* might more accurately have been entitled *The Inheritance of Useless Habits in Man and Animals* (2003: 168).

Darwin's Determinism

Additionally Dixon (2003) discusses how Darwin was opposed to mind-body dualisms and sided with the materialism of the British empiricists in terms of the association of ideas theories (see Hume in Chapter 3). Thus Darwin was a determinist in that he concluded that all actions 'are determined either by habits, hereditary character, by education or by chance' (Dixon, 2003: 161) and thus saw free-will as a mere delusion. And yet, against the grain of British empiricists' understanding of mental life beginning as a tabula rasa, Darwin used their notion of associationism and integrated it into his understanding of how habits (ideas) formed by individuals through the course of their lives, could then be inherited. In this way mental faculties could be both inherited and learnt. Thus he gave weight to the rationalist notions of *a priori* innate ideas and innate mental faculties. Dixon suggests that this was a transformative moment in the history of psychology wherein two opposing philosophical positions were conjoined in the new evolutionary paradigm.

And yet it is important not to throw the baby out with the bathwater. In contrast to Dixon's point, Darwin did write about some social elements of emotional expressions. Although he may have been obsessed in disproving creationist notions and thus emphasised some of the dysfunctionality of emotional expression, he also clearly makes the point that they also include essential communicative functions. For example, the following extract is from near the conclusion of *The Expressions*.

> The movements of expression in the face and body, whatever their origin may have been, are in themselves of much importance for our welfare. They serve as the first means of communication between the mother and her infant; she smiles approval, and thus encourages her child on the right path, or frowns disapproval. We readily perceive sympathy in others by their expression; our sufferings are thus mitigated and our pleasures increased; and mutual good feeling is thus strengthened. The movements of expression give vividness and energy to our spoken words. They reveal the thoughts and intentions of others more truly than do words, which may be falsified. (Darwin, 1872/2002: 194)

As we shall see, theories of facial expressions in this respect have received a great deal of attention in and around social psychological research on emotion. Indeed there is more room for manoeuvrability in Darwin's understanding of emotion than he is often (relatively recently) given credit for. Barrett (2011: 400) argues that the account that is often given of Darwin's theory of emotion may be an example of what Danziger (1997) calls 'presentism'. In other words, his writings are interpreted in such a way that they fit with the state of things today. For example, lesser recited points that Darwin made about emotion are firstly that there is within-category variability. This means that a given emotion can be expressed in a variety of ways by different people. Secondly, he stated that there is between-category similarity, meaning different emotions can have very similar expressions by different people. As Barrett (2011) suggests, and as we will come to look at in more detail, the jury is still out in relation to the universality of emotion but the impact of this thesis has been tremendous. Indeed his theories are still intriguing and were to set the scene for contemporary understandings of emotion in the newly forming biologies of emotion.

Neo-Darwinism

Darwin's cross-cultural analysis of emotion proposes that there are universal emotional expressions which are a product of evolution. Neo-Darwinists generally suggest that there are at least five hard-wired emotions, e.g. anger, fear, sadness, disgust and enjoyment. The leading neo-Darwinist in this field is Paul Ekman who has written prolifically. For an example see his very influential book entitled *Emotions Revealed: Understanding faces and feelings* (Ekman, 2004). In one study Ekman showed participants photographs of facial expressions of fear, anger, sadness, disgust, happiness, and surprise in 21 countries. He found a lot of support for the argument that these emotions are universal; for example, there was agreement of 19 out of 21 countries for fear, 18 out of 21 for anger, 20 out of 21 for surprise. He also went on to look at these expressions with people in New Guinea who had never been exposed to the Western media and found similar results; however, fear and surprise were not always clearly distinguished. Ekman's claim, however, is that when people experience strong emotion and do not attempt to mask the facial expression, the basic emotions will be expressed in the same way regardless of age, education, sex, race or culture.

Despite all of this evidence there are still very strong arguments against these claims. For example, we may ask why the various researchers come up with different amounts and kinds of basic emotions? Ekman names quite a large number: amusement, anger, contempt, contentment, disgust, embarrassment, excitement, fear, guilt, pride in achievement, relief, sadness/distress, satisfaction, sensory pleasure and shame, while Panksepp (2004) states that there are only four: fear, rage, panic, and expectancy. Plutchik (1980) and Izard (1971) state there are eight, but do not agree which they are. Plutchik includes fear, anger, sadness, joy, acceptance, disgust, anticipation and surprise in his list; while Izard includes fear, anger, joy, interest, disgust, surprise, shame, contempt, distress and guilt.

Identifying emotion can be quite a subjective matter. For example, what emotion would you suggest the Mona Lisa is portraying? Is it contentment, glee, pleasure, delight exhilaration, ecstasy? Many people suggest that her expression is enigmatic. However, as we will see in later chapters, many social scientists today suggest that we are likely to have subjective understandings of the emotion that we *feel* is being expressed. Our interpretation may be influenced by our present feeling states. Much research suggests that our interpretation of a phenomenon (what we read into a situation) are coloured by our mood (it is 'mood-dependent'). Not only is it mood-dependent, but our reading of a face may be influenced by our cultural experiences.

In relation to culture Ekman suggests that people in Papua New Guinea tended to understand emotional expressions in the same sort of way as people from other places, but evidence suggests that many cultures have very nuanced interpretation of emotion. Indeed some of the basic emotions are either missing or understood quite differently to each other. Here are some examples. Happiness is actually missing from the Chewong vocabulary, as is surprise for the Fore, Dani and Ifaluk peoples. Fear is missing in the Ifaluk, Ukta and Pintupi peoples as is sadness missing for the Tahitian and Chewong peoples (Wierzbicka, 1986). Disgust is missing for the Ifaluk and Chewong people. Anger overlaps with sadness or grief in the Luganda, Illingot and Ifaluk. The traditional Indian basic emotions are known as 8 main *rasas* (essences) each with a corresponding *bhava* (mood).

Erotic (*srngara*): love

Comic (*hasys*): amusement

Pathetic (*karuna*): compassion

Furious (*rudra*): anger

Heroic (*vira*): pride

Terrible (*bhayanaka*): horror

Odious (*bibhatsa*): disgust

Marvellous (*adbhuta*): amazement

There are also culturally specific emotion metaphors for emotion. For example the Zulu people tend to use a container type metaphor (Taylor and Mbense, 1998). They may use the term such as 'long heart' which is understood as a great capacity for love, or short heart which is understood as quick to anger.

The Triune Brain

Although Darwin and the neo-Darwinists are particularly interested in the expression of emotion, much of the research conducted in the biological sciences has been concerned with the neurobiological structure of emotion. One of the bedrocks underlying many of the structural theories of emotion is a relatively simplistic notion put forward by Paul MacLean (1990). In this theory we see another resurfacing of a tripartite notion of human functioning which breaks the human brain down into three fundamental parts. In accordance with theories of evolution each of these parts are seen to reflect a particular stage of human brain evolution: the reptilian brain, the mammalian brain and the primate brain. And as we saw way back in Plato's and Aristotle's theories, each of the three parts is correlated with a hierarchy of human functioning.

The lowest part is known as 'the reptilian brain', and is made up of the brain stem. The central nervous system has been compared to a tree (Badcock, 2000). The nerves that run through the body can be thought of as the roots. These then come together in the trunk, which corresponds to the spinal column and then move up to the top of trunk (just before the branches) the part that MacLean calls the 'reptilian brain' (the brain stem). MacLean claims that the brain stem had evolved in reptiles about 300 million years ago. It remains the basis of the brain in all animals that have evolved since and controls automatic functions like digestion and breathing. Behaviours which are associated with the brain stem are correlated with reptilian behaviour, such as, mating, aggression, territoriality, asserting dominance and self-defence.

The branches (limbs) of the tree trunk are known as the mammalian brain, otherwise known as the limbic system. The word limbic derives from the Latin *limbus* which means rim or margin. The limbic system has been associated with a number of functions, such as smell, temperature control (mammals are warm-blooded), vocal communication, parental care, and long-term memory (Badcock, 2000). Paul MacLean was actually the first to introduce the notion of the 'limbic system' in 1952. Before this in 1878, the famous French physician Paul Broca called this part of the brain *le grand lobe limbique* and then it came to be known as the 'papez circuit' after the American physician James Papez in 1937. Prior to Papez, Bard proposed that the hypothalamus was likely to play a critical role in emotion. This assumption followed the results of experiments which showed electrical stimulation of the hypothalamus induced sympathetic nervous system arousal which in turn was associated with rage. There were to follow a number of relatively rudimentary anatomical understandings of emotion, which, although important, were not able to articulate – as Papez went on to – the much more complex structures of the 'circuit'. Gainotti states that Papez proposed,

> (1) that the hypothalamus, the anterior thalamic nuclei, the cingulate gyrus, the hippocampus, and their interconnections may constitute a harmonious mechanism that elaborates the functions of central emotions and participate in emotional expression; and (2) that the hypothalimic component of the circuit might be mainly involved in functions of emotional evaluation and emotional expression, whereas the cortical component (namely, the cingulate gyrus) might be involved in the elaboration of emotional experience. (Gainotti, 2002, 216)

Of course MacLean's limbic system was very much influenced by the Papez circuit; however, his system incorporates brain activity made up of the hippocampus, amygdala, anterior thalamic nuclei, septum, habenula, limbic cortex and fornix. Following the work of Papez, MacLean understood the limbic system as being very much associated with emotion. Indeed this part of the brain is even today known by some as the emotional centre of the brain.

MacLean suggests that the primate brain, or the neocortex as it is usually referred to, is the top of the tree: the foliage. The neocortex has many deep folds and its surface area measures about 2,500 square centimetres crammed into the skull (which is on average only 20 centimetres across). In humans this part of the brain is concerned with problem-solving, conscious memory, learning, speech and verbal comprehension. It has also been called the 'word-brain' which is in contrast to the limbic system which is described by MacLean as 'illiterate'.

LeDoux's Amygdale

Through MacLean's account of the triune brain, one may be led to consider the evolution of the brain as heaping new layers of brain matter on to unchanged layers. However, contemporary understandings of brain evolution are quite different. The brain evolves by modifying the existing structures to present adaptive needs. Thus the three sections work in tandem with each other in a dynamic interplay of information, communicated through synaptic activity and neural chemicals. For example, if we take LeDoux's understanding of the amygdala, it is portrayed as receiving information not only from the brain stem but also from the neocortex. The amygdala in return sends information to virtually all the other parts of the brain, including the important decision making centre: the frontal lobes. Thus LeDoux is concerned with the relationship between the various parts of the brain. This is very much elaborated on in one of his books *Synaptic Self: How Our Brains Become Who We Are* (2002), wherein he looks at how the synaptic connections within the brain are of fundamental importance to the development of the self. However, LeDoux is much more noted for his empirical research which offers evidence for the central role of the amygdale (plural for amygdala) in relation to fear. The amygdala is a bilateral part of the limbic system which consists of two almond shaped components which are supposed to trigger fight or flight reflexes. In humans direct excitation of the amygdale through electrical stimulation is seen to evoke sensations of anxiety and apprehension (Gloor, 1986). Also researchers have been interested in looking at the fear responses of individuals who have lesions (damaged) amygdale. This has led to correlations between the amygdale and emotionally loaded memories, suggesting that they play a significant role in their storage and subsequent emotional responses (Allman and Brothers, 1994). One aspect of LeDoux's amygdale fear processing theory is that the messages sent from the amygdale to the neocortex are much stronger than the messages sent back from the neocortex to the amygdale. This suggests that the neocortex has limited influence upon amygdale processing and in turn provides some reasons as to why it is so difficult to control emotional states such as anxiety. This may also give some insight into why psychotherapy can be a long arduous process. When in psychotherapy, quite often one is consciously processing, through for example talking about feelings and experiences associated with anxiety. It is suggested while the amygdale may be sending multiple messages to various parts of the brain, the processing (cognition) which subsequently occurs in the neocortex has a difficult job of being turned back to the amygdale. This emphasises not only the multiple synaptic connections between the neocortex and limbic system, but importantly that there is at times a problematic relationship between them. In some respects, LeDoux's understanding of the amygdale-neocortex relationship reflects Darwin's theorisation of emotion as being vestigial. For LeDoux we are almost stuck with this domination of the amygdale (supposedly a more primitive part of the brain) in relation to fear and anxiety. It may be better if the relationship for fear processing was the other way (i.e. neocortex-amygdale), anxiety therefore would probably be much more controllable.

Triune Critiques

Thus the triune brain theory is not without its objectors. Indeed there are many contemporary theorists who see many problems with it. For example, Steven Pinker states that MacLean's triune brain theory is a romantic doctrine of the emotions which is largely incorrect (Pinker, 1997); additionally, LeDoux (1996; 2002) points out a number of criticisms of it. For example it has been known since the 1950s that damage to the hippocampus (a central structure within the so called limbic system) leads to deficits in long term memory, arguably cognitive function. According to LeDoux this runs against MacLean's supposition that the limbic system is made up of primitive architecture that is ill suited to participate in complex cognitive functions. In the 1960s it was found that the equivalent to the mammalian neocortex was present in nonmammalian vertebrates. LeDoux also points out that the 'limbic system itself has been a moving target' (2002: 211) in that after over half a century it is still not generally agreed what areas of the brain belong to it. In discussing some of the problems with the limbic system theory of emotion in relation to using it to predict how specific aspects of emotion work in the brain, LeDoux states:

> The problem is particularly apparent in recent work using functional imaging to study the human brain. Whenever a so-called emotional task is presented, and a limbic area is activated, the activation is explained by reference to the fact that limbic areas mediate emotion. And when a limbic area is activated in a purely cognitive task, it is often assumed that there must have, in fact, been some emotional component to the task. We are, in other words, at a point where the limbic theory has become an off-the-shelf explanation of how the brain works, one grounded in tradition rather than in facts. (LeDoux, 2002: 211–12)

Yet the limbic system is still widely used both as an anatomical concept and as a way of understanding emotion. For example, it is still widely thought that intellectual functions are carried out in the neocortex and emotional behaviour is dominated by functions in the limbic system. The eminent neuroscientist Jaak Panskepp wrote:

> I certainly affirm, however, that some critics unfairly treat MacLean's legacy; they sweep his sagacious and broad perspective away as if it were detritus of a pre-scientific past. MacLean's 'limbic system' concept (didactically sound though it is) and his enunciation of general patterns in the evolution of brain and emotions (sound though they are as well) have too commonly been the focus of recent attacks by those who seem to consistently ignore MacLean's abundant empirical contributions. Some senselessly gratuitous attacks reflect inadequate historical conceptual perspectives while misrepresenting MacLean's position, perhaps with opportunistic intent. (2002: iv)

Hemispheric Distinctions

Another rather interesting and popular discursive formulation of the location of emotion in the brain, which again tends to draw sharp distinctions between cognitive and emotion based processes, are the hemisphere specialisation theories. There are two general theories here; the first suggests that the right hemisphere is more efficient in mediating the recognition and expression of emotion while the left hemisphere is better suited to linguistic and analytical tasks (Cacioppo and Gardner, 1999; Stone et al., 1996). The second theory suggests that the left hemisphere predominantly mediates negative affect while the right predominantly mediates positive affect (Davidson, 1992). Rolls (2007) suggests that the reason for the lateralisation of emotional processing is that when a human function is not represented bilaterally in the brain, this is due to the topology of the body. For example, there are left and right hands, feet, eyes etc. and each have left and right representations in the brain. Emotional expressions, however, are not topologically manifest by the body. Thus it is understood to be evolutionarily advantageous to have all the neurons for emotion processing close together (without having to connect to the other side of the brain via the corpus callosum). This facilitates faster communication between the neurons and helps to minimise brain size and weight.

Rolls (2007: 200–2) points to various sources of evidence which suggest there is some form of hemisphere specialisation for emotion processing. For example, in right-handed people, lesions in the left hemisphere are more likely to affect language and lesions in the right hemisphere are more likely to affect emotional processing (Etcoff, 1989; Starkstein and Robinson, 1991). The identification of a facial expression when flashed rapidly is more accurately recognised when presented to the right hemisphere compared to the left. Another intriguing bit of research is that emotions are understood to be more clearly expressed on the left-hand side of the face compared to the right (Nicolls et al., 2004). And perhaps most famously of all, split brain theories often invoke evidence for the lateral specificity of emotion processing. Split brain patients are those people who have a rupture (or what's known as a callosotomy: a surgical incision) in their corpus callosum: a bundle of neural fibres which constitutes the main connecting point of the two hemispheres of the brain.

Split Brain

Although it was not until around the 1970s that split-brain research was given a lot of attention, the understanding of the role of the corpus callosum and its relation to epilepsy was theorised much earlier. In 1940 two neurologists (van Wagenen and Herren) wrote a paper on their observations of tumours and convulsions. They noted that at the early stage of a tumour's growth, convulsions are common. Generally they inferred that if the associated neural pathways were destroyed by the tumours then convulsions were reduced. Hence in an effort to stop a convulsive wave from spreading to the other half of the cerebrum, a callosotomy surgery was applied. However, these interventions produced only limited success on reducing the seizures, so they stopped performing the procedure.

Many years later Bogen and Vogel (1962) suggested that these had not worked because van Wagenen and Herren had not fully severed the corpus callosum. Vogen and Bogel therefore severed it completely and found success in controlling the seizures of an ex-paratrooper who previously had life-threatening seizures. Sperry (along with his colleagues Hubel and Wiesel) had been experimenting with some sophisticated callosotomy surgery with animals and eventually performed them on humans (Berlucchi, 2006). They went on to win the Nobel prize in physiology or medicine for their work with split-brain research in 1981.

Sperry was very much interested in the age old dichotomy of 'nature vs. nurture'. To get some answers to some of the questions this dichotomy invokes, Sperry set up a number of rather horrific but nonetheless intriguing experiments on rats. He took the motor nerves from their left and right hind legs and switched them over (right to left and left to right). He then placed each leg of the rat onto each of four sections on an electric grid and then a shock was administered to each section. When the shock was administered to the left hind leg via the electric grid, the right leg was lifted up and when administered to the right hind leg, the left was lifted. It was interesting to Sperry that the rats never actually learnt to lift up the leg that was receiving the shock. This was proof for him that some things are simply hardwired and cannot be relearned (Berlucchi, 2006).

Today, a lot of contemporary neuroscience seeking to further understand the possible lateralisation of emotion is conducted via brain imaging techniques, such as positron emission tomography (PET) and functional magnetic resonance imaging (fMRI). Pizzagalli et al. undertook a review of selected research papers that were published between 1993 and 2001. They concluded that there are presently many inconsistencies in the literature and these are likely to be

> a function of a multitude of causes including methodological issues in the statistical assessment of asymmetry, variability in affective responses that are elicited by particular stimulus conditions and the failure to utilize proper control conditions in the experiments. (2003: 23)

Cultural Factors

Although there has been some evidence for hemisphere specificity in emotion processing (particularly in relation to the right side of the brain), this does not necessarily mean that emotion is hard-wired in particular parts of the brain. Cultural factors are very likely to influence functional organization. For example, Racle (1980; 1986) discussed Tadonobu Tsunoda's research on Japanese people's brains and reported that they tend to process both linguistic and non-linguistic sounds (including emotional utterances) in the left hemisphere. This contrasts with people from Western countries who tend to process non-linguistic sounds within the right hemisphere. However, this does not appear to be the case for Japanese people raised in countries where Western languages are spoken. Thus it does not appear to be a hereditary (hard-wired) phenomenon. Additionally, left-handed individuals display a relatively greater ability to integrate the left and right hemispheres (Christman, 1995) and there is other evidence that some individuals show a greater capacity for interhemispheric integration than others (Hellige, 1993).

Affective Neuroscience

Affective neuroscience is a relatively new discipline in emotion research which has emerged alongside the technological advances that have been made in neuroimaging techniques. For example, these techniques include functional magnetic resonance imaging, computer tomography, positron emission tomography, and electroencephalography. Functional magnetic resonance imaging (fMRI) detects changes in blood oxygenation that occur in response to neural activity. When an area of the brain is more active it consumes more oxygen; to meet this demand there is increased blood flow in the area that is active. Computed tomography (CT) is a technique whereby a picture of the brain is created through the differential absorption of X-rays. The pictures created by the x-rays are dependent upon the amount the x-ray beams that are absorbed. Air and water absorb the x-rays very little while hard tissue absorbs them well. Positron emission tomography (PET) traces radioactive material in the brain to map its various functional processes. A short lived radioactive tracer (isotope) is injected into the blood circulation. The isotope then undergoes positron emission (decay) when it interacts with an electron. The interaction produces photons which can be picked up by the detector. Electroencephalography (EEG) measures the electrical activity within the brain. Electrodes are placed on the scalp which can pick up electrical signals from neurons. It is able to pick up changes in electrical activity in the brain.

Using these techniques, affective neuroscience literally attempts to look at the brain mechanisms which are seen to underlie emotional behaviour. Importantly, however, researchers in this field recognise how the subjective nature of experience is central to the configuration of the affect. Affective neuroscience has generally challenged a lot of the cognitive models of psychology by offering evidence to suggest that emotion influences a host of psychological processes such as attention, perception, learning and memory at many, if not all, levels. Dalgleish (2004) states that research in affective neurosciences has addressed a multitude of questions such as:

> Which brain systems underlie emotions? How do differences in these systems relate to differences in the emotional experience of individuals? Do different regions underlie different emotions, or are all emotions a function of the same basic brain circuitry? How does emotion processing

in the brain relate to bodily changes associated with emotion? And, how does emotion processing in the brain interact with cognition, motor behaviour, language and motivation? (Dalgleish, 2004: 583

Empathic Mirroring

An example of the kind of work that is being explored in this field which is quite important to social psychological understandings of emotion are the attempts to distinguish the neural mechanisms through which we understand other people. For instance, simulation of the behaviours of others is a way that we can experience, say, the intentions of others. Neuroscientists have presented some interesting insights into the processes of what they see as the central place for simulation in learning through finding what they term mirror neurons. These neurons are seen to be located within the premotor and motor cortices of primates. Rizzolatti and his colleagues found that these neurons respond when both performing a specific action and when viewing another performing that action; however, these studies were conducted on monkeys (Rizzolatti, Fadiga, Gallese, and Fogassi, 1996). Since these early studies, subsequent research also shows activity in the human brain which is seen as mirroring perceived actions. Human emotional empathy has also been correlated to the same brain region. For example, when observing one's partner in pain, neurons in the motor cortex are activated which leads to the suggestion that one is also, but to a different extent, experiencing the pain that the partner feels (Singer et al., 2004). However, importantly Singer et al. add that although the partners may have a similar affective experience of pain, emotional empathy does not involve the entire matrix of pain. Only 'that part of the pain network associated with its affective qualities, but not its sensory qualities, mediates empathy' (2004: 1157).

Harrison and colleagues similarly found that the brain activates unconscious autonomic somatic responses which mirror emotion that is being observed (Harrison et al., 2006). More specifically their findings suggest that our empathic responses are fundamental to our ability to share emotions with others. For example, unconsciously perceiving another person's pupil size can modulate our perception of the other's emotional facial expression. A diminishing pupil size enhances the ratings of emotional intensity for a perceived sad face (however, this was not the case for happy and neutral facial expressions). Interestingly they also found that the observed pupil size was mirrored by the observer's own pupil size. As stated in the previous chapter, some of this body of work in the affective neurosciences is beginning to shed some light into processes that evoke so called 'emotional contagion'. It can be suggested, therefore, that the observation of the emotions of others may be a more general unconscious feature of the human interaction which goes beyond the classical mirror neurons hypothesis. Research in the area of affective neuroscience has the potential to open many of the dark secrets concerning the communication of affective activity. This has been particularly taken up by neuroscientists who are interested in psychoanalysis, thus a new branch of thought has sprung up entitled neuropsychoanalysis.

Neuropsychoanalysis

Although Freud continued to use biological metaphors and concepts through his development of psychoanalysis, he is seen as formally breaking with neurology early on in his career. His attempt to link neurology with psychoanalysis can be seen in his incomplete work called *Project for a Scientific Psychology* (1895). At that time, just over 100 years ago, the neuron was only just beginning to be described and understood. Because of the lack of knowledge and technical abilities, Freud decided to abandon his project. It is argued, for example by Kaplan-Solms and Solms, that we now have the knowledge and the technical abilities to continue Freud's project (Kaplan-Solms and Solms, 2001). The method that they use is the 'clinico-anatomical method'. They use brain imaging techniques to look at localised brain lesions, such as tumours and strokes and surgical lesions, and correlate these to psychological (particularly psychoanalytic) functioning. These methods are regarded as further substantiating psychoanalysis as an empirical science. Indeed this method, albeit now more sophisticated, mirrors the early work that Freud conducted with the great French neurologist, Jean-Martin Charcot.

Although object-relations theory was initially developed through a reaction to Freud's biologisation of psychic processes, it has fore-grounded a number of neuro-biological developmental perspectives concerning the emotional interaction between the mother and baby; for instance, to look at ways that emotions are developed and constituted within the social world. In relation to this Alan Schore has developed a multidisciplinary view of affect development and regulation (Schore, 1994). Schore threads many psychological, biological and indeed social theories together to develop a theory exposing the infant's affect systems developing in a number of post-natal critical periods of cortical growth. Culture plays a vital role in this development, as attachment phenomena are reported to be central to processes through which a whole complex of emotional expressions are developed,

> ... the most powerful elicitor of affect [in the first years of an infant's life] is information emanating from an emotionally expressive face... These experiences would permanently shape the final critical period maturation of the dual circuit orbitofrontal cortex and thereby indelibly influence its appraisal capacities and the types of socioaffective stimuli to which it selectively attends or excludes... This psychoneurobiological process may underlie the mechanism of the child's induction into an 'emotional culture,' by which the child constructs out of social interaction a molar or complex unit of prototypical components for each emotion identified by the culture. (Schore, 1994: 281)

Schore points to ways in which idiosyncratic and cultural expressions are learnt by the child in the prelinguistic period of development. He suggests that emotions may at times be both more primitive than language and learnt through individual and cultural non-verbal expressions. Kaplan-Solms and Solms state,

> Shore's model focuses primarily on the ventromesial frontal cortex, which he conceptualises as the inhibitory component of a motivational system that originates in subcortical limbic and brain stem structures, the physical maturation of which he demonstrates is significantly guided by certain aspects of early mother-infant interaction. The ventromesial frontal cortex is thereby shown to almost literally embody an internalized, containing mother (2001: 234).

This concept is then both challenging to theories advocating basic emotions, which suggest that a number of emotions are evolutionary hard wired neural circuits, and also challenges cognitive appraisal models of emotion, which suggest that emotions are the expression of cognitive appraisals based within a language system, but very much supports the understanding that emotion is primitive.

Although Kaplan-Solms and Solms appear to be appreciative of the work that Schore has conducted, for example in his book *Affect regulation and the development of the self*, Schore tends to side with object-relations theories of affect regulation and thus the historical splits between the Kleinian and the Freudian schools of psychoanalysis begin to emerge. Kaplan-Solms and Solms argue that the notion that the baby is primarily object-seeking from birth,

> ignores the fact that what the 'object-seeking' infant is seeking is pleasure (or relief from unpleasure). And that the attraction to the object only arises because the object is capable of meeting the infant's needs (i.e. ultimately, of reducing drive tension). (2001: 235–6)

Kaplan-Solms and Solms are in the process of developing Freud's drive theory through further understanding neuro-chemicals such as dopamine and noradrenalin. For example, they suggest that there is compelling evidence that dopaminergic circuits in the brain can be associated with drive discharge. There is also compelling evidence to suggest that noradrenergic circuits in the brain are associated with the binding of libidinal energies (inhibition of drive discharge) which, in line with Schore's understanding, occur in the ventromedial frontal region. In other words, these processes are linked to learning to regulate emotion and are inextricably linked to the social.

Damasio's Somatic Marker Hypothesis

Another very popular theorist, who perhaps can be categorised under the affective neuroscience umbrella, is Antonio Damasio. Although Damasio and his colleagues have published a large number of high impact factor publications of their empirical research (for example see Bechara, Damasio, and Damasio, 2000), Damasio has also managed to publish a number of books which are very accessible to the general lay public. He has done very well to describe a neural system that integrates feelings, affect and cognition in relation to social processes. He proposes that much decision-making is influenced by marker signals (emotional signals) that arise in bioregulatory processes which may operate both consciously and non-consciously. The ventromedial (VM) sector of the frontal lobe of the brain is a critical connection in this system, as was suggested in the previous section. A number of studies have suggested that VM lesions significantly disrupt decision-making in social settings, whilst leaving intellectual faculties such as learning, memory, language and attention relatively unaffected. The classic case that is usually referred to is Phineas Gage who had a three centimetre tamping iron pass through his skull and frontal lobe in 1823 (today it is possible to observe his skull and tamping iron in a museum in Massachusetts). The accident caused him to show little intellectual, or linguistic impairment, but he became more egocentric, obstinate and capricious than before; in other words his ability to read the social world and act according to social norms was extremely diminished.

Damasio argues that there is a constant representational mapping of the bioregulatory state of the body within somatosensory parts of the brain. This body-state mapping is coupled with monitoring of the external social world. As new stimuli are encountered, maps previously associated with similar stimuli are inducted and the feelings associated with previously experienced stimuli are re-evoked. These feelings then act as a covert biasing system which facilitates rapid decision-making, marking options with valences according to whether the re-evoked feeling is negative or positive. In other words these somatic maps or what he coins 'somatic markers', are re-evoked feelings which help us to negotiate day-to-day social activity. Evidence for this 'somatic marker' hypothesis is derived both from clinical studies which reveal a 'double dissociation' between VM lesions, impaired decision making and flattened affect, and from experimental work with brain injured participants. In one study, participants tried to win money in a card gambling task (Iowa Gambling Task). A control group without lesions developed higher levels of skin conductivity before a high risk gamble. Skin conductivity is gauged through the discretion of sweat from the eccrine glands of the palms of the hands which are associated with autonomic nervous system activity and thus emotional arousal. The heightened emotional arousal, although often non-conscious, seemed to influence effective gambling strategies. However, participants with bilateral VM lesions were unable to find appropriate gambling strategies and avoid losses.

Bechara and colleagues thus propose that decision making may be dependent on the generation of somatic states, configurations of the 'internal milieu, visceral and musculoskeletal' activity (Bechara et al., 2000: 295), in other words emotional dispositions. The VM prefrontal cortex is necessary to form such links between factual knowledge and body-states. Although it is emphasised that these links are dispositional, they 'do not hold the representation of the facts or of the emotional state explicitly, but hold rather the potential to reactivate an emotion by acting on the appropriate cortical or subcortical structures' (Bechara et al., 2000: 296). Following repeated associations, the actual body-state is not always engendered, but instead may merely be re-presented as a somatosensory map. Damasio names this the *as-if body loop*, since the brain creates the feeling of a body-state without there being any actual body-state change.

> In numerous instances the brain learns to concoct the fainter image of an 'emotional' body state, without having to re-enact it in the body proper ... the activation of neurotransmitter nuclei in the brain stem and their responses bypass the body, the neurotransmitter nuclei are part and parcel of the brain representation of body regulation. (1994: 155).

Where formerly a somatic-state was induced, now a cortical representation of that profile is evoked instead (a body-state map), accelerating the process. Because of the advantages this acceleration provides, Damasio suggests that the as-if body loop will usually come to supersede the somatic state response. The fundamental component of the somatic marker hypothesis is that bioregulatory signals, including those that constitute feeling and emotion, provide the principal guide for decisions and are the basis for the development of the as-if body loop mode of operation (Bechara et al., 2000).

The as-if body loop, it is suggested, develops throughout maturation and environmental adaptation.

> The association between a certain mental image and the surrogate of a body state would have been acquired by repeatedly associating the images of given entities or situations with the images of freshly enacted body states. To have a particular image trigger the 'bypass device,' it was first necessary to run the process through the body theatre, to loop it through the body, as it were. (Damasio, 1994: 196)

Clearly, the movement from the somatic states to the as-if body loop reduces body-state changes and ANS activity. A stimulus which previously initiated a highly aroused body-state now calls out its surrogate instead, using this to inform executive activity. Thus they consider that there is a cognitive and social advantage gained by the increased speed of processing due to the as-if body loop. If Damasio and his colleagues are right, this really does complicate (or perhaps simplify?) age-old dichotomies and distinctions that we have discussed throughout this book between the mind and body.

There have been numerous critiques of Damasio's work. For example, Wetherell (2012) suggests that Damasio's theory is invalid as it includes the 'basic emotions thesis' discussed above. Wetherell offers some nice critique of this thesis, but perhaps is overly reliant on this critique to dismiss central aspects of Damasio's theory that we have described here. Indeed the somatic-marker hypothesis is not reliant upon the 'basic-emotions thesis'. The markers do not necessarily have to be maps of basic emotions but rather feelings, emotions or rather 'body states' that one has previously experienced. A number of more detailed critiques of Damasio's work are put forward by Bennett and Hacker (2003). Many of the critiques rest upon the following quote taken from Damasio through which he describes 'the essence of emotion as the collection of changes in the body state that are induced in myriad organs by nerve cell terminals, under the control of a dedicated brain system, which is responding to the content of thoughts relative to a particular entity or event' (1996: 139). Bennett and Hacker pick up on Damasio's understanding of what a 'thought' is which they suggest rests upon the outmoded British empiricist tradition encapsulated by David Hume (whom we looked at in Chapter 3). Thus they suggest that Damasio 'holds the view that if thought were not exhibited to us in the form of images of things and images of words signifying things, then we would not be able to say what we think' (2003: 211). In a footnote they describe their critique of this by stating that Damasio,

> fails to see that one could not find out what one thinks by mere attention to whatever mental images cross one's mind when one thinks. A mental image may, as it were, illustrate a thought, as a picture may illustrate a text. But it is the thought that makes the mental image the image of what it depicts, just as it is the text of the book that makes the illustration an illustration of the story. Without the text the picture of Lancelot in full armour could depict any knight whatsoever, illustrate how to sit in the saddle, or how not to sit in the saddle, illustrate armour of a given period, or depict the kind of horse used by knights in armour and so on. And what applies to the relation of picture to text applies similarly to the relation of mental image and thought. (2003: 211, fn 9).

However, this is perhaps a misrepresentation of Damasio's understanding of what he means by the term 'image'. In the introductory section of his book *The Feeling of What Happens* Damasio states,

> by image I mean a mental pattern in any of the sensory modalities, e.g., a sound image, a tactile image, the image of a state of well-being. Such images convey aspects of the physical characteristics of the object and they may also convey the reaction of like or dislike one may have for an object, the plans one may formulate for it, or the web of relationships of that object among other objects. (2000: 9)

Indeed, Damasio goes on to admit that presently there is an 'explanatory gap' in the neurosciences to sufficiently explain how these sensory qualities become mental patterns or what Damasio is referring to here as 'images'. For example it is not clear how 'the blueness of the sky or the tone of sound produced by a cello' (2000: 9) are converted from nerve cell endings to what he denotes as an image.

It is fair to say that Damasio does present some compelling evidence and theory in relation to the somatic marker hypothesis, which has been taken up by a variety of social scientists most notably outside the field of neurosciences. Of particular significance is that somatic markers affect individuals often in non-conscious ways. It is here that Damasio makes some very interesting distinctions which have not been included in mainstream psychology understandings of emotion since William James (see Chapter 4). Emotion for Damasio is related to body-state changes that occur which are not-conscious, it is not until we have the feeling of the emotion that we then may begin to know we have the emotion. It is how these non-conscious body-state maps (related to emotion) are socially constructed and how they subsequently influence decision making which may be of particular interest to the social psychologist and more particularly that emotion need not be some primitive force, but rather, and Hume would be proud of this, an intelligent guide.

Conclusion

One may ask the question: why should there be a chapter on biological under-standings of emotion within a book on the social psychology of emotion? Mainstream social psychologists would probably not be alarmed at this, as the biological sciences have, as we discussed in Chapter 4, been relatively dominant in psychology, and have helped it gain purchase as a science. 'Critical social psychologists' are more likely to be concerned, due to a view of biological theories as having a sordid history, in terms of an essentialising tendency that has, at times, been used to justify forms of social Darwinism which do not often favour equality and an appreciation of diversity. Indeed, why should we need to know about the brain to understand psychological functioning at all? Isn't it more valid to explore emotion through individual/socio-cultural expressions, subjective reportings, narratives, discourses, novels, music, behaviour and cultural artefacts? As we suggested in our introduction, the study of emotion requires, to some extent, intra/inter/trans-disciplinarity. It is undeniable that emotion, as well as having something to do with that which is outside of us and that which is between us, also has something to do with the within, that which is under our skin. Indeed it is a bit of an irony that the biological sciences, particularly the socially-aware affective neurosciences, should begin to help us to move away from the dominant thesis that emotion is animalistic, irrational and untrustwor-thy to views of it as at times providing us with non-conscious and yet intelligent information which appear to guide our everyday social activity. In the next section we move away from the focus on biological processes to the other end of the spectrum, to focus on the sociology of emotion.

FURTHER READING

Charles Darwin's book *The Expression of Emotions in Man and Animals* was published in 1872. It has been extremely influential and still today forms the bedrock of many theorisations of emotion. This book should be on the shelves of every emotion scholar and even the most vehement opponents of the universality thesis of emotion should find it a useful reference point.

Panksepp, J. (1998). *Affective Neuroscience: The foundations of human and animal emotions.* Oxford: Oxford University Press.
This book is part of the Series of Affective Science published by Oxford University Press. All of the books in the series would of course be of interest to scholars wanting to explore the affective neurosciences.

In the context of neuropsychoanalysis there have been two books that we find particularly helpful:

Schore, A. (1994). *Affect Regulation and the Development of the Self: The neurobiology of emotional development.* Hillsdale, NJ: Lawrence Erlbaum Associates.

and

Kaplan-Solms, K. and Solms, M. (2000). *Clinical Studies in Neuro-Psychoanalysis: Introduction to a depth neuropsychology.* New York: Other Press, LLC.

Antonio Damasio manages to put across some very complex neuroscientific concepts of emotion in a very accessible way. Indeed his books could be classed as more popular science than serious scholarship. For more detailed and scholarly renditions of his work one would do well to look for his journal publications. However, readers may be interested in his following two books which we have found useful:

Damasio, A. (1994). *Descartes' Error: Emotion, reason and the human brain.* New York: Putnam.

and

Damasio, A. (2000). *The Feeling of What Happens: Body, emotion and the making of consciousness.* London: Vintage.

7

Sociological Understandings of Emotion

Key Aims

In this chapter we will discuss the sociology of emotion. In doing so we will include:

- Discussion of some micro-sociological accounts concerning emotion based interaction
- An exploration of dramaturgical theory of Goffman focusing on his notion of face-work
- Details of Hochschild's view of emotion work
- A review of the research concerned with the social construction of emotion particularly in relation to gender

Introduction

The sociology of emotion is a growing sub-discipline of sociology which has been influenced by an eclectic mix of theories and concepts. Surprisingly, it was not until 1975 that sociologists started to become more interested in emotion. This is mainly due to the work of Erving Goffman and Arlie Hochschild, whose theories are among those we will discuss in this chapter. As one might expect, sociologists have tended to be more interested in emotion as an experience of social relations and social structures rather than a quality that individuals have. We have already seen, particularly throughout the historical sections of this book, how emotion has been theorised as important to state governance (for example, Aristotle and Hobbes) and to social-ethical decision-making processes (for example, Hume and Kant). Indeed, many of the theories of emotion we have looked at are concerned with, ultimately, how emotion is very much tied up with relational (and therefore social psychological) processes. In many respects it is quite obvious that the study of emotion should form a vital part of sociology. Indeed Shilling makes the point that concepts of emotion were importantly included in the early social theories of Comte, Durkheim, Simmel and Weber, who are regarded as founding and shaping the discipline of sociology (Shilling, 1997); subsequently theories of emotion became much more the domain of psychology and the biological sciences until relatively recently.

Like social psychology, there is no one theoretical or methodological framework which characterises sociology as a whole. The same can be said for the sociology of emotion: there is not one but a variety of, sometimes competing, theoretical and methodological perspectives. What is similar in many sociological accounts of emotion is that they differ from many early biological accounts (particularly evolutionary) by emphasising that the patterns of emotional expression are different from society to society and culture to culture and moreover, there is a concern for what emotion does rather than what it is. This does not mean that there is a denial that biological processes are involved – for example, many of the theories that we will consider below are concerned with facial expressions – but the emphasis is of course that emotion is more fundamentally socially constituted than it is biologically determined. Additionally, as we shall see throughout this chapter, sociologists are particularly interested in links between power and the politics of emotion.

A Two Factor Model

One of the underlying theories of emotion which have helped to pave the way for social accounts is Schachter and Singer's (1962) two factor model. The two factors are physiological arousal and social cognition. Very simply put this theory suggests that emotional states are a combination of a general arousal of the sympathetic nervous system coupled with a cognitive interpretation (appraisal) of the arousal (or feeling) that it produces. The cognitive appraisal is seen, therefore, to be coloured by the perception of the situation (the social context) from which we believe the arousal (feeling state) was brought about.

In a famous experiment, Schachter and Singer (1962) injected participants with adrenalin (epinephrine) which has an arousing effect on the sympathetic nervous system. Participants tended to act happily when they were put with a research accomplice who was generally larking about and happy. When they were put with an accomplice who acted angrily and generally insulted the participants and displayed anger, the participants also displayed similar kinds of angry emotions. These emotional effects occurred more vigorously when the participants were not informed about the physiological effects of the injection. The participants who were told that the injection would make them feel jumpy, did not display as much emotion (either happiness or anger) as the other participants. Schachter and

Singer went on to provide what they saw as three important propositions concerning emotion:.

1. Given a state of physiological arousal for which an individual has no immediate explanation he (sic) will label this state and describe his feelings in terms of the cognitions available to him...
2. Given a state of physiological arousal for which an individual has a completely appropriate explanation...no evaluation needs will arise and the individual is likely to label his feelings in terms of the alternative cognitions available...
3. Given the same cognitive circumstances, the individual will react emotionally or describe his feelings as emotions only to the extent that he experiences a state of physiological arousal. (1962: 381)

Generally the theory suggests that emotions are controlled through a very close interrelationship with the physiological arousal and the cognitive appraisal of the arousal; that is individuals will look for clues within the social context for the cause of psychophysiological excitation that they feel. The arousal is then interpreted accordingly with the perceived emotion. Although this theory has been quite influential and seemingly robust there are a number of criticisms of it.

Subsequent studies have not been able to replicate these findings (Manstead and Wagner, 1981; Reisenzein, 1983). Leventhal and Tomarken (1986) has presented a number of criticisms of the two factor theory, particularly in relation to the implication that emotion and feeling states therefore must be all subjectively learned. If this is the case then how is a young child capable of feeling anything before he or she knows the label for the feeling, if it is the label that promotes the feeling?

However, the two factor theory of emotion has allowed theorists to move away from biological accounts; to think more about, for example, the way that cultural definitions of the physiological arousal are produced and what the social functions are for which these serve. At times the reason for the physiological arousal is ambiguous and so therefore people tend to look for answers and clues to the arousal in the external environment to make sense of it. The causal relations that we attribute to the arousal which subsequently generates particular psychological emotional tones, Rosenberg argues, are developed through social consensus and social scripts that we have acquired through socialisation practices through particular 'emotion cultures' (Rosenberg, 1990) as will be discussed throughout this chapter.

The Dramaturgical Theory of Emotion

Erving Goffman has researched and written extensively about the cultural scripts and scenarios that make up emotion cultures. Goffman developed a dramaturgical approach; that is, he sees social interaction as a dramatic production performed between actors who draw on cultural scripts. Emotion is central to these performances in that we use them as cues in interaction.

In *The Presentation of the Self in Everyday Life* Goffman discusses in sometimes painful detail the kinds of rituals and performances that are played out when one enters the presence of another. Most particularly he stresses that individuals tend to (particularly when unacquainted) try to find out 'information' about the other to help 'define the situation, enabling others to know in advance what he will expect of them and what they may expect of him' (1959: 1). This then will help one to know how best to 'act' stereotypically in attempts to evoke a desired response. This works through then drawing on an appropriate cultural script to determine the interaction with the view of creating the right kind of 'impression' upon the other which is in his or her interest. For example, one may look at the appearance and behaviour of the other in relation to the context to guide the interaction and one's emotional display. This helps individuals to figure out what emotional and interactional dynamics are appropriate to achieve one's end. Thus individuals in interaction 'choose' particular culturally relevant scripts from their experiential storehouse which additionally determine the right type of emotion to display. However, Goffman states that there are limits to our abilities to keep up an act, and others will examine micro phenomena, for example facial expressions, to find cracks to 'find out' what the other 'really' feels. The following is a relatively extensive example given by Goffman:

> ... in Shetland Isle one crofter's wife, in serving native dishes to a visitor from the mainland of Britain, would listen with a polite smile to his polite claims of liking what he was eating; at the same time she would take note of the rapidity with which the visitor lifted his fork or spoon to his mouth, the eagerness with which he passed food into his mouth, and the gusto expressed in chewing the food, using these signs as a check on the stated feelings of the eater. The same woman, in order to discover what one acquaintance (A) 'actually' thought of another acquaintance (B), would wait until B was in the presence of A but engaged in conversation with still another person (C). She would then covertly examine the facial expression of A as he regarded B in conversation with C. Not being in conversation with B, and not being directly observed by him, A would sometimes relax usual constraints and tactful deceptions, and freely express what he was 'actually' feeling about B. This Shetlander, in short, would observe the unobserved observer. (Goffman, 1959: 6–7)

Goffman here pulls out of the above hypothetical interaction distinctions between the 'polite' surface expressions from the 'actual' underlying thoughts, detected through both extra-discursive activity (i.e. facial expressions and eating behaviours) and the almost covert surveillance of conversation. This, however, may appear as cold and calculated forms of impression management; but he states it need not be,

Sometimes the traditions of an individual's role will lead him to give a well-designed impression of a particular kind and yet he may be neither consciously nor unconsciously disposed to create such an impression. (1959: 6)

Goffman's understanding of the importance of emotion is also evident in his 1961 work on *Encounters*. Goffman's conceptualisation of 'encounters' can be described as the kinds of behaviour that occur through the interaction caused by what he called 'a focused gathering' or 'a situated activity system'. Thus 'encounters provide the communication base for a circular flow of feeling among the participants as well as corrective compensations of deviant acts" (1961: 18). In a later work, *Interaction Ritual*, Goffman discusses some of the rituals that are involved in 'correcting compensations of deviant acts' through his concept of 'face-work' (Goffman, 1967).

Face-work

The term *face* may be defined as the positive social value a person effectively claims for himself by the line others assume he has taken during a particular contact. Face is an image of self delineated in terms of approved social attributes – albeit an image that others may share, as when a person makes a good showing for his profession or religion by making a good showing for himself. A person tends to experience an immediate emotional response to the face which a contact with others allows him; he cathects his face; his 'feelings' become attached to it. (Goffman, 1967: 5–6)

In other words, people are emotionally attached to their faces. For example, people feel good when events have gone on to establish a face for the person that is better than expected. When being *in face* rather than *out of face* or having *the wrong face*, the feelings associated with the responses by that person, according to Goffman, are that of confidence and reassurance (1967: 8). Conversely, *loss of face* leads to emotional pain; for example through feeling ashamed (*shamefaced*) and inferior. In such situations the person presents with 'no useable line' in other words, there is no cultural script in one's storehouse to draw upon. Goffman adds that 'this creates disorder to the expressive organization of the situation' (1967: 9). Therefore we need to perform various social acts to *save face*, indeed Goffman points out that within Chinese culture one can say to *give face*, this is a cultural ritual that is employed to facilitate the saving of face of the other, in other words they get *face given back* (1967: 9). The process of saving face, in any culture, is often employed to sustain 'the expressive order' to regulate the flow of events and because of 'the emotional identification with the others and with their feelings', otherwise one may appear to be 'heartless' (1967: 9–11).

But this given face is only 'on loan' and may be taken back if the other does not correspond accordingly. The kinds of rituals that are involved here are named *face-work* by Goffman.

This was described in two general ways by Goffman as 'the avoidance process' and 'the corrective process'. The avoidance process concerns avoiding discussing certain topics to maintain a positive face. For example, I often choose not to discuss either religion or politics at extended family gatherings. This is because I have often experienced arguments and feelings of anger and frustration that arise through such discussions which may negatively impact upon extended family relationships. Thus conversations are often constructed in such a manner to avoid topics that may be controversial or raise anxiety. Goffman suggests that we will often suppress feelings in conversation until we have knowledge about 'what kind of line the others will be ready to support' (1967: 16).

The corrective process involves what Goffman considers as 'four classic moves'. Firstly, persons may call to attention the form of misconduct that was committed: 'the challenge'. Secondly, in 'the offering', the person being challenged may be offered the chance to apologise or account for the inappropriate behaviour, to 're-establish the expressive order'. Goffman discusses a number of ways that the offering may occur. For example, a joke may be made of it so it isn't taken seriously, or the person may claim not to be accountable for the activity (e.g. 'this wine has got to my head!'). An offering of penance and punishment may be made in a bid to uphold the expressive order; for example, accept the loss of face and the loss of pride that comes with that, promising not to do it again. Thirdly, the person who has been offended may then accept the 'ritual offering' as a satisfactory means of restoration. Lastly the offender offers 'thanks' for being forgiven. Goffman also hypothesises a number of departures from these 'classic moves' (1967: 19–23). Goffman stresses the central role of emotions throughout these moves.

> It is plain that emotions play a part in these cycles of response, as when anguish is expressed because of what one has done to another's face, or anger because of what has been done to one's own. I want to stress that these emotions function as moves, and fit so precisely into the logic of the ritual game that it would seem difficult to understand them without it. In fact, spontaneously expressed feelings are likely to fit into the formal pattern of the ritual interchange more elegantly than consciously designed ones. (1967: 23).

Feeling Rules

These kinds of 'rituals of politeness' are used by people in cooperation to maintain each other's faces. This Goffman calls 'impression management' that people use 'to make positive impressions on others and to help others and ourselves save face when interaction goes awry' (Stets and Turner, 2006). Impression management is highly emotional as it is seen as guiding these encounters and so facilitating the maintenance of social arrangements, it incorporates 'feeling rules'. These feeling rules which create forms of 'ritual care' produce and reproduce a moral order. However, this does not mean that we are therefore always concerned about saving the other's face; Goffman recognises that there are those who will aggressively manipulate the feeling rules for personal gain. Thus actors are both heroes and villains (and sometimes simultaneously both). Fineman (2008) points out, however, that people for Goffman

> belong neither to the sacred nor the profane but continually cross boundaries – sometimes cynical, sometimes sincere, sometimes the hero, sometimes the villain, but all always present to some degree. They are image-makers rather than mere images and their emotions are agential experiences and not cultural artefacts. (Fineman, 2008)

Emotion Work

In her paper *Emotion Work, Feeling Rules, and Social Structures*, Arlie Hochschild asks,

> Why is the emotive experience of normal adults in daily life as orderly as it is? Why, generally speaking, do people feel gay at parties, sad at funerals, happy at weddings? (Hochschild, 1979: 87)

Of course, there are cultural scripts or feeling rules concerning what we ought to feel in given situations. Often, however, we do not feel as we ought in a given situation and then quite often we have to engage in what Hochschild called 'emotion work' in attempts to manage our feelings as the cultural script and feeling rules demand. This process Hochschild described as 'the act of trying to change in degree or quality an emotion or feeling' (Hochschild, 1979: 94). For example, if you attended a funeral of somebody who was not that close to you, and for some reason you felt quite happy, for instance because you had just inherited a lot of money from that person, you would be expected to engage in emotion work to evoke sadness, at least to give the impression to others that you are feeling sad.

Emotion work may involve what Hochschild called either 'surface acting' or 'deep acting'. Surface acting involves simply changing one's outward expressions to appear as if one were feeling in a particular normative way which was socially desired. Deep acting, by contrast, involves not only deceiving others that you are feeling a certain way, but involves deceiving the self that you are feeling a certain way. In this way it is not only the expression that is manipulated, but also one's emotional experience. Hochschild also identified two forms of work that are involved in emotion work: body work (altering the physiological aspect) and cognitive work (altering thoughts and ideas) (Hochschild, 1990). These changes are brought about through both evocation and suppression. One attempts to either evoke a socially desirable feeling or suppress a socially undesirable feeling.

Hochschild (1983) also looked at how businesses have commercialised emotional management or what she termed 'emotional labour'. Emotional labour is theorised as being performed in the workplace to manipulate the emotions of customers or clients to facilitate desired reactions. For example, flight attendants are taught to express particular emotions so as to help the customers feel safe and happy. When the aeroplane hits an air pocket which produces turbulence, the flight attendants are taught not to produce any anxious expressions, but rather to express happiness and calmness in a mothering manner. Of course this relates to forms of emotional contagion that we discussed earlier. This will help the passengers to feel at home and comfortable with the view that they will use the airline again. Another example of this that perhaps many parents will recognise, is when a young child has an accident, for example falling off a sofa. Commonly, the child will look at the parent to 'read' her/his facial expression. If some kind of worried expression is read, it is likely that the child will start crying, even if he or she has not been hurt. The parent then learns not to pull an anxious expression on occasions when it is felt that it is unlikely that the child is hurt. Instead perhaps the parent will smile and say some words of comfort or joke so that the child does not start crying. However, Hochschild went on to argue that in some cases too much sustained emotional labour can lead to feelings of self-estrangement, alienation and inauthenticity (I should note!). So, the feeling rules of emotional labour can be learned by people from when they are young children. Hochschild (1983) argues that some families teach their children to value feelings that will help them to become good emotional labourers. For example, children are often taught that the feelings of their superiors are extremely important, this is then transferred to the workplace and can engender a contoured world of emotional inequality as we saw when we looked at Aristotle. Hochschild also notes that children need also to be taught that their own feelings are important and importantly that emotions can be managed.

The Constructions of Gendered Emotion

This next section is very much indebted to Stephanie Shields and her colleagues who have extensively researched the socially produced meanings of emotion in relation to gender. Shields has written an influential book entitled *Speaking from the Heart* through which she discusses the prevailing stereotypical beliefs (or what we have alluded to as cultural scripts) which suggest 'she is emotional and he is not' or what she calls 'the master stereotype'. She draws on examples from popular culture, everyday life and empirical research which reinforce the belief that women are emotionally expressive while men are not. The supposed emotional inexpressivity of men, Shields argues, is often understood as a trait, that is a fairly stable (measurable) personality factor that may be innate, learned, or both (2002: 121).

For example, the manly man needs to learn to avoid expressing emotion as this will lead to vulnerability and moreover signs of femininity and weakness.

Shields argues that these beliefs are contradictory; for example, masculine traits include a host of emotion related components; such as 'sexual interest, aggressiveness, competitiveness, anger' (2002: 120). Masculine emotional inexpressivity seems to be much more about the inability to talk about emotion or a disinterest in it as something to be discussed, rather than the ability to show emotion; when men display it 'emotion is not often counted as emotion' (2002: 124). Shields et al. look at a number of studies that tend to demonstrate the contradiction of the gender-emotion stereotype. For example, Robinson and Johnson (1997) found that participants described female targets as more 'emotional' than male targets even though they saw male targets as more 'stressed' than females. Shields goes on to argue that,

> Given that participants believe men express more anger more often than women (Timmers et al., 2003), believe men express positive emotions more often than women in certain contexts (Johnson and Schulman, 1988), it seems contradictory that participants would also describe women as 'more emotional' than men. Essentially, participants are labelling female, but not male, emotion expression as 'emotional'. (Shields et al., 2006: 69)

Gendered Assumptions

Individuals are prone to resort to the gender stereotypes of emotion to guide judgments when faced with ambiguous situations. It was found that when presented with photographs of a combination of ambiguous angry and sad faces, the participants tended to rate the males as being more expressive of anger and the females as more expressive of sadness (Plant et al., 2000). However, when the faces were less ambiguous the stereotyping was not as prominent. Shields et al. (2006) state that other studies have similarly gone on to suggest that when we do not have enough information to make a judgment concerning a person's emotional state, we tend to draw on gender stereotypes to formulate judgments.

Relatedly, there is quite a strong tendency advanced by these cultural scripts that suggests that men express *powerful* emotions and women express *powerless* emotions (Fabes and Martin, 1991; Fischer, 1993). Gender and emotion therefore are seen to have strong associations with issues of power. Powerless emotions are related to feminine vulnerability (low power), whereas powerful emotions are related to masculine dominance (high power). Masculine powerful emotions are associated with, for example, anger and pride; whereas feminine powerless emotions are associated with, for example, sadness and fear. Shields argues that the powerful and powerless emotions can often be subverted, men are often expected to express sadness in achievement-related contexts and powerless emotional expressions can often have powerful impacts. Additionally men are often expected to display controlled emotions, or what she calls 'manly emotions' (Shields, 2002). This control is seen as subtly displaying emotion in a very controlled way. We can see this in forms of sadness when a man may secrete tears or moistened eyes but is also quiet and calm. This is often viewed positively as being a sensitive yet controlled person.

The Subordination Hypothesis

Shields et al. (2002) discuss how there has also been much research into looking at different emotional responses between genders which is related to both power and status. Forms of non-verbal expressive behaviour are thought to highlight gender differences. Women tend to smile more than men (Hall et al., 2000) and also make more eye contact than men (Dovidio et al., 1988). These types of non-verbal emotional expressive differences between the genders have been argued as being a result of subordination, or what is otherwise known as the 'subordination hypothesis' (Henley, 1973). The hypothesis suggests that because women often have a low-power status in relation to men, they are more aware of non-verbal expressions and cues. People of a low-power status are seen as paying more attention to people of higher power to better predict their thoughts and feelings in an attempt to increase their own power (Fiske, 1993). Anger is associated with status because high-status individuals are more likely to experience violations to what they perceive as their entitlements, which is popularly referred to as the basis for anger. Coincidentally, as we saw in Chapter 1, Aristotle put forward a similar argument. He was very much interested in the relationships between status and emotion. These uneven relationships, if you remember, are what were referred to as a *contoured world of emotional investment* (Gross, 2006). The point is, however, that anger is thought to be a more acceptable expression in men than women because of the perceived entitlement of status.

Sexual Desire and Emotional Connectedness

Many studies that have been conducted in the Western world (particularly in the United States) have unsurprisingly found that heterosexual men and women desire to express both their 'sexuality' and 'emotional closeness' when in romantic relationships. Shields et al. (2002) state, however, that men report that they tend to place more emphasis on 'sexual desire', whereas women report placing more emphasis on 'emotional connectedness' (see Peplau, 2003). Shields lists a number of studies which produce evidence that men report to be

> expecting to engage in sex earlier in relationships ... expecting sex regardless of physical attractiveness of their partner and in the absence of emotional closeness ... and desiring more frequent sexual activity than they are currently experiencing, particularly in the earlier stages of their relationships (Shields et al., 2006: 75).

An argument as to why this is the case is that men are simply less able to express their emotional closeness (Levant, 1996). Levant argues that this is not because of biological differences between men and women but because societal cultural scripts expect men to suppress contact which promotes emotional closeness. He also goes on to suggest that these cultural scripts promote a form of mild alexithymia in men.

Research on women on the other hand has suggested that they desire more affection from their partners than men in sexual encounters and desire more emotional closeness (Hatfield et al., 1989). Shields et al. (2006) argue that women are caught in a sort of catch–22 when it comes to emotional matters that concern relationships. On the one hand, women are seen to be more authentically female if they draw on cultural scripts which position them as emotional experts in relationships. Therefore women are required to champion emotional closeness in a relationship through emotional talk. However, the catch is, when they participate in these cultural scripts they at the same time are undermined by the normative belief that 'women are overly emotional'.

Restraint and suppression of sexual desire is also a cultural script which women are expected to draw on. Women are discouraged from 'admitting, recognizing, or acting on sexual impulses' (Shields et al., 2006). Men therefore tend to be admired for sexual activity while women are generally stigmatised. According to Tolman (2002) women are quite conflicted around the double standards of the normative cultural scripts. On the one hand, women are led to believe that it is healthy to have sexual desires but on the other hand they are under social pressures not to act on them. Thus sexual activity can often lead to experiencing conflicting emotions, although they may be enjoying the sex, there is also the concern about how society will judge them. Additionally, cultural scripts encourage women to be sexy but not sexual (Crawford and Popp, 2003).

Conclusion

Although we have drawn extensively from the work of Shields and her colleagues here, we cannot do it justice in this small section. Indeed Shields' book tackles some complex and fundamental questions in relation to gender and emotion. For example she asks '[W]hy do emotion stereotypes sometimes fill the gaps of memory or inform one's answer to a vague and general question?' (2002: 61). Although the answer to this question is complex and discussed by Shields throughout a number of the chapters of her book, her discussion includes the claim that beliefs about gendered emotions facilitate the socially-constructed definitions of what it is to be male and female.

Within the broad cultural context, beliefs about emotion serve to define the difference between masculine and feminine, male and female. Whether explicitly represented in statements of beliefs about emotion or more subtly transmitted via judgments about the appropriateness of others' emotions and emotional display, gender limits are clearly delineated by emotional standards. In our lived experiences, beliefs about emotion are among the more powerful guides by which we understand ourselves as women and men.

Hence *the sociology of emotion* largely breaks from the classic discourses concerned with positioning emotion as a lower aspect of the self, to look at how the various discourses of emotion position the self. As we have seen, it is very useful in looking at such social psychological phenomena as the constructions of gender that have come about through these discourses. One could equally apply this logic to constructions of race, sexual orientation and class for example. Additionally we have looked at some of the micro-sociology through the work of Goffman and Hochschild and discussed how we draw on these discourses (or what has been denoted above as social and cultural scripts) in everyday situations. Of interest here is that these cultural scripts determine activity rather than the underlying emotional disposition itself. In a way there is a form of what the Stoics denoted as *apatheia*, although it is not learning to suppress all emotion but rather learning to 'perform' the socially desirable type of emotion, through, for example, Goffman's notion of face-work. Additionally, we may also relate the underlying notion of emotion here, as something controllable and suppressible to the kind of discourse that we saw Aristotle advocated and went on to be understood as, for example, rational affects as opposed to the more bodily oriented and uncontrollable passions. Hochschild is keen to point out the incongruence that can come about through the drama and the arising negatives that may ensue. In the following chapter we look further at representations and constructions of emotion in language and follow up understandings of the effects of performing emotion in talk.

FURTHER READING

We started this chapter by discussing some relevant concepts from Erving Goffman. Although we discussed a number of his works, of particular interest was his notions of face-work taken from the following:
Goffman, E. (1967). *Interaction Ritual: Essays on face-to-face behaviour*. New York: Doubleday.

No account of the sociology of emotion should overlook the work of Arlie Hochschild, particularly the following book:
Hochschild, A. (1985). *The Managed Heart: Commercialization of human feeling*. Berkeley: University of California Press.

Throughout this chapter we are heavily indebted to the work of Jan Stets and Jonathan Turner (2006) in relation to their extensive *Handbook of the Sociology of Emotion* and Stephanie Shields (2002) in relation to her book *Speaking from the Heart*. The former book is an excellent reference to this developing field of work. Turner and Stets have also, however, written a much more accessible abridged paperback version simply entitled *The Sociology of Emotion*.

Turner, J. and Stets, J. (2005). *The Sociology of Emotion.* Cambridge: Cambridge University Press.

Shields, S. (2002). *Speaking from the Heart: Gender and the social meaning of emotion.* Cambridge: Cambridge University Press.

The following two edited books are also recommended as they include some key theorists in this area:

Harré, R. (1996). *The Emotions: Social, cultural and biological dimensions.* London: Sage Publications.

Spencer, D., Walby, K. and Hunt, A. (2012). *Emotions Matter: A relational approach to emotions.* Toronto: University of Toronto Press.

8

Emotion Talk: Theories and Analysis

Key Aims

In this chapter we will discuss the various ways that emotion in talk is both theorised and analysed. In doing so we will include:

- A critical discussion of the emotional disclosure paradigm and its theorisations of inhibition confrontation and cognitive reappraisal
- Reflection on Bucci's theorisation of referential activity
- Exemplification of a mixed methods approach to studying emotion talk

Introduction

The importance of the ability to express the self through emotion talk is not only confined to publicly inaccessible journal articles, books and lecture theatres but relatively recently has become a bit of a popular cultural obsession. Many social theorists today talk about the rather narcissistic therapeutic culture (for a prime example see Lasch, 1991) that much of the Western world finds itself within. Popular self-help books, reality television shows, magazines, chat-shows, advertising and political agendas (among other forms of popular culture) draw on the theories and terminology of psychology to enlighten the public as to the right way to live one's life. This is often referred to as the 'psy-complex' (for example see Rose, 1979), which denotes the way that neoliberal agendas of psychological health and well-being permeate society. The ability to overcome repression, suppression and more particularly emotional inhibition is often at the heart of such advice. Being able to express our emotion through talk (or indeed through some other media such as writing) seems to be self-evidently 'good' for the self. And yet evidence for its benefits is difficult to quantify and measure. Indeed Freud himself was accused of not being able to produce sufficient evidence to substantiate his psychoanalytic theory; he may even be accused of anecdotalism as he only used case-studies to provide evidence for his theories. But there have been new ways of looking at emotional talk that have sprung up over the last three or so decades particularly in relation to social psychology's 'turn to language'.

So, in this chapter we are going to look at some of the ways that emotion is understood and analysed through text, particularly in relation to understanding psychological health and well-being. Emotion in 'text' here is understood as words, phrases, narratives, expressions and representations that in some way symbolically refer to emotion which are thus available to undergo analysis through the transcriptions of, for example, talk, interviews, films, radio pro- grammes, lyrics, poems, newspaper articles, novels, autobiographies, websites, magazines, television programmes and arguably anything that is visual such as photographs, artwork and space itself. A radical understanding of the 'text' has its roots in the influential post-structuralist Jacques Derrida, who suggested that 'everything is text'. This rather profound assertion is often referred to as 'pan- textualism' which advocates the primacy of language in understanding culture and subjectivity. Thus emotion in text can be thought of as a structure through which meaning is made by a system of signification through which cultural meanings are produced.

Emotional Disclosure

There have been a number of ways that psychologists have attempted to under- stand the potential effects of emotional disclosure (talking about emotional experiences related to the self). One way of course to do this is by conducting case study analysis of clients undergoing psychotherapy. There are a number of quite well established methods for undertaking this form of analysis. In the UK, most Masters and Doctoral students of clinical psychology, psychotherapy and coun- selling tend to have to conduct case study analysis of one of their clients as part of their dissertation or thesis. However, social psychology has tended to be rela- tively dissatisfied with these methods to look at the effects of emotional disclosure as there are too many variables to account for in the psychotherapy context. To address this a methodological framework has been established to further investi- gate this phenomenon generally within the experimental (social and health) psychology traditions, entitled the emotional disclosure paradigm (EDP).

In an article of a research project that one of the authors of this book (Ellis) wrote with John Cromby (Ellis and Cromby, 2012) we noted that there is a considerable body of literature exploring the associations between the inhibition or non-expres- sion of emotion and various forms of pathology and ill-health. Emotional inhibition is seen to have a negative effect on psychological processes, for example, problems of anxiety, mood and dissociation. Additionally emotional inhibition has been thought to straddle the terrains between the body and the mind (see Ellis and Cromby, 2009). Researchers, as well as looking at *psychological* processes, have been interested in the possible links to *physiological* processes. For example, emotional inhibition has been associated with raised physiological arousal and with increased illness (see Ellis and Cromby for references: 2009; 2012).

Typically, to discover these possible associations, researchers within the EDP ask participants to complete a disclosure task (usually, writing or talking about emotional experiences) on a number of occasions. Pre- and post-variables are assessed (Pennebaker, 1997); for example, one of the more common measures is the frequency of reported visits to general practitioners before and after the disclosure period. These studies have shown that those who disclose negative affect laden memories subsequently make fewer visits to their general practitioner compared both to a control group and to the amount of visits that they made prior to the task. This is because the immune system functionality can be negatively affected by too much emotional inhibition.

Inhibition Confrontation

One of the main explanatory models that is utilised by researchers within the EDP context to account for the associations between emotional disclosure and health outcomes is the inhibition-confrontation model. This model suggests that inhibition of trauma-related thoughts, feelings and behaviours requires psycho-physiological work to keep them from surfacing into consciousness. In this way emotional inhibition is understood as an active process that produces autonomic arousal in the short term and places cumulative stress on the body in the long term. Confronting this inhibition, for example through talking or writing about the inhibited memories of the experiences, which is understood as a relatively safe way of confronting them, reduces associated autonomic nervous system activity, and reduces associated stress on the body which in turn facilitates health benefits.

Arguably the inhibition confrontation model is limited because it does not appropriately consider other forms of emotional inhibition which might be the outcome of passive or automatic processes (Ellis and Cromby, 2009; 2012). Of course just a cursory glance over the previous chapter on the sociology of emotion shows that emotional expressions may not always be sincere for a variety of societal constraints. Additionally, it excludes the possibility that some ways of talking about emotional memories might not be beneficial, because they involve simply re-rehearsing the trauma or highly charged event, effectively re-living it in the present, rather than making new links between what happened and how the person now feels. Moreover, this view of inhibition does not appropriately account for the impact that social relations, material circumstances, life events and situations have upon a person.

Early theorisations of the relationship between emotional inhibition and psychological illness can be traced back to Breuer and Freud's early theorisations of psychosomatic processes. Subsequently, following Anna Freud's work, psychoanalysts have conceptualised two modes of emotional inhibition, suppression and repression: the former being a conscious process while the latter operates unconsciously (see Ellis and Cromby for reviews, 2009; 2012). Erdelyi (2006) attempts to further clarify this distinction by proposing two types of repression: inhibitory or subtractive processes ('degrading the signal'), and elaborative or additive processes ('adding noise to the signal'). A related distinction is made by Dalgleish et al. (1999) through what they term active (or controlled) processes of emotional inhibition and passive (or automatic) processes. Ellis and Cromby (2009) elaborate on this by suggesting that active inhibition could be understood as being deliberate but operating on the edge of consciousness to constrain thoughts, feelings and behaviours (what Freud would have termed the pre-conscious), while passive inhibition could be conceived of as the wholly non-conscious inhibition of affect.

Cognitive Reappraisal

Another model that is often used to supplement the former model is the cognitive reappraisal model. Cognitive reappraisal can be allied to Erdelyi's (2006) second subclass division of his unified theory of repression. Memories here are understood to also incorporate elaborative or additive process, e.g., adding noise to the signal. This relates to Bartlett's (1932) notions of memory being fundamentally revisionistic in nature and to Freud's understanding of how psychic defence mechanisms distort repressed memories; for example, through rationalisation, condensation, displacement, and reaction-formation etc. Of course these defences are understood to be particularly prominent when a person has undergone a significantly upsetting event (trauma) which has been repressed so deeply that aspects of the memory are extremely difficult to recall. In this respect disclosure stories are often changed in various ways so that they are more understandable to the self and indeed to others; for instance, by making them more rational and coherent.

So in these cases, according to the cognitive reappraisal model, benefits are seen to flow primarily from the creation of a coherent narrative of the trauma, an activity which might have multiple therapeutic effects. Ellis and Cromby explain,

> First, coherent narratives may increase perceived self-mastery, enabling participants to understand their experiences as more controllable (Páez, Velasco, and González, 1999). Lepore and colleagues suggest that 'When people feel more control over their emotional experience, negative moods should dissipate, resulting in less chronic subjective stress' (Lepore, Greenberg, Bruno and Smyth, 2002). Second, reappraisal may also change the meaning of events, reducing their associated negative effect. For example, a person's narrative may come to include the statement 'I considered how much worse things could have been' (Lazarus and Folkman, 1984), so emphasising positive aspects of a negative event.

Finally, constructing a new narrative of a traumatic episode may also generate insight into the experience (Meichenbaum, 1977), giving the memory more meaning again reducing associated negative effect. (Ellis and Cromby, 2009: 320)

The Multiple Code Theory

To further understand some of the processes related to emotional inhibition and disclosure, Bucci (1997) develops what she calls a 'multiple code theory' and a theory called 'referential activity'. The multiple code theory is described as:

> a psychological theory of emotional intelligence and emotional informa-
> tion processing. The theory concerns the interactions among diverse
> sensory, motoric, somatic, cognitive, and linguistic representations and
> processes their integration in the organisation of the self, and their adap-
> tive or maladaptive functioning in relation to the individual's goals.
> (1997: 12)

In a chapter in her book *Psychoanalysis and Cognitive Science* headed *The Architecture of Cognition* Bucci refers to 'the general structures underlying human information processing' (1997: 77). She suggests that cognition is divided into two major processes, those of the symbolic order and those of the sub-symbolic order. The symbolic order is cognition which is theorised to be subjugated by two particular mental processes: the imagery processing theory and the verbal processing theory, termed a dual code theory in Bucci's initial work, which emphasised the two symbolic forms of cognition (Bucci, 1985). This work was based on the work of Paivio among others, who highlighted a distinction between psychological information processing utilising images (imagery dominance) and psychological information processing utilising words (verbal dominance) (Paivio, 1979). In the verbal dominance theory, language is viewed as determining, mediating, or even constituting thought (Carroll et al., 1964; Chomsky, 1959). Some cognitive psychologists, interested in computer simulations of cognitive processes, tend to model the mind as being populated with propositions to create information (the proposition-attitude-school). They downgrade imagery as having little or no part in the underlying representation of knowledge in the mind. Visual (perceptual) dominance theories attempt to demonstrate that the categorical organisation of information processing is based on properties of the perceptual system itself without mediation by language (Berlin and Kay, 1991; Rosch, 1975).

Bucci (1997) incorporates both of these models of mental processing into her understanding of the architecture of cognition, but adds an extra dimension which underlies her multiple code theory, called subsymbolic processing. Her subsymbolic processing theory draws on a wide range of concepts which emphasise information processing as involving more than simply images and words. The subsymbolic modes may be associated with what psychoanalysts suggest is primary process thought (the unconscious). These modes display images that tend to become fused and can readily replace and symbolise one another, ignoring the categories of space and time and are governed by what Freud termed the pleasure principle. However, the subsymbolic mode of processing is seen by Bucci to represent a broader range of functions than the psychoanalytic concept of primary process. These include representations and processes in which the elements are not discrete, organisation is not categorical, processing occurs simultaneously in multiple parallel channels, higher level units are not generated from discrete elements, and explicit processing rules cannot be identified (Bucci, 1997: 13). Subsymbolic information, therefore, is registered in specific modal formats in visceral and motoric forms and all sensory systems. Hence, this form of processing is seen to be rapid and made up of complex computations, 'based on principles that are analogic and global without formation of discrete categories and without explicit metrics' (Bucci, 1995: 96).

So, according to the multiple code theory, there are three general forms of mental information processing. Other research, which has focused on cognitive and non-cognitive processes, is similar to Bucci's distinction between symbolic and subsymbolic emotional processing (as we have discussed elsewhere). For example, LeDoux's finding that there is a neural distinction within the processing of fear: the fast implicit amygdala processing and the slower explicit declarative hippocampus processing (LeDoux, 1996). Similarly, Gibson outlines two forms of knowing within the study of cognition: *knowledge-by-acquaintance* and *knowledge-by-description* (Gibson, 1986). And Tucker (1981) distinguishes between syncretic processing (affect cognition) and analytic processing (rational cognition). These conceptualisations of emotional processing both complicate and simplify understandings of the relationships between cognition and emotion. On the one hand we may state that the faster types of emotional processing are subtle forms of cognition and on the other hand we may state that they are not cognitions at all. Others have suggested that the concept of 'cognition' in this context is by and large anachronistic (Buck, 2000; Robinson, 2004). One of the problems that these theories of emotion leave us with is that if emotion can be thought of as subsymbolic and preceding symbolic forms of processing, it is likely to be quite difficult to be detected in language, for example in both in the psychotherapy and the EDP context.

Referential Activity

In response to this problem, Bucci describes ways in which emotion-related information (in other words, memories of emotional events) may be recalled; this is explained through a process she names 'referential activity' (Bucci, 1995). Referential activity is described as a cycle of 'organizing nonverbal experience and connecting it to words' (Bucci, 1997: 185). The connecting process is described as a referential cycle that is configured in three states. Firstly, highly charged emotional memories are expressed subsymbolically; for example, through somatic activity like heightened autonomic nervous system activity and detected through a high use of emotional vocal tone (the related speech acts are likely to be incoherent and affectively charged). Secondly, they are symbolised figuratively in some way (for example, pictorially or linguistically). Thirdly, they are symbolised through concrete language (for example, in narrative form); through which further insight and meaning is given. Thus, the referential activity process is the increasing integration of affective experiences into narrative form. Of course the referential activity occurs over time and is seen to mirror psychotherapy and EDP processes.

Content Analysis of Emotion

Surprisingly, very little attention has been paid to the qualitative structure or function of the narratives produced by participants within the EDP context. Instead researchers tend to conduct analyses using computer content analysis assisted programmes. A commonly used programme is the Linguistic Inquiry and Word Count (LIWC) application (e.g. Pennebaker and Francis, 1996). The LIWC is an application that calculates the percentage of words used in particular categories. For example when looking at emotional expression or inhibition confrontation, 'affect words' are counted. These are words that are seen to be explicitly associated with emotion, such as 'hate', 'love', 'feeling' and the like. Thus a narrative considered to have a relatively high amount of affect words is said to display a significant amount of inhibition confrontation and, of course, a high amount of emotional inhibition if the narrative contains a low amount of affect words. It is claimed that the LIWC can categorise a large percentage (86%) of words within a disclosure narrative (Pennebaker, Chung, Ireland, Gonzales and Booth, 2007) but it is, nevertheless, limited in what it can actually reveal about the affective content of narrative or indeed how emotional inhibition/expression may be operating. For example, Ellis and Cromby (2012) argue that it fails to account for the context of the words it categorises, it has a limited index of what may be considered emotional within a text, and it decomposes and then quantifies the narrative and so is unable to include the ways in which a narrative's form and function might contribute to both the construction of meaning and the expression – or inhibition – of emotion.

Discourse Analysis of Emotion

Arguably a more fruitful form of textual analysis of emotion within social psychology and beyond is discourse analysis. There are a variety of forms of discourse analysis which one may use to analyse representations of emotion in text. Derek Edwards in his book *Discourse and Cognition* (Edwards, 1997) writes a particularly helpful chapter on analysing emotion through a form of discourse analysis entitled 'discursive psychology'. Discursive psychology is essentially a form of discourse analysis which is focused on deconstructing 'psychology talk'. It is a methodological tool to help researchers analyse the ways so called 'psychological facts' are constructed through language (Edwards and Potter, 1992). Discursive psychologists tend to understand language as 'performative' in that it produces (or socially constructs) our understandings of the world. Edwards argues that discursive psychology is a good tool to analyse emotion in text, as emotion talk tends to be 'rich and various, full of contrasts and alternatives, and marvellously useful in working up descriptions of human actions, interpersonal relations, and in handling accountability' (Edwards and Potter, 1992). For example, we have already looked at how emotion is often constructed as being defined as opposite to rational thought, primitive and agentic, and determining particular forms of behaviour. These views of emotion have derived from a variety of discourses that we saw historically emerge in the earlier chapters.

One of the things Edwards focuses on is how emotion categories are often used in everyday talk as excuses/to account for particular kinds of behaviours. In other words, representations of emotion in talk are often used in descriptions of one's behaviour as rhetorical devices to lower one's accountability; in this way emotion is seen as a cause for actions that would otherwise be deemed inappropriate, immoral or unreasonable in some way. To facilitate analysis in looking at the ways that emotion concepts are evoked as rhetorical devices, Edwards lists ten of what he calls 'rhetorical positions and contrasts'.

1. Emotion versus cognition
2. Emotions as irrational versus rational
3. Emotion as cognitively grounded and/or cognitively consequential
4. Event-driven versus dispositional
5. Dispositions versus temporary states
6. Emotional behaviour as controllable action or passive reaction
7. Spontaneous versus externally caused
8. Natural versus moral
9. Internal states versus external behaviour (private versus public)
10. Honest versus faked

(Edwards, 1997: 194)

You may want to have a look at Edwards' (1997) chapter on emotion to further understand how he develops these ten contrastives. Most of them will be fairly obvious given that we have discussed many of these contrastive views of emotion in earlier chapters.

We can see how some of these constrastives might work in the following extract, taken from some interview data (Ellis, 2012). Here emotion is portrayed as undermining cognition, irrational, event driven, temporary, passive and requiring control.

> and it was almost like (1) my emotions were (.) were CHARGED that's how I could (.) feel I was ALMOST BUZZING with my emotions (.) but SOMEWHERE in the back of my mind (.) the sensible part of me (.) the LOGICAL part of me (.) TOOK OVER to SAY (.) you've got to do this you've got to do that (.) you've got to stop these people going into the road

The above is a description of a road accident which is portrayed as being extremely emotional or perhaps traumatic. There is a juxtaposition between what is seen as the sensible 'logical' part of the self and the part of the self 'buzzing' with emotions; there is the sense that each of these parts of the self can take control. The emotionally charged state is portrayed as almost all encompassing, or much larger than the rational part, there is the invocation of the phrase 'somewhere in the back of my mind'. The self is then positioned as being able to take control of the incongruent 'buzzing' somatic state, by the 'logical', symbolised through a set of linguistic commands: 'you've got to do this, you've got to do that'. Emotional, more bodily, oriented states are depicted as a hindrance to decision making. They are not constituted in language, thus are not rational and need to be curtailed through language which organises these somatic states.

It must be stated that Edwards and Potter would disagree with utilising discursive psychology for further understanding processes of emotional inhibition and confrontation; they are more likely to use this form of analysis to 'deconstruct' the psychological notion of 'emotional disclosure'. Indeed, they would probably suggest that trying to understand embodied processes through discursive psychology is beyond its remit as one will then be assuming that which is beyond the text.

Indeed emotion is a tricky concept as we have discussed at length throughout these chapters. Its representation in text can sometimes be quite elusive as it is often bound up in the detail and narrative of the text. Perhaps no one word, phrase or sentence conveys emotion, but the rhythm of the text, the story, the intonation etc. facilitates the expression. Sarbin suggests that emotion in text is best understood through the 'narrative-emplotments' (Sarbin, 1989). In this account emotion is interwoven dynamically within events, plots and happenings of a text. Indeed Craib goes as far to argue that when looking at the ways in which narratives attempt to signify emotion it is found that they cannot capture emotional life as they 'are too complex and contradictory to enable a story that makes sense ... to be grasped in a coherent way' (Craib, 2000: 71).

Combining Methods

Beyond the debates between realist and relativist philosophies concerning the ontological status of a text, we have found discourse analysis generally and discursive psychology particularly useful in looking at emotion and affective activity within texts in relation to social, psychological and even biological phenomena. The data that we presented above of a fatal road accident, was interesting to the authors of the study as the narratives that she recounted (emotional disclosures) would be viewed by researchers within the EDP context who use the LIWC as representing a high amount of inhibition confrontation as the narratives contained a high amount of affect words (as demonstrated through the LIWC). However, results for the participant throughout the study suggested otherwise. The study (Ellis and Cromby, 2012) measured autonomic nervous system (ANS) arousal, which is known to be associated with the inhibition of emotional memories (discussed above). This is specifically linked to increased skin conductance activity. The disclosing of emotional experiences tends to decrease skin conductance levels (SCLs); conversely, individuals higher in emotional inhibition who find it difficult to disclose such experiences tend to have increased SCLs. Yet this participant's conductance levels increased throughout the study periods even though a high amount of so-called affect language was recorded.

Although the EDP is a relatively well established model within and around social and health psychology for looking at the effects of emotional expression and inhibition, what Ellis and Cromby were interested in was that a number of meta-analyses of studies within this context suggested that the outcomes of emotional disclosure are not straightforward. It seems that research in this area does not always find an association between emotional disclosure and positive outcome measures. In 1998 Smyth meta-analysed 13 EDP studies and found that emotional disclosure was reported as improving health through a number of indicators. A later study by Frisina, Borod and Lepore in 2004 meta-analysed nine EDP studies and suggested that emotional disclosure in this context does improve health, but was more effective for physical rather psychological health outcomes. But by far the most comprehensive meta-analysis conducted by Meads and Nouwen in 2005, who looked at 61 studies, found that there was no clear benefit associated with emotional disclosure. Indeed they suggested that the paradigm was in need of reassessment.

One of the ways that the paradigm could be reassessed, argued Ellis and Cromby (2012) is through utilising a much more complex and sophisticated form of analysis of the disclosure data (such as discursive psychology) in relation to possible links to expression and inhibition. Thus they developed a mixed methods model wherein statistical analysis was performed upon the psychophysiological activity data (skin conductance activity) collected from the participants (throughout disclosure tasks) and then subsequently subjected the narrative disclosure data to discourse analysis. One of the pitfalls of conducting discourse analysis is that it takes a lot of time. It would have been impossible to conduct this on all of the 93 narratives that were recorded. Hence, sampling techniques were utilised to select case studies of the narrative data set. Selection was based upon participants who produced significant increases or decreases of skin-conductance activity.

Indeed, the case study from which the above extract was taken was a participant who actually produced the most significant increases in skin-conductance activity, suggesting that the disclosure tasks were having a rather negative effect on this participant's autonomic nervous system (related to decreased health outcomes), although clearly a lot of what we may call affect language was being used.

Among the number of conclusions that were formed through this study was that emotional inhibition takes on many forms in relation to emotional disclosures, at least within the EDP context. Firstly, the social setting of the interview context is not the same as, for example, the psychotherapy setting. There is very little space to develop a more meaningful relationship between the interviewee and interviewer. There can be some pressure to present the self as a good psychological subject; for example, to give to the interviewer what they believe is required. We found that quite often the narratives followed social scripts of what was thought to be culturally acceptable in the interview context. This is not to argue that the narratives of the memory of the emotional experiences consciously deviated from the actual emotional experience, but rather what is perceived as socially acceptable can also become what Sartre calls a 'bad-faith' narrative or what Hochschild understood as 'emotional work' (see previous chapter). In other words to some degree there is deception of the self to the self (and the other). Of course, psychoanalysts are all too aware of these processes and have conceptualised a number of defence mechanisms to account for them.

Incongruent Rationalisation

One defense mechanism that appeared to be relevant for the above participant's narrative was what Freud denoted as the 'rationalisation' defence mechanism. Although the participant produced detailed articulations of what she portrayed herself as feeling at the time of the experience, as we can see from the small extract above, she is quick to denigrate the affective components to display a subject that has the ability to gain control of her emotional self. This is likely to relate to a number of 'subject positions' that she takes on throughout. One particular example of this is that of (ex)police officer. Positioning the self within speech acts is something that is of particular interest to many who employ discourse analysis; for example, how is one positioned in relation to others within the narrative, to emotion, to gender and so on. Discursive psychologists discuss a form of positioning theory which they refer to as 'category entitlements' (Potter, 1996). Category entitlements can discursively work to further legitimise the factuality of a particular account. For example, the participant's category entitlements of (ex)police officer and psychology student work to legitimate her feelings of suspicion that she portrayed throughout the account. Additionally, a police officer is often involved in highly charged events, such as she described. Moreover, a police officer is often understood as a person who one expects would not get 'carried away' or 'overwhelmed' by emotion. Indeed police officers learn to describe, through reporting events such as arrests, in ways that are understood to be rational and devoid of emotion. For example, Howard, Tuffin and Stephens (2000) found that police officers in New Zealand tend to resort to what they describe as a discourse of 'unspeakability' in relation to emotion. Emotions here are often 'framed as dangerous and threatening to performance, demanding management and control' which would then enable the police officers 'to present themselves as both culturally and professionally competent' (2000: 295). Hence rationalisation here is not so much a psychic defence mechanism that one has adopted through early childhood experiences, but something which is culturally normative for this profession and likely to be cultivated through police officer training. For example Gergen and Gergen (1988) have looked at how stories in legal contexts are required to be clear, with rational causal links, to be considered believable.

Additionally, what seems of particular relevance to the participant's narrative that it appeared to be what Kehily (1995) describes as a 'well worn story'. Although her narrative was far from what a police officer may write up in a report, she was being a good psychological subject in describing the emotion which she saw as relating to the experience. She also spoke about how she had to tell this story to a coroner's court, and again she most probably then reverted to 'police-talk' to do this. Well worn stories are those narratives that we tend to wheel out when socially appropriate; thus they have been rehearsed on numerous occasions. In this way it is rather the memory of the story as told which is recalled rather than the actual experience itself. As discussed above, this may add what Erdelyi (2006) describes as 'noise to the signal' through elaboration, and as Bartlett (1932) would suggest, memories tend to have a 'revisionistic' nature to them. In other words they are cognitively reappraised. Haaken and Reavey (2009) discuss how there are complex issues at stake here on how 'virtual' affectively charged events can get re-told or 'actualised' on subsequent occasions. To some degree the continued repetition of the story may become relatively emotionally incongruent with the actual experience.

Conclusion

This chapter demonstrated one way through which various concepts and methods can be brought together to develop a multimodal analysis of emotion. The two concepts that were discussed here in relation to the EDP (the inhibition confrontation model and the cognitive reappraisal mode), as you may have noticed, subtly draw on often opposing views of emotion. The former conceives of emotion as relatively primitive, residing in the body and either needing to be suppressed or expressed, the latter is concerned with emotion being much more of a cognitive mental phenomenon that can be manipulated through forms of linguistic rationalisations. Both of these models can be broadly allied to the Platonic-Aristotelian emotion dichotomisation thesis that we have discussed. As was argued, this is broadly a false dichotomy, as indeed is the distinction between emotional inhibition and cognitive reappraisal. We have attempted to describe how these are not separate processes but necessarily overlap. Indeed, elsewhere Prinz (2004) has argued that the distinctions between cognition and emotion present us with anachronistic understandings of the terms, something that some of the affective neuroscientists have begun to address, for example through Damasio's somatic marker hypothesis wherein so-called rational decision making is shot through with emotion. However, the use of a mixed methods approach, for example where embodied psychophysiological processes are considered alongside external linguistic representations and expressions, does go some way to augment a more holistic analysis of this thing we call emotion. We are here, for example, able to investigate the embodied micro activity alongside the macro structural features that are represented in social discourse.

However, the overarching thesis of language being able, to some degree, to organise emotion can be understood as in need of some form of restraint. This is a necessary result of the need to express emotion, to take what is primarily embodied and render it linguistic. Of course, this is a completely understandable endeavour. And yet, it has come under increasing pressure due to what is deemed to be lost through a move to discourse as the primary site for analysis. This critique has catalysed a shift to (re)focus on the body and its relation to emotion, with particular reference to notions of affect, and what can be gained from (re)distinguishing affects and emotions. This move has come to be known as the 'affective turn', and has to a large extent become a key site for critical social psychological theory and practice, for many in place of the aforementioned 'discursive turn'. Not only do contemporary theories of affect seek to engage with the material as well as discursive aspects of affect, they also seek to present affective activity and experience not as stable properties of individuals, but as relational processes that shift in and through bodies, objects and spaces. This distinguishes them not only from the discursive theories of emotion but also from the mixed methods approaches, which, whilst attempting to incorporate both embodied and discursive elements, still present emotions as relatively stable forms. In the next chapter we cover a range of theories featuring prominently in the affective turn, and consider them in a wider context of post-structuralism.

FURTHER READING

James Pennebaker is the most widely known researcher within the emotional disclosure paradigm. There are two edited books that we have used that he has been involved in. These books will supply a good overview of the theories and research that has been conducted in this field.

Pennebaker, J. (1995). *Emotion, Disclosure and Health*. Washington, DC: American Psychological Association.

Traue, H. and Pennebaker, J. (1993). *Emotion, Inhibition and Health*. Seattle: Hogrefe & Huber Publishers.

We discussed the use of discursive psychology for looking at emotion in text. One book that would be of particular interest here is the following:
Edwards, D. (1997). *Discourse and Cognition*. London: Sage.

Some of the chapter also drew on the work of one of the present authors (Ellis) and Cromby to illustrate both critiques of the EDP and a mixed methods approach to empirically investigating emotion:
Ellis, D. and Cromby, J. (2009). 'Inhibition and reappraisal within emotional disclosure: the embodying of narration', *Counselling Psychology Quarterly*, 22 (3): 319–31.
Ellis, D. and Cromby, J. (2012). 'Emotional inhibition: A discourse analysis of disclosure', *Psychology and Health*, 27 (5): 515–32.

9

Affect Theory: Post-Structuralist Accounts

Key Aims

In this chapter we discuss some of the post-structural developments of emotion studies known as 'affect theories'. In doing so we will include:

- A view of Freud's and later Tomkins' affect theories
- A discussion of Deleuze's process of philosophy and affect
- A critical review of Massumi's notions of affect
- A consideration of the place of affect in subjectivity and social psychology

Introduction

What is post-structuralism? Let us briefly remind ourselves. It can be described as a body of work which was essentially a response to structuralism. Structuralism viewed human culture as being understood through the signs and symbols which structure it. Structuralists tend to reject notions of human freedom, autonomy and free will, instead there is a focus on the ways that human behaviour is determined by various structures, like language systems. Indeed the very term 'subjectivity' tends to be concerned with the way that systems of language are related to power and shape the individual's outlook on the world; in other words, the individual is *subject to* structures of language (for example discourses) which speak through the person. For Karl Marx (1818–1883) human existence could be understood by analysing economic structures. Freud has also been claimed to be a structuralist as he described human functioning in terms of the structure of the psyche. Although Michel Foucault (1926–1984) is often considered to be allied with structuralism because his philosophy tends to agree with the notion that language and society are governed by various systems, he was sceptical of the endeavour to find underlying structures and was also concerned that we could never put ourselves outside of the power of discourse to think through these systems objectively. Jacques Derrida (1930–2004) argued against this latter point through his pioneering work on the critical theory known as 'deconstructionism'. He felt that all texts have ambiguities, paradoxes and binary oppositions entailed within them which facilitate interpretation through a careful textual analysis, or a questioning of the so-called metaphysics of presence. For Derrida, texts do not naturally or simply reflect the world that they speak of, but exhibit 'différance' which allows for multiple interpretations. They tend to be produced by a hierarchy of binaries; for example, man vs. woman, good vs. evil, cognition vs. emotion and so on. Thus, many of the forms of qualitative linguistic analysis draw on the deconstructive philosophy of Derrida. Indeed, in Chapter 8 we looked at Edwards' ten emotional constrastives when looking at how discursive psychology deconstructs the structure of emotion in language (Edwards, 1997).

Affect Theory

Theories of affect have become a hot topic in the humanities and social sciences in recent years. The concept of affect is fashionable again as part of post-structuralist responses to the tendency for reductionist thinking in relation to emotions and the body in mainstream humanities and social scientific theory. As we have previously discussed, theories derived from structuralism (and indeed post-structuralism) in the humanities and social sciences have been extremely dissatisfied and critical of bio-psychological reductionist accounts of human functioning. This is largely due to the tendency to biologise psychosocial phenomena. Critiques of the naive realism of the biological sciences in relation to social and psychological phenomena became heavily focused on the deconstruction of language. One of Derrida's most quoted sayings is that 'there is nothing outside the text' (Derrida, 1988). The so-called 'discursive turn' has addressed the creative and productive role of language in a plethora of ways across the whole range of social and cultural theory. To some extent, the (re)emergence of theories of affect has led to an 'affective turn' that is taking up the baton from discourse theory as the primary tool for critical theories of emotion (Brown and Stenner, 2009). It has been said that the interest and focus on emotion in the turn to language acted as a catalyst for the subsequent turn to affect (Greco and Stenner, 2008). In general, affect theories argue that deconstructionism tends to be stuck in analysing that which is socially produced, it does not have the capacity and theoretical capability for looking beyond to what constitutes the very fabric of our being (Hemmings, 2005). Affect theories attempt to understand our experiences of the social world as not completely socially determined. In this way they attempt to overcome the pessimism of social determination by offering versions of social processes that are not completely subject to social constraint.

Given the range of disciplines that have become interested in affect, it is difficult to provide a neat summary of all their definitions and empirical explorations of and with affect. In this chapter we aim to draw attention to key themes and points of similarity, as well as differentiation, across the affective turn. Our focus though is primarily social psychological so we will develop our argument in the direction of affect theories in psychology.

Affect in Tomkins

So what is this affect that affect theory proposes? Hemmings states that '[A]ffect broadly refers to states of being, rather than their manifestation or interpretation as emotions' (Hemmings, 2005: 551). In this respect, to some extent, we can see the roots of affect theory in Freudian notions of affect, in which affect is the qualitative expression of the quantity of the drive's mental energy. The affects of the drives can be tied to objects in the world through the pleasure principle, which allows for the drive discharge. These may be manifest and tied to what we consider to be particular emotions such as love and hate. The work of Sylvan Tomkins is an important part of the history of affect theory in psychology, particularly in how it has been taken up in contemporary non-cognitive social psychology. Tompkins took up the affect theory of Freud, but was not satisfied with the central place of the drives (Tomkins, 1962). Instead, he theorised the affects as at times having their own rewards (autotelic). Similar to Darwin, Tomkins suggests there are a number of basic (hard wired) affect systems: interest/excitement, enjoyment/joy, surprise/startle, distress/anguish, disgust/contempt, anger/rage, shame/humiliation, and fear/terror. These, he stated, were mainly expressed through the face and form feedback loops which are likened to amplifiers, enhancing the volume of the affect and in turn increasing motivation. However, although the affects may be biological and evolutionarily hard-wired, they are understood as being socially malleable through the development of motivational narratives (scripts), with which the affects interact. These scripts are developed through ongoing experiences, not just deterministic forms of cultural scripts, and they can become quite idiosyncratic and help us to negotiate the social world in our own unique ways. Hence, similar to Damasio's (1994) somatic marker hypothesis (Chapter 6), past emotional experiences mark and flavour the way that individuals re-experience a new emotional situation.

Additionally, Tomkins was interested in the forms of affective contagion that occur in social encounters with others. He uses the contagious nature of a smile, yawn or blush to illustrate this. Once one smiles for example, it may transfer to others and then double back to the self but increases in its original intensity in a circuitry form. So the affect that is transferred to others can be understood as a narration of our own inner life. Gibbs states that it is very difficult not to respond to a spontaneous smile with a smile of one's own, and one's own smile provides sufficient feedback to our own bodies to activate the physiological and neurological aspect of joy (Gibbs, 2010). Hemmings states that this is one of the main reasons that affect theory has been taken up as an alternative to social determinism (Hemmings, 2005). The individual is theorised here has having a degree of control over his or her life.

Affect in Deleuze

Whilst psychoanalytic accounts of affect have been very influential in social psychological and psychosocial accounts of affect, in cultural studies (and human geography) the work of Gilles Deleuze (1925–1995) has been a primary reference point. Hemmings describes the main distinction between Tomkins' and Deleuze's affect theories as the former breaking it down 'into a topography of myriad, distinct parts' while the latter understands it as 'the passage from one state to another, as an intensity characterized by an increase or decrease in power' (Hemmings, 2005: 552). Affect for Deleuze is always active, never passive, as it moves (or flows) from one state to the next. It is forever 'becoming', it has no fixed identity. The times affect becomes fixed are when it forms into prefigured emotional categories. At these times a line is crossed from affect to emotion, and a knowledge associated with classifications of emotion can be used. Deleuze's own account of affect draws influence from the seventeenth century work of Spinoza that we discussed in Chapter 3. Principally it is the notion that human experience is not about knowing the world, but rather 'the way the world affects us' (Brown and Stenner, 2009: 112) that is important. Deleuze never really marks a clear distinction between affect and emotion, and indeed, his explicit mentions of affect are not as frequent as his subsequent influence suggests. Nevertheless, the notions of moving from models of stable categories of the subject that are defined according to specific sets of inherent properties, towards an understanding of affect as action (verb) rather than a thing (noun) have spread across cultural theory. This has led to thinking of experiences of feeling and intensity not as emotions that are defined according to linguistic grids of meaning, but as creative and contingent practices that are relational and processual. Indeed, Deleuze draws on early Greek process philosophies, which emphasised the ever changing nature of so called reality: being as becoming. Deleuze then understood life as characterised by such things as connections, disjunctions and flows.

For Deleuze, affect escapes representation, 'it cannot be converted into or delimited by the discursive, by images or representations, by consciousness or thought' (Seigworth, 2005). For Deleuze affect has a form of bodily meaning that can pierce social interpretations by often undoing social expectations and logic. He illustrates this well through Lawrence of Arabia's account of being gang raped in the desert: while in the midst of the torture of being raped he has an erection. For Deleuze, this demonstrates the autonomy of the body in relation to the tragic event. Lawrence feels shame but not because he was raped but because of his own body's response to the rape. The unruly body therefore cannot, according to Deleuze, be understood in terms of its social organisation. This particular excerpt of shame is analysed by Deleuze in the light of Lawrence's autobiographical writings, through which he looks at Lawrence's subjective disposition (Deleuze, 1998). 'Subjective', in this context for Deleuze, does not denote the analysis of a single body, but rather he thinks in terms of, as Probyn puts it, an 'affective assemblage of bodies of different orders and elements' (2010: 142). Deleuze notes that Lawrence's subjective disposition of his writings is 'inseparably political, erotic and artistic' (Deleuze, 1998: 118). Deleuze looks at the way that shame is configured or in Deleuzian terms, 'assembled' and 'territorialised' through the writings. He is in awe of Lawrence's writing concerning the flows of shame. Deleuze states, '[N]ever before has shame been sung like this, in so proud and haughty a manner' (Deleuze, 1998: 120). Probyn commenting on Deleuze's understanding of shame states,

> Lawrence's shame is not the result of a simple psychological quality that is to be explained by some aspect of his person, such as his putative homosexuality. Deleuze makes such characterizations of Lawrence's shame beside the point. Shame is a product of the machine of subjective disposition, which produces shame as both idea and affect. The subjective, in Lawrence's case, is deeply connected to the context in which he writes. (2010: 122)

Probyn discusses a number of affects considered to be connected to this particular assemblage of shame; for example, his having to betray the Arabs because of his role during that war and many experiences of shame that were related to his family background. Deleuze's main focus, however, is more philosophical, more precisely, a philosophy of the body. Deleuze looked at his experiences of shame in the light of the pride he has of his physical strength. He has a particular relationship with his body, in that he, Deleuze writes, has shame because he thinks

> the mind, though distinct, is inseparable from the body ... The mind depends on the body; shame would be nothing without this dependency, this attraction for the abject, this voyeurism of the body. Which means that the mind is ashamed of the body in a very special manner; in fact, it is ashamed for the body. It is as if it were saying to the body: you make me ashamed, You ought to be ashamed ... 'A bodily weakness which made my animal self crawl away and hide 'till shame was passed' ... The mind begins by coldly and curiously regarding what the body does, it is first of all a witness; then it is affected, it becomes an impassioned witness, that is, it experiences for itself affects that are not simply effects of the body, but veritable critical entities that hover over the body and judge it. (1998: 123–4)

Probyn states that for Deleuze affect seems to be concerned with ideas but ones that are not particularly of the mind.

> They are a violent collision of mind and body. As such they are not, properly speaking, of either; they are a particular combination of thought and body in which a distinction between the two is no longer important. (2010: 125).

In the analysis of Lawrence's affective experience of shame, a whole raft of affects ensued. We first see the autonomous affectivity of the body: the surprised erection; secondly, there arises the affect of shame of the body; thirdly the affective subjective dispositions which include: relations of shame with the Arabs (whom he betrays) and a family background of multiple shames. Here we begin to see how Deleuze uses concepts of affect in multiple ways to form a rhizomatic network of roots that comes together as an assemblage of shame in that particular event.

Elsewhere one of the co-authors (Tucker) discusses how Deleuze's idea of bodies is not concerned with form (e.g. an individual subject), but it is more concerned with thinking bodies as constituted through flows of relation (2010). Deleuze's theory of affect was far removed from cognitive psychological accounts, as it focuses on the body as a relational form, produced as part of processes incorporating other 'objects' (human and non-human) from which affects come to be felt and experienced. The point is that the starting point for analysis should be relational processes rather than stable traits. For Deleuze, affects need to be considered through context rather than individuated and abstracted. That is why so much of Deleuze's focus on affect is really a consideration of bodies, and how they move and interact with other bodies in the production of everyday life. They are the products of any 'given relations of movement and rest, speed and slowness (longitude); the sum total of the intensive affects it is capable of at a given power or degree of potential (latitude)' (Deleuze and Guattari, 1987: 287). Thus Tucker states that '[A]ffect is this very aspect, the potential that exists in any set of relations to shift direction, to form new relations, to spin off in new directions' (2010: 521). The Deleuzian school of affect offers a more expansive concept, moving away from what it sees as the restrictive and limited explanatory power of biological and cognitive accounts of emotion. Indeed, this is key to the subsequent influence of Deleuze on contemporary turns to affect. Dominant theories of emotion are seen as at best inflexible and insufficient, and at worst, ignorant of the social and political forces that constitute modern subjective life.

Actual Selection

One key concept that keeps cropping up in Deleuze's writings in relation to affect is the notion of two separate realms of experience: 'the virtual and the actual', a concept originally formulated by the process philosopher Henri Bergson (1896/1991). This is the notion that emphasises experience of the world as always necessarily selective. That which we select, that which we experience through our perceptive capacities, is that which is actualised through, for example, semantic organisation. However, there is a whole realm which we do not attend to through perceptive selection: this is the realm of the virtual. That which is not actualised through selection does not undergo social organisation and thus remains virtual. The virtual always exists as a capacity for new connections beyond those that we have formed (Tucker, 2010). In other words, the virtual is that which has not yet become. The virtual represents a potentiality for experience to spin off in new directions, along new lines of flight.

Deleuze seeks to frame the actual as masking virtuality as we get a sense of concrete reality as existing in states of relative stability. These perceptions are illusions; they are snapshots, points in time and space, of a much wider field. Think of a pearl necklace. Perception, as Bergson would have it, can be likened to a singular pearl, rather than the view of the whole necklace. The perception of the pearl may affectively move us in more or less ways, but it is necessarily limited through the process of selection. It is not possible to select the whole. The thing in-itself is shaded in the virtual realm and has more potentiality emitted (affectivity) than can be picked up in perception. For example, a bee's perceptions of a flower are quite different from a human's perceptions. Hence there is always an excess to experience. It is the excess of the virtual that Deleuze is interested in. It is here that change can be affected. It is here where potentiality exists.

Affect in Massumi

Brian Massumi takes up many concepts of Deleuze to produce what is now a very popular form of affect theory in his chapter *The Autonomy of Affect* (Massumi, 2002, pp. 23–45). In this chapter, Massumi develops a useful conceptual distinction between emotion and affect. Firstly drawing on the Bergsonian/Deleuzian notions of the actual and the virtual he suggests that the affective excess (the virtual realm) is conceived of as a realm of intensity. It is intensity, in that it is non-conscious autonomic experiences. When the virtual is experienced (non-consciously) it does not need to conform to the rules of conscious dictations.

> An emotion is a subjective content, the socio-linguistic fixing of the quality of an experience which is from that point onward defined as personal. Emotion is qualified intensity, the conventional, consensual point of intersection of intensity into semantically and semiotically formed progressions, into narrativizable action reaction circuits, into function and meaning. It is intensity owned and recognized. (Massumi, 2002: 28)

Massumi, along with a new wave of post-structuralist thinkers interested in developing affect theory, is often not afraid of (critically) drawing on the findings of some experimental psychology and neuroscience to help him develop his theories and concepts. For example, Massumi looks at some research conducted where children were shown three versions of a film of a melting snowman (Robinson and Sturm, 1987). Previously this film was shown on German television and it received a number of complaints as it was seen as frightening the children. The film concerned a snowman melting in somebody's garden. The person then takes the snowman to the cold mountains where it stops melting. He then says goodbye and leaves it. There were three versions of the film made for this particular study, which included the original wordless version and two versions with voiceovers added. One of the voiceovers was 'factual' in that it narrated a step by step account of the activity of the film, the second version was 'emotional', which was more or less the same as the factual version but included some words which amplified the emotional tone. The children were asked to recall the film and rate the three films based on 'pleasantness'. The factual version was rated by the children as the least pleasant and was the worst remembered, the most pleasant was the wordless version which received slightly higher ratings than the emotional version, while the emotional version was the best remembered. The confusing thing about the study, however, was that the children were then asked to rate the film on a 'happy-sad' scale. When compared to the 'pleasantness scale', it was found that the sadder scenes were rated as the most pleasant. In fact it seems that the sadder the scene the more pleasant it was rated!

Massumi's explanatory hypothesis for this finding was that the children were equating arousal with pleasure. Yet the children were also 'wired up' so that their autonomic nervous system (ANS) activity could be simultaneously monitored. Of course, increased ANS activity is correlated with emotional arousal (or per-haps we should use the term affective arousal in this context). They found that the factual account elicited the highest level of arousal, even though it was the most unpleasant (therefore rated happy) and generated the least lasting impres-sion. However, Massumi states that there was a physiological split: although the factual account correlated with increased heart rate and deepened breathing, their skin conductance level fell. Skin conductivity is also a way of measuring ANS activity as increased affective arousal generates the secretion of sweat from the eccrine glands within the skin of the palms of the hands. When secretion occurs there is increased conductivity of electrical impulses between two elec-trodes placed on the hand. Also of interest was that it was the non-verbal account which elicited the highest skin conductance response.

Massumi suggests that the researchers were a bit perplexed by the findings and stated that the difference between sadness and happiness 'was not all that it was cracked up to be'. Massumi adds that 'it would appear that the strength or dura-tion of an image's effect is not logically connected to the content in any straightforward way' (2002: 84). So what we have here, in Massumi's terms is: the image (in this example the film), its impact on the person (affectivity or what Massumi calls intensity), and the socio-linguistic qualification (the social mean-ing applied to it). Massumi suggests that there does not seem to be any conformity between 'quality and intensity'; in other words the socio-linguistic qualification did not match the affect. Instead, Massumi thinks there appears to be a crossing of semantic wires through which sadness was pleasant. It seems therefore that intensity does not fix semantically ordered distinctions. Also, although both the qualification and the intensity are immediately embodied:

intensity (that which was non-verbal, and presumably for Massumi therefore not qualified in a language system) created reactions at the surface of the body (skin). Qualifications (that which is indexed in language) are registered in deeper levels (heart rate and breathing).

Massumi argues that intensity is directly manifested at the surface of the body, where it interfaces with things. This level is purely autonomic reactions. The depth reactions are associated with expectations which line themselves with a narrative continuity. These are mixed with consciousness, which he calls a 'conscious-autonomic mix'. Intensity, in contrast, is a 'never-to-conscious' (non-conscious) autonomic remainder which is outside of expectation and adaptation. 'It is narratively de-localized, spreading over the generalized body surface, like a lateral backwash from the function meaning...' (2002: 85).

Like Deleuze, Massumi's writings can be difficult to digest. From reading his text, it is possible to get the gist of his arguments, but he attempts to conflate discourses and develops neologisms which make it very tricky to hold onto his arguments. Bell suggests that it is a 'neo-psychology' 'that seeks to move beyond current psychological conceptualizations of people' which

> highlights 'affect', the 'virtual', 'movement' and 'sensation' which the author believes will oblige theorists to transcend (or to alter at least) the banal and reductionist physicalism and hedonistic psychogenesis of empirical psychology. (Bell, 2002: 445)

However, Massumi's philosophical writing style, although it is extremely poetic and has quite a performative effect for the reader, is difficult to follow for someone who is used to more scientific forms of research. Some of his terms interchange and so following a line of argument is difficult, even through a close reading. For example, in *Parables for the virtual* Massumi (2002) begins the snowman analysis by describing an aspect of the study. He states that the 'children were tested for recall' and he states which version was the worst remembered and then which version was the 'best remembered': this is extremely straightforward. A couple of sentences later he states that 'The factual version elicited the highest level of arousal, even though it was the most unpleasant (i.e., happy) and made the least long-lasting impression'. Now, one is not quite sure exactly what 'long-lasting impression' refers to here. It is presumed that it refers to the 'remembered'. Then he states that 'the strength or duration of an image's effect is not logically connected to the content in any straightforward way.' Now, one would expect strength, perhaps, to be associated with autonomic arousal, and duration with recall. But it is now becoming increasingly unclear. Then, however, he states 'the strength or duration of the image's effect could be called its intensity'. Intensity, of course, is important for this particular chapter as it is a term he uses as a synonym for affect. So if our presumptions are right, it seems that intensity (affect) is both autonomic arousal and recall, and recall must be understood as qualification. However, much of the focus of the chapter is concerned with the ways that intensity is set up as quite different to processes associated with qualification!

This is just an example of how it can be confusing to follow an argument when the concepts become too fluid and slippery. In saying this, it must be remembered that Deleuze states that the task of philosophy is the invention of concepts (Deleuze and Guattari, 1994). This small section of Deleuze's and Massumi's work must be put into that context. In this section we have only begun to think about these great writers, a single section cannot do justice to the complexity of their work. One really needs to go and read, for example, Deleuze, to get a flavour of his writing and his writing style. Deleuze and Massumi should be read for this very reason; their writings invoke new concepts and new ways of understanding emotion and indeed what it is to be human.

Affect and Subjectivity

The drive of much affect theory has focused on a de-subjectification of emotion and bodily activity. It has been concerned to point to the many ways that affective activity operates outside of pre-conceived notions of emotion and embodied experience. This endeavour is seen as important for the potential utility and value of contemporary theories of affect, for if they cannot tell us something about forces potentially at work outside our current frame(s) of understanding, how can they bring about valid change in thought? Wetherell, in her comprehensive review and critique of the 'affective turn' in respect of social psychology, raises this question as central to her engagement in the area; '[S]ubjectivity becomes a no-place or waiting room, through which affects as autonomous lines of force pass on their way to somewhere else' (2012: 123). Wetherell's concern is that subjectivity is written out of accounts, particularly those emanating from human geography and cultural studies, that expend considerable theoretical effort to unravel some of the multiplicity of non-human relations at work in the constitution of patterns of affect. For Wetherall, key geographers of affect, such as Nigel Thrift, tend to 'construe affect as "becoming", as unspecific force, unmediated by consciousness, discourse, representation and interpretation of any kind' (2012: 123). Wetherell's accusation is that such moves de-subjectify affect, through placing it outside of a range of realms usually seen to operate at the level of the subject (e.g. biology, consciousness, discourse). Wetherell sees social psychoanalysis as a potential way to keep the subject at the centre of affect theory (e.g. Layton, 2004), but claims it ultimately falls short through a reliance on depth psychology processes from which a viable 'affective intersectionality' is not possible. In its place Wetherell offers a 'minimal subjectivity' as the starting point for empirical and theoretical accounts of affect. Here there are no prefigured categories of the subject present, but rather a commitment to see the subject as an 'organising site contributing pattern and order to affective practice' (2012: 139). Wetherell's concerns resonate with wider questions regarding the strand of post-structuralist accounts that are heavily influenced by the work of Deleuze (Hemmings, 2005). Whilst we share the view that it can be easy to forget about the subject at times when reading the intricate and nuanced accounts of relationality, fluidity, power and process in Deleuzian work, we feel it provides some valuable theoretical support when one is primarily concerned with the role of emotionality in human activity. Furthermore, such models of affect prepare us for a journey into exploring the collective expression of emotional experience, which has for a long time been a concern of crowd psychology.

Conclusion

Contemporary theories of affect have proved valuable for understanding the context from which emotional activity, both individually and collectively, emerges. As we have seen, models of affect have been varied and differentiated, particularly in relation to the role and constitution of the subject. Nevertheless, the socialising of emotion that features throughout the affective turn helps us to consider the multiplicity of ways that emotional experience is produced in and through relations between bodies and materialities, with shifting flows of power. Affect theory is useful for demonstrating links between classic and contemporary theories of emotion, e.g. from Spinoza to the 'affective turn'. Furthermore, it demonstrates how theories of emotion have recruited past conceptions of affect and feeling, which have been used to (re)position our understandings of emotion. They demonstrate some of the value of mining historical concepts of emotion and affect, which is something we have been keen to do throughout the book. For instance, Deleuze specifically draws his theory of affect from the work of Spinoza we saw in Chapter 3, which itself was positioning itself against (although not in entire opposition to) the work of Descartes.

A trajectory can then be seen from some of the earliest thinking on emotion and contemporary theories that are focused empirically on modern social worlds that take a very different form than those in which classic theories were written. We want to address some of this in the next, and final, chapter that addresses a question as to the potential impact/s of living in social environments that involve increasing amounts of technological and informational activity. This reality has been said to be a contemporary threat to emotion, in the sense that increased digital activity may mean reduced bodily activity. We use an exploration of digital media and emotion to consider one example of what is at stake for contemporary social psychology accounts of emotion. Namely, creating, organising and managing social relations in and through digital media, which is often framed as 'virtual', as opposed to the 'real' world of face to face interactions. Digital media has the potential to exhibit a significant impact on social psychological experience and activity, which is one reason we think them a worthwhile topic for our final chapter.

FURTHER READING

It is very much worth the effort to have a read through some of the work Gilles Deleuze produced with the psychoanalyst Felix Guattari. However, his writing on Spinoza will be of particular interest to those who are interested in how he draws on Spinoza's notion of *affectus*.

Deleuze, G. (1988). *Spinoza: Practical Philosophy*. (trans. R. Hurley). San Francisco: City Light Books.

We have discussed the work of Brian Massumi, particularly in relation to a chapter that he wrote entitled *The Autonomy of Affect*. This can be found in the following title:

Massumi, B. (2002). *Parables for the Virtual: Movement, affect, sensation* Durham, NC: Duke University Press Books.

The various contemporary affect theories are well illustrated in the following Reader which one of the present authors (Tucker) has contributed to:

Greggs, M. and Seigworth, G. (2010). *The Affect Theory Reader*. Durham, NC: Duke University Press.

10

Digital Emotion

Key Aims

In this chapter we look at some of the ways that emotion may be theorised in relation to technological advancements and the digitisation of human activity. In doing so we include:

- Discussion of the value of the work of Gilbert Simondon to theorising relationships between bodies and technologies
- Conceptualising the role of emotion as central to people's experiences of digital media
- Discussion of societies of mass information, individuation and emotion

Introduction

As we have seen throughout the preceding chapters, emotional activity has been defining how we feel our way through our everyday lives, with such feeling unravelling as part of the multitude of relationships we have. In relatively recent times we have formed an increasing amount of relationships with technologies, e.g. from televisions in the mid-late twentieth century, to the rapidly expanding set of information technologies that exist today (e.g. internet, smart phones, social media, smart watches). This technological advancement has raised questions for social scientists, in terms of what increased usage of technologies means for humanity, and the core categories of emotion, perception and sense. The impacts that digital technologies can have on perception have been a focus of attention (Hansen, 2004), but there has been less consideration of the possible impacts of such technologies on emotional activity, and specifically how experience is shaped through connecting with digital technologies. It is fair to state that sensory activity has also received scant focus (one exception being Tucker and Goodings, 2014), but it is emotion that is subject to our attention here.

The starting point for thinking about modern human-technology relations is often to consider the extent to which bodies are becoming *determined* by technologies. That is, given the increasing power of technologies to seek control over aspects of daily life, is agency shifting from bodies to technologies? For instance, the extent to which people's thoughts, preferences and feelings come to be known to commercial and state organisations when they are discussed and/or disclosed through digital media use, e.g. internet shopping and social media. The ability for digital communication to be tracked, recorded and stored has fast become a mainstay of contemporary living (Harper et al., 2013). This has led to claims that control over activity traditionally seen as personal is shifting from individuals to the huge databases of government and commercial organisations (e.g. Google, Apple). This has been framed as an expansion of the 'surveillance society' (Tucker, 2013), with its effects on affective activity recently beginning to come under scrutiny (Ellis et al., 2013a). However, there is limited exploration of the wider shaping of emotional activity through stronger relationships with digital technologies. In this chapter we explore the work of Gilbert Simondon in considering how emotional activity can be limited and/or innovated by digital technologies.

Simondon's Technics

Simondon is perhaps best known for his philosophy of technology (technics), and is increasingly cited in a trajectory that takes in Heidegger, Leroi-Gourhan and Bernard Stiegler. His work has only recently started to be translated into English (e.g. special issue of the journal Parrhesia, 2009), although as yet only one published translation of a sole authored Simondon work (*Two Lessons on Animal and Man*, 2012), which covers two of his lectures. His major works have yet to be translated into English, although there is a growing body of secondary sources (e.g. Scott, 2014; Combes, 2013). His work is increasingly referenced in relation to critical philosophies of technology focusing on the potential growing agency of technologies, e.g. computer algorithms. Simondon had an interesting take on the relationship between individuals and technologies, which rather than being defined as a philosophy of technology was actually part of his broader theory of individuation. Seen in this light, it will come as little surprise that Simondon saw neither human nor technology as dominant. Technologies do not come to determine human behaviour and neither can technical activity be fully understood through knowledge of human capabilities. Instead, Simondon saw technologies as transformative elements in human activity to respond to their presence and potential, once realised through human design and innovation. For Simondon it is possible to have fully technical individuations (e.g. mail sorting machine), fully human individuations (e.g. a dream), and any combination in between. The important point is not the technology itself, or the original human desire in creating the technology, but rather how technologies and humans intersect and unfold as part of processes of individuation. Simondon is therefore not talking about technologies *per se*. For Simondon, individuating events (e.g. a person feeling sadness at a funeral) are produced in and through connections that are always-already embodied and technological.

To suggest one is dominant is theoretically problematic as it gets in the way of analytic understanding. This is his solution to avoiding technological determinism, which he captures in stating:

> It is the individual, as a constituted individual, that is the interesting reality, the reality that must be explained. The principle of individuation will be sought as a principle capable of explaining the characteristics of the individual, without a necessary relation to other aspects of being that could be correlatives of the appearance of an individuated reality. Such a research perspective gives an ontological privilege to the constituted individual. It therefore runs the risk of not producing a true ontogenesis— that is, of not placing the individual into the system of reality in which the individuation occurs. (Simondon, 2009: 4)

For Simondon, technologies should not be ontologically separated from bodies. Technologies are instead thought of as one of two primary constituents of individuation, which is the formation of individual experience (e.g. a person's specific emotional reaction), and the human body. For Simondon, there is a tension between technologies and bodies, as they form two distinct (and yet inherently related) parts of experience. The tension occurs as any mode of individuation involves the 'coming together' of these two distinct elements. Moreover, any event of individuation can produce a new 'coming together', which always involves a tension (or anxiety) as it is new and as such has not been 'known' before. This tension is 'managed' through information, which passes from the two parts, and subsequently, comes to act as the primary constituent of experience itself. Of interest here is that Simondon places a primacy on information, not the body. Although he is interested in the development of individual action manifest as embodied activity (although individuation does not have to be human), it is information that he focuses on, as the mediating force at work in attempting to resolve the tension between bodies and technologies.

Simondon's work is experiencing something of a revival due to the growing prominence of information in contemporary society (Combes, 2013; Tucker, 2013; Toscano, 2006). Social scientists are looking for viable philosophies of technology and information to help develop understanding of living in digital societies. Simondon offers a comprehensive theoretical account of the relationship between bodies and technologies, with his concepts of information and individuation. This develops through one of the central concerns for Simondon, namely the relationship between individual and collective. Simondon sees what he calls the 'psychic' (i.e. individual subjectivity) as a problem, which cannot be defined as a set of internal properties. Simondon's relational philosophy instead sought to overcome a dualistic model in which individual and collective has two distinct sets of properties. In its place, Simondon thought of individual and collective as *produced* through processes rather than categories *from* which analysis of relationality would occur.

Affective Collective Baggage

What Simondon needed was a conceptual vocabulary through which to make sense of the co-production of individual and collective expression. Core to this was the notion of affectivity which Simondon conceptualised as the layer through which individuals have a relation with themselves, whilst simultaneously recognising their relation(s) with others. Managing this dual-aspect individuality occurs through an affectivity, which in effect, works to continue an individual's perception of self (i.e. personal life history) as well as its role in continuing to act as part of the collectivity (i.e. its role in collective life history). Combes sums this up as 'Affectivity includes a relation between the individuated being and a share of not-yet-individuated preindividual reality that any individual carries with it' (2013: 31). This is the crux of the matter for Simondon. His theory of affect holds that an individual always-already carries some of the collective with it, and as such, its experience cannot be entirely reduced to its own individual being. This 'collective baggage' that is carried through individual bodies is experienced as a tension, which at a psychological level operates as an anxiety. It is an anxiety because the individual is simultaneously experiencing itself as a subject as well as part of an ongoing collective, or what Simondon calls *preindividual*. The awareness that the subject exists through forces of individuation as well as realising the vast potential of preindividuality is felt as an anxiety. This resonates with Foulkes' notion of the collective unconscious and the primary horde we discussed in Chapter 5, and is summed up well by Combes:

> In Simondon's view, anxiety is thus not a passive experience; it is the effort made by a subject to resolve the experience of tension between preindividual and individuated within itself; an attempt to individuate all of the preindividual at once, as if to live it fully. (2013: 32)

Anxiety, as an affective psychic experience, is not then a reaction to challenging life experiences, but rather is an active process of continually trying to resolve the 'problem' of being presented with the collective possibilities of preindividuality, whilst not being able to realise them in entirety. The problem for Simondon here is that anxiety arises as a direct result of the attempt to resolve the tension of the subject at the level of the individual, e.g. by and in oneself. If, on the other hand, the tension is taken on at a collective level, then it may be possible to pose an alternative solution, one that is not anxiety. Simondon invents the concept of the *transindividual* to try to do this. In doing so Simondon is presenting the 'problem' of the relationship between subject and collective in terms of perception and affectivity. The 'perceptual problem' concerns the need to continuously deal with multiple 'requests' to form a perception of something that exists outside of oneself *from* the position of the individual. The subject is faced with a multiplicity of perceptual worlds, and therefore needs to invent perceptual forms to bridge the incompatibilities between different worlds that it faces on a day to day basis.

More broadly, the perceptual problem relates to the fact that when considering individuality it is commonly assumed that an individual exists that we need to account for. For Simondon, this 'mistake' occurs, because of the 'affective problem', which is the reality that the individual experiences itself as a unique subject, but at the same time recognises itself as partially collective.

Simondon argues that the tension between individual and preindividual cannot be resolved 'in' the subject, but must be found in the collective. And yet, Simondon does not want to reify a level of 'collective' *from which* the subject is formed. Instead, a quite densely ontogenetic argument unfolds. Simondon tries to help the reader though this density by inventing a concept to define the philosophical point he is making, namely the *transindividual*. Simondon uses this concept to define how previous incompatibilities can be unified, for a time at least, before they become actualised in the subject's everyday experience. In inventing the transindividual, Simondon was not identifying a space as such, somewhere that can be pointed to and observed. Instead it was more about a 'phase of being' (Combes, 2013), in the process of individuation (similar to how Aristotle discussed the hypothetical substance he named 'prime-matter' that we discussed in Chapter 1). Doing so allowed Simondon to avoid framing individuation in relation to categories of interior and exterior (to the subject). These categories are often used as reference points for debates regarding individuality and collectivity, and yet, for Simondon, such a distinction should be avoided. This is because he sought to see interiority and exteriority as *products* of processes of individuation, not as pre-defined categories.

Transindividuality suggests that to define a subject (i.e. an individual) we have to understand that which took place in advance of its forming, e.g. the *preindividual*, which was neither interior or exterior to it. As such, transindividual names the reality of a subject always carrying with it something that came before, and that it cannot realise in entirety in its individuated form. Instead, we can think of transindividuation as the boundary between interiority and exteriority; that which works across their limit, whose being becomes present at the level of both individual and collective. Simondon works hard to avoid thinking transindividuation as only collective (which its name may imply), because again, he does not want to reify the collective or the individual. It is *trans* because it works across preconceived boundaries of collective and individual, and consequently cannot be said to reside in entirety in either (as they are not stable bounded entities). Indeed, Simondon does not like the notion of relation, as it is most commonly used to define activity between two (or more) prefigured states: 'relation can never be conceived as a relation between preexisting terms but as a reciprocal regime of exchanges of information and of causality in a system that individuates' (cited in Combes, 2013: 47). We can see from this quote why Simondon thinks *information* is the primary source of being. It is not to be thought of merely as the content of communication between individuals, but is the productive and creative source of individuation. It *produces* individuals, rather than representing aspects of their predefined self.

Techno-Biological Emotion

With regard to technologies, for Simondon we are always operating in contexts in which technological and biological are at work as elements in the production of individual affective experience. His emphasis on information as a creative rather than a representative force makes it potentially valuable for understanding the emotional activity at work in and through digital technologies. It potentially allows us to think about 'digital emotion' without having to utilise common notions of 'real' and 'virtual', which can ultimately devalue activity seen as 'virtual' (e.g. social media, online) as less 'real' than 'face to face' contact. What Simondon offers is an inventive set of concepts, through which to understand how emotional activity works across the boundaries of individual and technological (collective) and individuates subjects, who see themselves as individuals with discrete sets of emotion. Indeed, Simondon considers emotion and affective activity as central to the process of individuation. Simondon uses the term 'emotive latency' to refer to the way that emotion is the core disruptor between individual and collective (Krtolica, 2009). Emotive latency refers to the incompatibility between experiencing oneself as a subject as well as part of something greater than one's own individual self (i.e. the collective). Simondon defines emotion as latent as it remains so until transindividual relation takes hold through processes that are always-already collective. This means that emotion cannot be entirely reduced to the level of the individual, however personal it may feel, but is always the product of processes that are collective.

Emotion is the concept that Simondon uses to define the process of psychic individuation, although this is not to suggest that emotion can be seen or captured in any individual instance of subjective experience. Furthermore, psychic individuation can only take place in relation to the collective, and will never operate purely at the level of the individual. Emotion, for Simondon, marks the reality of the subject experiencing itself as 'more than individual', whilst simultaneously facing the pressure to try to actualise this 'more than' as an individual, which for Simondon, is not possible. This is why it's a tension, an anxiety. Simondon's philosophy of individuation is an ontogenesis that considers all 'nature' as part of processes of individuation. When we consider an individual being (human or technology), what we see is the result of a transformation, through an innovative process of trying to resolve the tension between two previously heterogonous dimensions. Core to the psychological dimensions of these processes is emotion, or what, as we have seen, Simondon refers to as 'emotive latency'. When we consider what we have called 'digital emotion', we suggest that it is useful to frame such activity as part of processes of individuation, in which people are attempting to set the parameters of their individual self online. For instance, there is widespread use of emoticons to try to express emotion textually in digital communication. However, emoticons offer only rather limited possibilities to present a range of emotions as they refer to predefined categories of facial expressions that portray feelings of happiness, sadness, frustration etc. This does not mean that emotional activity is limited though in digital spaces, as may be suggested if arguing that emotional expression only occurs through specifically designed technical tools (e.g. emoticons). Following Simondon's argument leaves us with a broader notion of 'digital emotion', which sees the concept of emotion as a core part of our relationships with technologies. For sure, things like emoticons facilitate emotional activity in online spaces, but they are only one small part of the role of emotion in the production of individuated experience, which is formed through relational processes incorporating bodies and technologies.

What this viewpoint allows us to do is to frame technologies as working in concert with bodies in the production of emotional and affective activity. It does not privilege one realm over another in terms of creating emotional activity, and therefore emotion deemed to be 'within' technologies, such as social media profiles, is not categorised as 'virtual', or somehow less valid or real than non-technological emotional activity. In this sense, Simondon raises the profile of technologies, and gives them potential equal weighting in the formation of psychological experience. This allows an understanding to develop that people can and do *feel* in and through technological activity and expression. This is not to suggest that bodies *use* technologies to feel *with*, e.g. as a prosthetic. Instead, technologies are seen as relational forces that co-produce emotional activity with bodies (Goodings and Tucker, 2014). One view of this is that Simondon is offering an ontology that gives non-human objects the same billing as humans in the formation of psychological experience, and imbues them with notions of agency. This position has been well rehearsed in Science and Technology Studies, particularly through Actor-Network Theory. We think that Simondon's position is in effect quite subtle with regard to the ontological status of technologies. In writing *Psychic and Collective Individuation* he was focused on the production of individuated psychological experience and activity (Scott, 2014). He was not suggesting that technologies can feel or think. These are individuated human activities. However, Simondon was arguing that technologies can play a prominent role in their individuation *in feeling*. Furthermore, the idea that online activity is somehow false or 'not real' is troubled by a Simondonian reading. Whilst online activity can be distinguished from offline experience, neither is privileged in terms of its legitimacy. Online media (e.g. social media) have become a new forum for the production of emotional and affective activity. Online experience is no less valid than offline, and given its increase in prominence, we think a Simondonian account is a potentially valuable way of understanding digital emotion. This is because we follow the line set out by Toscano, which is 'to know the individual through individuation rather than individuation through the individual' (2006: 136). To understand individual emotional activity then requires us to address the processes of individuation through which it is produced. Increases in digital activity in our everyday lives mean that technologies are playing an increasingly prominent role in processes of individuation, and as such, a viable and realistic social psychology of emotion needs to understand that emotional activity realised at an individual level has been produced in a context of bodies and technologies working together in multiple and increasingly mobile spaces and times.

The potential value of the concept of individuation is that it presents individual experience as simultaneously individual and collective, which fits well with the reality of interacting with digital technologies. The widespread capture, storage and recording of our digital activity is now well known, e.g. through recent (2013) media coverage of the extent of the US National Security Agency's surveillance of everything from individuals' emails to the German Chancellor Angela Merkel's mobile phone. We already know that engaging with internet technologies, such as online shopping and social media involves leaving a trace of our activity (e.g. shopping habits, Facebook Timeline), that is stored in the vast databases of large technology corporations (e.g. Amazon, Apple, Google). For many people this is not experienced as a concern (Harper et al., 2013). However, there can be moments when anxiety arises through the recognition that one's online activity is tracked and stored: for instance, when an organisation uses past activity to tailor its advertising to users. At moments like this people can become aware of their presence as part of the 'informational collective' that shapes online activity. This is just as Simondon suggested, namely that recognising one's reality as an individual whilst simultaneously collective can be anxiety producing. A similar point is made through thinking about the form of what Ellis et al. (2013a) have distinguished as affective atmospheres of digital forms of surveillance and the particular forms of distrust and paranoia that these may give way to (Ellis et al., 2013b; Harper et al., 2012).

The presence of a set of information online that relates to individual activity has been coined a 'data double' (Lyon, 2006). We prefer the concept of individuation as it captures more of the processes at work in body-technology assemblages, rather than presenting the two as distinct. This culminates in our proposition to define digital emotion as processual and produced through relations and activity that operate across levels from international corporate databases to individual posts on social media sites. Separating these levels out theoretically is problematic, as to do so limits the context in which emotional activity is understood. Simondon offers us a way of framing emotion that can account for how people *feel* in and through connections between their individual bodies and mass technologies. It is not just about defining what kinds of 'technological spaces' are emerging that people can experience emotions *within*, but rather how digital technologies are allowing people to produce new and innovative emotional solutions and to feel in ways that address the tensions and anxieties of living in 'societies of mass information'.

FURTHER READING

Very little of Simondon's work is translated in English, so we recommend reading some very good secondary sources:

Combes, M. (2013). *Gilbert Simondon and the Philosophy of the Transindividual.* Cambridge, MA: The MIT Press.
Combes' book is probably the most accessible of current secondary Simondon texts. It provides a broad overview of his core concepts (for example, individuation and affectivity). It is a strong introduction that allows a good engagement with Simondon's thought to develop.

De Boever, A., Murray, A., Roffe, J. and Woodward, A. (eds) (2012). *Gilbert Simondon: Being and technology.* Edinburgh: Edinburgh University Press.
This is an edited collection that includes a translation of one of Simondon's chapters, along with chapters from a range of critical theorists exploring the value of Simondonian philosophy. It's a good introduction as it covers Simondonian thinking in considerable breadth, as well as including primary sources.

Conclusion

It seems that the scientisation of psychology as a discipline has to some extent repressed its emotional history. This is not a unique contemporary phenomenon but history tells the story of the ways in which ideas are suppressed and superseded. For example emotion theories throughout the medieval period drew on the philosophy of Plato, but tended to reframe it through a Christian doctrine; later the enlightenment period attempted to reframe Christian doctrine through for example natural law theory; and contemporary psychology attempts to reframe former theorisations through inductive (scientific) methodologies. As Freud would have it, however, there is always a return of the repressed and thus we see similar discourses and questions emerge but in different guises through the various epochs and disciplines. However, we can (and perhaps should) learn something from the early theories of emotion. For example, distinctions between passions and affect were quite important to many pre-scientific conceptualisations. In many accounts the passions were less voluntary than the affects; but we no longer have such a distinction, perhaps because psychology has attempted to move away from these theologically loaded conceptualisations, such as *affectus* being part of the higher (intellectual) soul. In this way it dismisses some very rich theorisations that could be reinvigorated for contemporary purposes. Indeed it is argued by some scholars that today many of these early concepts that were bound up with theology have found their way through to psychology in disguised form (either consciously, or perhaps more likely, unconsciously or rather non-deliberately) (see Dixon (2003) for a review). For example, we still see distinctions between cognition and emotion, one often understood as more rational than the other, more intelligent and more suitable to human behaviour. Even the post-structuralist theories of affect resort to dichotomising the virtual with the actual in a way that is reminiscent of Plato's distinction between *doxa* and *episteme* or Kant's *phenomena* and *noumena*. This is not to say that there is no value in the development of thought, just as the ego must supersede the id, there is a requirement for psychology to become a rational discipline. Indeed it required disciplining! Yet, and if we are to continue with the metaphor of psychoanalysis, there is the danger of over-socialising the discipline through which the superego can become too overbearing.

Just as individuals have been in need of taming the primitive and animalistic aspects of the self, one could argue that the discipline of psychology attempts to disentangle itself from the more emotional, subjective, messy and undesirable parts of itself. For instance, in the UK social cognition is the primary approach for social psychology, and is a core part of the British Psychological Society undergraduate curriculum, whereas emotion is not. Whilst we are not in any way denying the importance of cognitive processes in human activity (as we have not denied biological approaches), we feel that emotion as a topic features far too rarely in approaches that seek to toe the rationalist line. One could argue that this is because, whether consciously or not, mainstream social psychology's desire to operate a primarily cognitive approach has been, in part at least, to avoid engaging in aspects of the psychological self that emerge in and through emotional activity. Emotion's existence as messy, contradictory, complex, difficult to pin down and understand seemingly makes it problematic for mainstream rationalist approaches. We argue though that such messy activity is of prime concern for psychology, and although it may trouble its scientific credentials, should not be played down or taken out of the social psychological gaze.

Thus in this book we have attempted to engage with the messy from Ancient Greek understandings right through to contemporary philosophies of digital media and technologies. Our aim has been to cover those theories and empirical accounts of emotion that we argue are important for a social psychological understanding of emotion, past and present, not because they fit into some form of social psychological paradigm. Some of the theories we've covered have featured in existing psychological histories of emotion, for instance, Aristotle, Aquinas, Hume, Darwin and James. However, we have drawn out aspects of their work that is valuable when following a 'social' psychological account. We have also discussed theories that have not traditionally featured in histories of emotion, for instance, the social psychology of Kurt Lewin and the philosophy of technology of Gilbert Simondon. This is because we have wanted throughout to revisit well known theories of emotion, and point to what a modern social psychology of emotion can learn from them, as well as supplement them as and when appropriate. In doing so we hope to have avoided producing yet another potted history of emotion, and instead present a social psychological understanding of emotion, which has often been absent from previous accounts.

Contemporary psychologies of emotion tend to be dominated by biological and cognitive accounts, which attempt to model the underlying biological and/or cognitive processes of emotion. We have not focused extensively on existing models of this kind, as our concern has been to address what is important for social psychological understandings. Our reason for wanting to write about specifically social psychological understandings of emotion, and what is important for them, is due to a desire to broaden psychological focus on the emotions, away from some of the potentially reductive beliefs that can form when focusing only on single disciplinary thinking. This can be exacerbated when one's approach aims to identify processes as causally underpinning emotional activity (e.g. biological models). Taking a social approach usefully facilitates an alternative starting point for analysis, in terms of thinking about the multiple relationships between objects and spaces that constitute the inner and outer realms of our social worlds. Doing so obliges one to think interdisciplinarily from the start. We know this from the success of social psychology as a field. We seek to add to this through an explicit focus on emotion, which we feel has, rather surprisingly, remained a minor part of existing social psychology.

To date social psychology has been dominated by focus on concepts that are seen to be central to social behaviour. A glance through most social psychology textbooks will find chapters on attitude, prejudice, inter-group processes, social identity etc. These have, in the main, been studied experimentally and in accordance with the dominant theoretical paradigm of the time, e.g. social cognition. Since the 1980s an alternative stream of social psychological research has emerged, often called 'critical social psychology', which focuses on unpacking some of what it thought of as overly individualistic and reductive thinking in mainstream social psychology, and instead points to the social and historical contingency of social psychology categories, rather than simply accepting that they relate to specific and inherent psychological realities. This alternative stream has been for a lot of its time concerned with various forms of textual analysis, focusing empirically on the ways people orient to and/or construct their own understandings of identity and subjectivity. To a degree, 'critical social psychology' has been a less rational and more nuanced and complex sub-discipline, not without its own contradictions and internal debates. In writing this book we are addressing what we see as a gap in both mainstream and 'critical' social psychology, namely providing a sustained and substantive historical and contemporary account of emotion. In doing so, we are claiming that 'emotion activity' remains in need of continued theoretical and empirical social psychological focus. Moreover, battle lines do not need to be drawn between mainstream and critical approaches, but a course can be navigated that draws out the important antecedents and influences from across psychology as a whole, and beyond.

So, in writing this book we have not set out to offer a new 'social psychology of emotion', theoretically and/or empirically. Instead we have presented a range of theories that we argue are important for social psychological understandings of emotion. As we stated in the Introduction, such a history has not been completed before in this context, and therefore the book is hopefully a timely offering. Moreover, a strength of this approach, namely not offering a specific social psychological approach itself, is that it allows us to present a set of concerns that we think should shape social psychology, and its multiple engagements with emotion. The discipline needs to be free to draw on theories from a range of disciplines where appropriate, and should not feel restricted through fear of entering existing debates that require one to take a specific position in relation to, for example, biology, discourse etc. Throughout the book we have sought to point out the importance of emotion for social psychology, yet we see drawing territorial lines around for instance, specific topics, paradigms, and approaches as unhelpful. This is why we argue that whilst it is useful for social psychology to have a distinct disciplinary identity, and therefore justify its existence in the world, in its practice it needs to be able to draw on theories from multiple disciplines.

Reference List

Allman, J. and Brothers, L. (1994). 'Faces, fear and the amygdala', *Nature*, 372 (6507): 613–4.

Aquinas (1964–80). *Summa Theologiae*. (ST) Ed. and trans, the Fathers of the English Dominican Province, 30 vols. London.

Aristotle (1961). *De Anima*. W. Ross (ed.). Oxford: Clarendon Press.

Aristotle (1984). *Rhetoric, The Complete Works of Aristotle*. J. Barnes. (ed.). Princeton: Princeton University Press.

Aristotle (1988). *Ethica Nocomachea*. I. Baywater (ed.). Oxford: Clarendon Press.

Augustine (1972). *City of God*. D. Knowles (ed.). Harmondsworth Press.

Averill, J. (1974). 'An analysis of psychophysiological symbolism and its influence on theories of emotion', *Journal for the Theory of Social Behaviour*.

Badcock, C. R. (2000). *Evolutionary Psychology: A critical introduction*. Cambridge: Polity.

Barrett, L. (2011). 'Was Darwin wrong about emotional expressions?', *Current Directions in Psychological Science*, 20 (6): 400–6.

Bartlett, F. C. (1932). *Remembering*. Cambridge: Cambridge University Press

Bechara, A., Damasio, H., and Damasio, A. R. (2000). 'Emotion, decision making and the orbitofrontal cortex', *Cerebral Cortex*, 10 (3): 295–307.

Beebe, B. and Lachman, F. (1988). 'The contribution of mother-infant mutual influence to the origins of self-and-object representations', *Psychoanalytic Psychology* 5 (4): 305–37.

Bell, P. (2002). 'Neo-psychology or neo-humans? A critique of Massumi's Parables for the virtual', *Continuum*, 17 (4): 445–62.

Bennett, M. and Hacker, P. (2003). *Philosophical Foundations of Neuroscience*. Oxford: Blackwell Publishing.

Bergson, H. (1896). *Matter and Memory*. Trans. N.M. Paul and W.S. Palmer [1991]. New York: Zone Books.

Berlin, B. and Kay, P. (1991). *Basic Color Terms: Their universality and evolution*. Berkeley: University of California Press.

Berlucchi, G. (2006). 'Revisiting the 1981 Nobel Prize to Roger Sperry, David Hubel and Torsten Wiesel on the occasion of the centennial of the prize to Golji and Cajal', *Journal of the History of the Neurosciences: Basic and Clinical Perspectives*, 15 (4): 369–75.

Bertrand, I. and Hughes, P. (2004) *Media Research Methods: Audiences, Institution*: New York: Palgrave MacMillan.

Bettelheim, B. (1982). 'Freud and the soul', *The New Yorker*, 6: 52–75.

Bion, W. (1961). *Experiences in Groups and Other Papers*. New York: Tavistock Publications Limited.

Bogen, J. E. and Vogel, P. J. (1962). 'Cerebral commissurotomy in man', *Bulletin of the Los Angeles Neurological Society*, 27 (4): 169–72.

Bower, G., Gilligan, S. and Monteiro, K. (1981). 'Selectivity of learning caused by affective states', *Journal of Experimental Psychology*, General, 110(4): 451–73.

Brennan, T. (2004). *The Transmission of Affect*. Ithaca, NY: Cornell University Press.

Brown, S. and Stenner, P. (2009). *Psychology Without Foundations*. London: Sage.

Bucci, W. (1985) 'Dual coding: A cognitive model for psychoanalytic research', *Journal of the American Psychoanalytic Association*, 33: 571–607.

Bucci, W. (1995). 'The power of the narrative: A multiple code account', in J. W. Pennebaker (ed.), *Emotion, Disclosure and Health*. Washington, DC: American Psychological Association. pp. 71–92.

Bucci, W. (1997). *Psychoanalysis and Cognitive Science: A multiple code theory.* New York: The Guilford Press.

Buck, R. W. (2000). 'The epistemology of reason and affect', in J. Borod (ed.) *The Neuropsychology of Emotion.* New York: Oxford University Press. pp. 31–55.

Cacioppo, J. and Gardner, W. (1999). 'Emotion', *Annual Review of Psychology,* 50 (19): 191–214.

Carroll, J. B., Whorf, B. L. and Press, M. (1964). *Language, Thought, and Reality: Selected writings.* Cambridge, MA: The MIT Press.

Chalmers, T. (1853). *On the Power, Wisdom and Goodness of God as Manifested in the Adaptation of External Nature to the Moral and Intellectual Constitution of Man.* London: Bohn.

Chomsky, N. (1957). *Syntactic Structures.* The Hague: Mouton.

Chomsky, N. (1959). 'Review of verbal behavior by BF Skinner', *Language,* 35: 26–58.

Christman, S. (1995). 'Independence versus integration of rights and left hemisphere processing: effects of handedness', in F. Kitterle (ed.) *Hemispheric Communication: Mechanisms and models.* Hillsdale, NJ: Lawrence Erlbaum Associates. pp. 231–53.

Combes, M. (2013). *Gilbert Simondon and the Philosophy of the Transindividual.* Cambridge, MA: The MIT Press.

Cooper, J. (1999). 'An Aristotelian theory of the emotions', in A. Rorty (ed.) *Essays on Aristotle's Rhetoric.* University of California Press. pp. 238–58.

Copleston, F. (1985). *A History of Philosophy: Vol. 4. Descartes to Leibniz.* New York: Image Books.

Craib, I. (2000). 'Narratives as bad faith', in M. Andrews (ed.) *Lines of Narrative: Psychosocial perspectives,* London and New York: Routledge. pp. 64–74.

Crawford, M. and Popp, D. (2003). 'Sexual double standards: A review and methodological critique of two decades of research', *Journal of Sex Research,* 40 (1): 13–26.

Dalal, F. (1998). *Taking the Group Seriously. Towards a post-Foulkesian group analytic theory.* London: Jessica Kingsley.

Dalgleish, T. (2004). 'The emotional brain', *Nature Reviews Neuroscience,* 5 (7): 583–9.

Dalgleish T., Matthews, A. and Wood, J. (1999). 'Inhibition processes in cognition and emotion: A special case?', in T. Dalgleish and M. Power (eds) *Handbook of Cognition and Emotion.* Chichester: John Wiley. pp. 243–65.

Damasio, A. R. (1994). *Descartes' Error: Emotion, Rationality and the Human Brain.* New York: Putnam.

Damasio, A. R. (2000). *The Feeling of What Happens: Body and emotion in the making of consciousness.* London: Vintage.

Danziger, K. (1997). *Naming the Mind: How psychology found its language.* London: Sage.

Darwin, C. (1872). *The Expression of the Emotions in Man and Animals.* New York: Oxford University Press. [3rd edition 2002]

Davidson, R. J. (1992). 'Emotion and affective style: Hemispheric substrates', *Psychological Science,* 3: 39–43.

De Boever, A., Murray, A., Roffe, J. and Woodward, A. (2012). (eds) *Gilbert Simondon: Being and technology.* Edinburgh: Edinburgh University Press.

Deigh, J. (1994). 'Cognitivism in the theory of emotions', *Ethics,* 104(4): 824–54.

Deleuze, G. (1998). 'The shame and the glory: T.E. Lawrence' in G. Deleuze: *Essays Critical and Clinical* (trans. D. W. Smith and M. Greco). London: Verso. pp. 115–25.

Deleuze, G. and Guattari, F. (1987). *A Thousand Plateaus: Capitalism and schizophrenia.* Minneapolis: University of Minnesota Press.

Deleuze, G. and Guattari, F. (1994). *What is Philosophy?,* trans. Hugh Tomlinson and Graham Burchell. New York: Columbia University Press.

Derrida, J. (1988). *Limited Inc.* Evanston, IL: Northwestern University Press.

Dixon, T. (2003). *From Passions to Emotions: The creation of a secular psychological category*. Cambridge: Cambridge University Press.

Dovidio, J. F., Ellyson, S. L., Keating, C. F., Heltman, K. and Brown, C. E. (1988). 'The relationship of social power to visual displays of dominance between men and women', *Journal of Personality and Social Psychology*, 54 (2): 233–42.

Edelman, G. M. (1993). 'Neural Darwinism: selection and reentrant signaling in higher brain function', *Neuron*, 10 (2), 115–25.

Edwards, D. (1997). *Discourse and Cognition*. London: Sage.

Edwards, D. and Potter, J. (1992). *Discursive Psychology*. London: Sage.

Edwards, P. (1967). (ed.) *Stoicism, The Encyclopedia of Philosophy*, vol. 8. New York: MacMillan. pp.19–22.

Ekman, P. (1980). *The Face of Man: Expressions of universal emotions in a New Guinea village*. New York: Garland STPM Press.

Ekman, P. (2004). *Emotions Revealed: Understanding faces and feelings*. London: Phoenix.

Ellis, D. (2010). 'Stop and search: Disproportionality, discretion and generalisations', *The Police Journal*, 83 (3): 199–216.

Ellis, D. and Cromby, J. (2004). 'It's not always good to talk'. *The Psychologist*, 17 (11): 630–1.

Ellis, D. and Cromby, J. (2009). 'Inhibition and reappraisal within emotional disclosure: the embodying of narration', *Counselling Psychology Quarterly*, 22 (3): 319–31.

Ellis, D. and Cromby, J. (2012). 'Emotional inhibition: A discourse analysis of disclosure', *Psychology and Health*, 27 (5): 515–32.

Ellis, D. and Tucker, I. (2011). 'Virtuality and Ernst Bloch: Hope and subjectivity', *Journal of Subjectivity*, 4: 434–50.

Ellis, D. Tucker, I. and Harper, D. (2013a). 'The affective atmospheres of surveillance', *Theory and Psychology*, 23 (6): 716–31.

Ellis, D., Harper. D. and Tucker. I. (2013b). 'The dynamics of impersonal trust and distrust in surveillance systems', *Sociological Research Online*, 18 (3): 8.

Erdelyi, M.H. (2006). 'The unified theory of repression', *Behavioral and Brain Sciences*, 29: 499–551.

Etcoff, N. (1989). 'Asymmetries in recognition of emotion', in F. Boller and J. Grafman (eds) *Handbook of Psychology*, Vol. 3. Amsterdam: Elsevier. pp. 363–82.

Fabes, R. A. and Martin, C. L. (1991). 'Gender and age stereotypes of emotionality', *Personality and Social Psychology Bulletin*, 17 (5): 532–40.

Fineman, S. (2008). *The Emotional Organization: Passions and power*. Oxford: Wiley-Blackwell.

Fischer, A. H. (1993). 'Sex differences in emotionality: Fact or stereotype?', *Feminism & Psychology*, 3(3): 303–18.

Fiske, S. T. (1993). 'Controlling other people', *American Psychologist*, 48(6): 621–8.

Foulkes, S. (1948). *Introduction to Group Analytic Psychotherapy*. München: Heinemann.

Foulkes, S. H. (1971). 'Access to unconscious processes in the group analytic group', in *Selected Papers*. London: Karnac, 1990. pp. 209–22.

Foulkes, S. H. (1971). The group as matrix of the individual's mental life. In: *Selected Papers* (pp. 223–34). London: Karnac, 1990.

Frazer, M. (2010). *The Enlightenment of Sympathy: Justice and the moral sentiments in the eighteenth century and today*. Oxford: Oxford University Press.

Freud, S. (1895). 'Project for a scientific psychology'. *The Standard Edition of the Complete Psychological Works of Sigmund Freud*, 1966. London: Hogarth Press. pp. 335–46.

Freud, S. (1900). 'The interpretation of dreams'. *The Standard Edition of the Complete Psychological Works of Sigmund Freud, Volume IV 1966*. London: Hogarth Press. pp. ix–627.

Freud, S. (1915). 'The unconscious'. *The Standard Edition of the Complete Psychological Works of Sigmund Freud, Volume XIV* 1966. London: Hogarth Press. pp. 159–215.

Freud, S. (1919). 'Group psychology and the analysis of the ego'. *The Standard Edition of the Complete Psychological Works of Sigmund Freud, Volume XVIII*. 1966. London: Hogarth Press. pp. 67–143.

Freud, S. (1923). 'The ego and the id', *The Standard Edition of the Complete Psychological Works of Sigmund Freud*, 1966. London: Hogarth Press. pp. 1–66.

Freud, S. (1942). *Psychopathische Personen auf der Bühne*. GW, Nachtragsband, 655–61.

Frisina, P.G., Borod, J.C. and Lepore, S. J. (2004). 'A meta-analysis of the effects of written emotional disclosure on the health outcomes of clinical populations', *Journal of Mental Disorders*, 192(9): 629–34.

Frosh, S. and Baraitser, L. (2008). 'Psychoanalysis and psychosocial studies', *Psychoanalysis, Culture & Society*, 13 (4): 346–65.

Gainotti, G. (2002). 'Neuropsychological theories of emotion', in J. Borod (ed.) *The Neuropsychology of Emotion*. Oxford: Oxford University Press. pp. 214–36.

Gergen, K. J. and Gergen, M. M. (1988). 'Narrative and the self as relationship', in L. Berkowitz (ed.) *Advances in Experimental Social Psychology*, V. 21, New York: Academic Press. pp. 17–56.

Gibbs, A. (2010). 'After affect : sympathy, synchrony, and mimetic communication', in M. Gregg and G. J. Seigworth (eds) *The Affect Theory Reader*. Durham, NC: Duke University Press. pp. 186–205.

Gibson, J. J. (1986). *The Ecological Approach to Visual Perception*. Hillsdale, NJ: Lawrence Erlbaum Associates.

Gill, C. (2010). 'Stoicism and epicureanism', in P. Goldie (ed.) *The Oxford Handbook of the Philosophy of Emotion*. Oxford: Oxford University Press.

Gloor, P. (1986). 'Role of the human limbic system in perception, memory, and affect: Lessons from temporal lobe epilepsy', in B. Doane and K. Livingston (eds) *The Limbic System: Functional organization and clinical disorders*. New York: Raven. pp. 159–69.

Goffman, E. (1959). *The Presentation of Self in Everyday Life*. Penguin: Harmondsworth.

Goffman, E. (1961). *Encounters: Two studies in the sociology of interaction*.

Goffman, E. (1967). *Interaction Ritual: Essays on Face-to-Face Behaviour*. New York: Doubleday.

Goldberg, E. (2001). *The Executive Brain*. Oxford: Oxford University Press.

Goodings, L. and Tucker, I. M. 'Social media and the co-production of bodies online: Bergson, Serres and Facebook timeline', *Media, Culture & Society*, 36 (1): 37–51.

Gould, S. (1981). *The Mismeasure of Man*: New York: Norton.

Greco, M. and Stenner, P. (2008). *Emotions: A social science reader*. London: Routledge.

Greenberg, J. R. and Mitchell, S. A. (1983). *Object Relations in Psychoanalytic Theory*. Cambridge, MA: Harvard University Press.

Gregg, M. and Seigworth, G. J. (2010). *The Affect Theory Reader*. Durham, NC: Duke University Press.

Griffiths, P. (1997). *What Emotions Really Are*. Chicago: University of Chicago Press.

Gross, D. (2006). *The Secret History of Emotion: From Aristotle's rhetoric to modern brain science*. Chicago: University of Chicago Press.

Haaken, J. and Reavey, P. (2009). (eds) *Memory Matters: Understanding Recollections of Sexual Abuse*. London: Psychology Press.

Habib, M. (2005). *A History of Literary Criticism: From Plato to present*. Oxford: Blackwell Publishing.

Hall, J. A., Carter, J. D. and Horgan, T. G. (2000). 'Gender differences in nonverbal communication of emotion', in A. Fischer (ed.) *Gender and Emotion: Social psychological perspectives*. Cambridge: Cambridge University Press. pp. 97–117.

Hansen, M. B. N. (2004). *New Philosophy for New Media*. Cambridge, MA: The MIT Press.

Harper, D., Tucker I. M. and Ellis, D. (2013). 'Surveillance and subjectivity: Everyday experiences of surveillance practices', in K. Ball and L. Snider (eds) *The Surveillance-Industrial Complex: A political economy of surveillance*. Abingdon: Routledge. pp. 175–90.

Harré, R., and Parrott, W. (1996). *The Emotions: Social, cultural and biological dimensions*. London: Sage.

Harrison, N. A., Singer, T., Rotshtein, P., Dolan, R. J. and Critchley, H. D. (2006). 'Pupillary contagion: central mechanisms engaged in sadness processing', *Social Cognitive and Affective Neuroscience*, 1 (1): 5.

Hartmann, G. (1935). *Gestalt Psychology: A survey of facts and principles*. New York: Ronald Press Company.

Hatfield, E., Cacioppo, J. and Rapson, R. (1994). *Emotional Contagion: Studies in emotional interaction*. Cambridge: Cambridge University Press.

Hatfield, E., Rapson, R. and Le, Y. (2009). 'Emotional contagion and empathy', in J. Decety and W. Ickes (eds) *The Social Neuroscience of Empathy*. Cambridge, MA: The MIT Press. pp.19–30.

Hatfield, E., Sprecher, S., Pillemer, J. T., Greenberger, D. and Wexler, P. (1989). 'Gender differences in what is desired in the sexual relationship', *Journal of Psychology & Human Sexuality*, 1 (2): 39–52.

Held, V. (1993). *Feminist Morality: Transforming culture, society, and politics*: Chicago: University of Chicago Press.

Hellige, J. (1993). *Hemispheric Asymmetry: What's right and what's left*. Cambridge, MA: Harvard University Press.

Hemmings, C. (2005). 'Invoking affect: cultural theory and the ontological turn', *Cultural Studies*, 19 (5): 548–67.

Henley, N. M. (1973). 'Status and sex: Some touching observations', *Bulletin of the Psychonomic Society* 2 (2): 91–3.

Hess, U. and Philippot, P. (2010). *Group Dynamics and Emotional Expression*. Cambridge: Cambridge University Press.

Hillman, J. (1992). *Emotion: A comprehensive phenomenology of theories and their meaning for therapy*. Evanston, IL: Northwestern University Press.

Hinshelwood, R. D. and Klein, M. (1991). *A Dictionary of Kleinian Thought*. London: Free Association Books.

Hochschild, A. R. (1979). 'Emotion work, feeling rules, and social structure', *American Journal of Sociology*, 85 (3): 551–75.

Hochschild, A. R. (1983). *The Managed Heart: Commercialization of Human Feeling*. Berkeley: University of California Press.

Hochschild, A. R. (1990). 'Ideology and emotion management: A perspective and path for future research', in T. Kemper (ed.) *Research Agendas in the Sociology of Emotions*. Albany, NY: State University of New York Press. pp. 117–42.

Hogan, P. (2000). *Philosophical Approaches to the Study of Literature*. Gainesville: University Press of Florida.

Howard, C., Tuffin, K. and Stephens, C. (2000). 'Unspeakable emotion: A discursive analysis of police talk about reactions to trauma', *Journal of Language and Social Psychology*, 19 (3): 295–314.

Hume, D. (1740/1978). *A Treatise of Human Nature* (T). Oxford: Oxford University Press.

Hume, D. (1748/1975). *An Enquiry Concerning Human Understanding* (EHU). Oxford: Oxford University Press.

Hume, D. (1751/1975). *An Enquiry Concerning the Principles of Morals* (EPM). Oxford University Press.

Izard, C. E. (1971). *The Face of Emotion*. New York: Appleton-Century-Crofts.

James, S. (2003). *Passion and Action: The emotions in seventeenth-century philosophy*. Oxford: Oxford University Press.

James, W. (1884). 'What is an emotion?', *Mind*, 9 (34): 188–205.

James, W. (1890). *The Principles of Psychology*. New York: Dover [reprint 1950].

Jarrett, C. (2007). *Spinoza: A guide for the perplexed*. London: Continuum.

Johnson, J. T. and Shulman, G. A. (1988) 'More alike than meets the eye: Perceived gender differences in subjective experience and its display', *Sex Roles*, 19 (1), 67–79.

Kant, I. (1785). *Groundwork of the Metaphysics of Morals*, 1785 (G) trans. H. Paton 1985. London: Hutchinson University Library.

Kant, I. (1974). *Anthropology from a Pragmatic Point of View*, 1798 (APV). KGS 7:119–333. Translated by Mary Gregor. The Hague Martinus Nijhoff.

Kant, I. (1783). *Prolegomena to Any Future Metaphysics that Will be Able to Come Forward as Science* (PFM). KGS 4: Trans. P. Carus, revised by J. Ellington [1977]. Indianapolis. Hackett. pp. 255–386.

Kant, I. (1996). *Religion within the Boundaries of Mere Reason*, 1793 (RBR). KGS 6. Trans. G. di Giovanni, in *Religion and Rational Theology. The Cambridge Edition of the Works of Immanuel Kant*, trans. and ed. A. Wood and G. di Giovanni. Cambridge: Cambridge University Press. pp. 3–202.

Kant, I. (1996). *The Metaphysics of Morals*, 1797 (MM). KGS 6. Trans. M. Gregor, in *Practical Philosophy. The Cambridge Edition of the Works of Immanuel Kant*. Cambridge: Cambridge University Press. pp. 203–493.

Kant, I. (1997). *Lectures on Ethics* (LE). KGS 27. Trans. by Peter Heath. Edited by Peter Heath and J. Schneewind. *The Cambridge Edition of the Works of Immanuel Kant*. Cambridge: Cambridge University Press.

Kant, I. (2000). *Critique of the Power of Judgment*, 1790 (CJ). KGS 5. Trans. P. Guyer and E. Matthews. Edited by Paul Guyer. *The Cambridge Edition of the Works of Immanuel Kant*. Cambridge: Cambridge University Press. pp. 167–484.

Kaplan-Solms, K., and Solms, M. (2001). *Clinical Studies in Neuro-psychoanalysis: Introduction to a depth neuropsychology*. New York: Other Press, LLC.

Kellenberger, J. (1980). 'Faith and emotion', *Sophia*, 19 (3): 31–43.

Kehily, M. (1995). 'Self-narration, autobiography and identity construction', *Gender and Education*, 7 (1): 23–31.

Kemal, Salim (2003). *The Philosophical Poetics of Alfarabi, Avicenna, and Averroës*. London and New York: Routledge.

Knuuttila, S. (2004). *Emotions in Ancient and Medieval Philosophy*. New York: Oxford University Press.

Konstan, D. (2006). *The Emotions of the Ancient Greeks: Studies in Aristotle and classical literature*. Toronto: University of Toronto Press.

Krtolica, I. (2009). 'The question of anxiety in Gilbert Simondon', *Parrhesia*, 7: 68–80.

Laplanche, J. and Pontalis, J. B. (1988). *The Language of Psycho-analysis*. London: Karnac Books.

Lasch, C. (1991). *The Culture of Narcissism: American life in an age of diminishing expectations*. New York: Norton Paperback.

Layton, L. (2004). 'A fork in the royal road: On "defining" the unconscious and its stakes for social theory', *Psychoanalysis, Culture and Society*, 9: 33–51.

Lazarus, R. S. and Folkman, S. (1984). *Stress, Appraisal, and Coping*. New York: Springer.

LeDoux, J. (1996). *The Emotional Brain: The mysterious underpinnings of emotional life*. New York: Simon and Schuster.

LeDoux, J. (2002). *Synaptic Self: How our brains become who we are*. New York: Viking.

Lepore, S. J., Greenberg, M. A., Bruno, M. and Smyth, J. M. (2002). 'Expressive writing and health: Self-regulation of emotion-related experience, physiology, and behaviour', in

S. J. Lepore and J. M. Smyth (eds) *The Writing Cure: How Expressive Writing Promotes Health and Emotional Well-being.* Washington, DC: American Psychological Association.

Levant, R. F. (1996). 'The new psychology of men', *Professional Psychology: Research and Practice,* 27, 3: 259–65.

Leventhal, H., and Tomarkin, A. J. (1986). 'Emotion: Today's problems', *Annual Review of Psychology,* 37: 565–610.

Lewin, K. (1936). *Principles of Topological Psychology.* New York: McGraw Hill.

Lewin, K. and Gold, M. (eds) (1999). *The Complete Social Scientist: A Kurt Lewin Reader.* Washington, DC: American Psychological Association.

Ludescher, T. (1996). 'The Islamic roots of the poetic syllogisim', *College Literature,* (23) 1, 93–9.

Lundqvist, I. (1995). 'Facial EMG reactions to facial expressions: A case of facial emotional contagion?' *Scandinavian Journal of Psychology,* 36: 130–41.

Lyon, D. (ed.). (2006). *Theorising Surveillance: The panopticon and beyond.* Cullompton: Willan Publishing.

MacKenzie, A. (2002). *Transductions: Bodies and machines at speed.* London: Continuum.

MacLean, P. D. (1990). *The Triune Brain in Evolution: Role in paleocerebral functions.* New York: Plenum Press.

Manstead, A. S. R. (2012). 'A history of affect and emotion research in social psychology', in A. W. Kruglanski and W. Stroebe. (eds) *Handbook of the History of Social Psychology.* New York: Psychology Press. pp. 177–98.

Manstead, A. S. R. and Wagner, H. L. (1981). 'Arousal, cognition and emotion: An appraisal of two-factor theory', *Current Psychological Reviews,* 1(1): 35–54.

Massumi, B. (2002). *Parables for the Virtual: Movement, affect, sensation.* Durham, NC: Duke University Press Books.

McDougall, W. (1908). *An Introduction to Social Psychology.* [33rd Edition 1960]. London: Morrison and Gibb.

McDougall, W. (1920). *The Group Mind: A sketch of the principles of collective psychology with some attempt to apply them to the interpretation of national life and character.* Cambridge: Cambridge University Press.

Meads, C. and Nouwen, A. (2005). 'Does emotional disclosure have any effects? A systematic review of the literature with meta-analyses', *International Journal of Technology Assessment in Health,* 21(2): 153–64.

Meichenbaum, D. (1977). *Cognitive-behaviour Modification: An Integrative Approach.* New York: Plenum.

Middleton, D. J. and Brown, S. D. (2005). *The Social Psychology of Experience: Studies in remembering and forgetting.* London: Sage.

Miner, R. (2009). *Thomas Aquinas on the Passions.* Cambridge: Cambridge University Press.

Nicholls, M., Ellis, B., Clement, J. and Yoshino, M. (2004). 'Detecting hemifacial asymmetries in emotional expression with three-dimensional computerised image analysis', *Proceedings of Comparative and Physiological Psychology,* 87: 1–15.

Nightingale, D. and Cromby, J. (1999). *Social Constructionist Psychology: A critical analysis of theory and practice.* Buckingham: Open University Press.

Norton, D. (1993). *The Cambridge Companion to Hume.* Cambridge: Cambridge University Press.

Nussbaum, M. (1986). *The Fragility of Goodness: Luck and Ethics in Greek Tragedy and Philosophy.* Cambridge University Press.

Nussbaum, M. (2001). *Upheavals of Thought.* Cambridge: Cambridge University Press.

Oatley, K., Keltner, D. and Jenkins, J. M. (2006). *Understanding Emotions.* Chichester: Wiley-Blackwell.

Paez, D., Velasco, C. and Gonzalez, J. L. (1999). 'Expressive writing and the role of alexithymia as a dispositional deficit in self-disclosure and psychological health', *Journal of Personality and Social Psychology,* 77: 630–41.

Paivio, A. (1979). *Imagery and Verbal Processes.* Hillsdale, NJ: Lawrence Erlbaum Associates.

Panksepp, J. (2002). 'Foreword: The MacLean legacy and some modern trends in emotion research', in G. Gory and R. Gardner (eds) *The Evolutionary Neuroethology of Paul MacLean.* Westport, CT: Praeger. pp. ix–xxvii.

Panksepp, J. (2004). *Affective Neuroscience: The foundations of human and animal emotions.* Oxford: Oxford University Press.

Parker, I. (1999). Varieties of discourse and analysis. in I. Parker and the Bolton Discourse Network (eds) *Critical Textwork: An introduction to varieties of discourse and analysis.* Buckingham: Open University Press. pp. 1–12.

Penelhum, T. (1993). 'Hume's moral philosophy', in D F Norton (ed.) *The Cambridge Companion to Hume.* Cambridge: Cambridge University Press. pp 117–47.

Pennebaker, J. W. (1997). 'Writing about emotional experiences as a therapeutic process', *Psychological Science,* 8 (3): 162–66.

Pennebaker, J. W. and Francis, M. (1996). 'Cognitive, emotional, and language processes in disclosure', *Cognition and Emotion,* 10 (6): 601–26.

Pennebaker, J. W., Chung, C. K., Ireland, M., Gonzales, A. and Booth, R. J. (2007). *The Development and Psychometric Properties of LIWC 2007.* Austin, TX: LIWC.net.

Peplau, L. A. (2003). 'Human sexuality', *Current Directions in Psychological Science,* 12 (2): 37–40.

Petrides, K., Furnham, A. and Martin, G. N. (2004). 'Estimates of emotional and psychometric intelligence: Evidence for gender-based stereotypes', *The Journal of Social Psychology,* 144 (2): 149–62.

Pinker, S. (1997). *How the Mind Works.* New York: Norton.

Pizzagalli, D., Shackman, A.J., Davidson, R.J. (2003). 'The functional neuroimaging of human emotion: Asymmetric contributions of cortical and subcortical circuitry', in K. Hughdal and R.J. Davidson (eds) *The Asymmetrical Brain.* Cambridge, MA: The MIT Press. pp. 511–32.

Plant, E. A., Hyde, J. S., Keltner, D. and Devine, P. G. (2000). 'The gender stereotyping of emotions', *Psychology of Women Quarterly,* 24 (1): 81–92.

Plato (1997). *Phaedrus* (Phae). Trans. Alexande Nehamas and Paul Woodruff. Edited by John M. Cooper. *Plato: Complete Works.* Cambridge: Hackett Publishing.

Plato (1997). *Philebus* (Phil). Trans. Dorethea Frede. Edited by John M. Cooper. *Plato: Complete Works.* Cambridge: Hackett Publishing.

Plato (1997). *Republic* (Rep). Trans. G. M. A. Grube, rev. C. D. C. Reeve. Edited by John M. Cooper. *Plato: Complete Works.* Cambridge: Hackett Publishing.

Plato (1997). *Timeus* (Tim). Trans. Donald J. Zeyl. Edited by John M. Cooper. *Plato: Complete Works.* Cambridge: Hackett Publishing.

Plutchik, R. (1980). *Emotion: A psychoevolutionary synthesis.* New York: Harper & Row.

Plutchik, R., Eisenberg, N. and Strayer, J. (1987). 'Evolutionary bases of empathy', in N. Eisenberg and J. Strayer, *Empathy and its Development.* Cambridge: Cambridge University Press. pp. 38–46.

Potter, J. (1996). *Representing Reality: Discourse, rhetoric and social construction.* London: Sage Publications.

Price, A. (2010). 'Emotions in Plato and Aristotle', in P. Goldie (ed.) *The Oxford Handbook of Philosophy.* Oxford: Oxford University Press. pp. 121–42.

Prinz, J. (2004). 'Embodied emotion', in R. Solomon (ed.) *Thinking About Feeling: Contemporary philosophers on emotions.* Oxford: Oxford University Press.

Probyn, E. (2010). 'Writing shame' in M. Gregg and G. Seigworth (eds) *The Affect Theory Reader.* Durham, NC: Duke University Press. pp. 71–93.

Racle, G. (1980). 'Civilizations of the left cerebral hemisphere?', *Journal of the Society for Accelerative Learning and Teaching,* 5: 267–74.

Racle, G. (1986). 'Book review: The Japanese brain, uniqueness and universality, by Tadanobu Tsunoda', *Journal of the Society for Accelerated Learning and Teaching*, 11: 57–9.

Reicher, S. (2001). 'The psychology of crowd dynamics', in M. Hogg and S. Tindale (eds) *Blackwell Handbook of Social Psychology: Group Processes*. Oxford: Blackwell. pp. 182–208.

Reicher, S. and Stott, C. (2011). *Mad Mobs and Englishmen*. London: Robinson.

Reisenzein, R. (1983). 'The Schachter theory of emotion: Two decades later', *Psychological Bulletin*, 94 (2): 239–64.

Richards, B. (2004). 'The emotional deficit in political communication', *Political Communication*, 21(3), 339–52.

Ricoeur, P. and Savage, D. (1970). *Freud and Philosophy*. New Haven, CT: Yale University Press.

Rizzolatti, G., Fadiga, L., Gallese, V., and Fogassi, L. (1996). 'Premotor cortex and the recognition of motor actions', *Cognitive Brain Research*, 3(2): 131–41.

Robinson, G. J. (ed.) and Sturm, H. (1987). *Emotional Effects of Media: The work of Hertha Sturm*. Montreal: McGill University.

Robinson, J. (2004). 'Emotion: Biological fact or social construction', in R. Solomon (ed.) *Thinking About Feeling: Contemporary Philosophers on Emotions*. Oxford: Oxford University Press. pp. 28–43.

Robinson, M. D. and Johnson, J. T. (1997). 'Is it emotion or is it stress? Gender stereotypes and the perception of subjective experience', *Sex Roles*, 36(3): 235–58.

Rolls, E. T. (2007). *Emotion Explained*. New York: Oxford University Press.

Rosch, E. (1975). 'Cognitive representations of semantic categories', *Journal of Experimental Psychology: General*, 104 (3): 192–233.

Rose, N. (1979). 'The psychological complex : mental measurement and social administration', *Ideology and Consciousness*, 5: 5–68.

Rosenberg, M. (1990). 'Reflexivity and emotions', *Social Psychology Quarterly*, 53 (1): pp. 3–12.

Ruckmick, C. (1936). *Psychology of Feeling and Emotion*. New York: McGraw Hill.

Russell, J. (1994). 'Is there universal recognition of emotion from facial expressions? A review of the cross-cultural studies', *Psychological Bulletin*, 115, 1: 102–41.

Russell, J. and Fernandez-Dols, J. (1997). *The Psychology of Facial Expression*. Cambridge: Cambridge University Press.

Sampson, T. (2012). *Virality: Contagion theory in the age of networks*. Minneapolis: University of Minnesota Press.

Sarbin, T. R. (1989). 'Emotions as narrative emplotments', in M. Packer and R. Addison (eds) *Entering the Circle: Hermeneutic Investigation in Psychology*. Albany: State University of New York Press. pp. 185–201.

Schachter, S. and Singer. J. (1962) 'Cognitive, social, and physiological determinants of emotional state', *Psychological Review*, 69 (5): 379–99.

Schore, A. N. (1994). *Affect Regulation and the Origin of the Self: The Neurobiology of Emotional Development*. Hillsdale, NJ: Lawrence Erlbaum Associates.

Sclater, S., Jones, D. and Price, H. (2009). *Emotion: New Psychosocial Perspectives*: Basingstoke: Palgrave Macmillan.

Scott, D. (2014). *Gilbert Simondon's Psychic and Collective Individuation: A critical introduction and guide*. Edinburgh: Edinburgh University Press.

Seigworth, G. J. (2005). 'From affection to soul' (ed.) in C. Stivale (ed.) *Gilles Deleuze: Key Concepts*. Montreal: McGill-Queen's University Press. pp. 159–69.

Sherman, N. (1990). 'The place of emotions in Kantian morality', in O. Flanagan and A. Rorty (eds) *Identity, Character and Morality: Essays in Moral Psychology*. Cambridge, MA: The MIT Press. pp. 149–70.

Shields, S. A. (2002). *Speaking From the Heart: Gender and the social meaning of emotion*. Cambridge: Cambridge University Press.

Shields, S. A., Garner, D., Di Leone, B. and Hadley, A. (2006). 'Gender and emotion' in J. Stets and J. Turner (eds) *Handbook of the Sociology of Emotions*. New York: Springer. pp. 63–87.

Shilling, C. (1997). 'The undersocialised conception of the embodied agent in modern sociology', *Sociology*, 31 (4): 737–54.

Simondon, G. (2009). 'The position of the problem of ontogenesis', *Parrhesia*, 7: 4–16.

Simondon, G. (2012). *Two Lessons on Animal and Man*. London: Univocal Publishing.

Singer, T., Seymour, B., O'Doherty, J., Kaube, H., Dolan, R. J. and Frith, C. D. (2004). 'Empathy for pain involves the affective but not sensory components of pain', *Science*, 303 (5661): 1157–62.

Smyth, J.M. (1998). 'Written emotional expression: Effect sizes, outcome types, and moderating variables', *Journal of Consulting and Clinical Psychology*, 66(1): 174–84.

Solomon, R. (1976). *The Passions: The myth and nature of human emotion*. Notre Dame, IN: University of Notre Dame Press.

Sorabji, R. (2002). *Emotion and Peace of Mind: From stoic agitation to Christian temptation*. New York: Oxford University Press.

Spencer, H. (1863). 'The physiology of laughter', in H. Spencer, *Essays: Scientific, Political, and Speculative*, 2nd series. London: Williams and Norgate. pp. 105–19.

Spinoza, B (1677). *Ethics Including the Improvement of the Understanding*. Trans. R. H. M. Elwes [1989]. New York: Prometheus Books.

Squire, C. (2001). 'The public life of emotions', *International Journal of Critical Psychology*, 1: 27–38.

Starkstein, S. and Robinson, R. (1991). The role of the frontal lobes in affective disorder following stroke, in H. Levin, H. Eisenberg and A. Benton (eds) *Frontal Lobe Function and Dysfunction*. Oxford: Oxford University Press. pp. 288–303.

Stenner, P. (2005). 'An outline of an autopoietic systems approach to emotion', *Cybernetics and Human Knowing*, 12 (4): 8–22.

Stets, J. E. and Turner, J. H. (2006). *Handbook of the Sociology of Emotions*. New York: Springer.

Stone, V. E., Nisenson, L., Eliassen, J. C. and Gazzaniga, M. S. (1996). 'Left hemisphere representations of emotional facial expressions', *Neuropsychologia*, 34 (1): 23–9.

Stotland, E. (1969). 'Exploratory investigations of empathy', *Advances in Experimental Social Psychology*, 4: 271–314.

Taylor, J. R. and Mbense, T. G. (1998). 'Red dogs and rotten mealies: How Zulus talk about anger', in A. Athanasiadou and E. Tabakowska (eds) *Speaking of Emotions: Conceptualisation and expression*. Berlin: de Gruyter Mouton. pp. 191–226.

Timmers, M., Fischer, A. and Manstead, A. (2003). 'Ability versus vulnerability: Beliefs about men's and women's emotional behaviour', *Cognition & Emotion*, 17 (1): 41–63.

Tolman, D. L. (2002). *Dilemmas of Desire: Teenage girls talk about sexuality*. Cambridge, MA: Harvard University Press.

Tomkins, S. S. (1962). *Affect Imagery Consciousness*. New York: Springer.

Toscano, A. (2006). *The Theatre of Production: Philosophy and individuation between Kant and Deleuze*. Basingstoke: Palgrave.

Tucker, D. M. (1981). 'Lateral brain function, emotion, and conceptualization', *Psychological Bulletin*, 89 (1): 19–46.

Tucker, I.M. (2010). 'The potentiality of bodies', *Theory & Psychology*, 20 (4): 511.

Tucker, I. M. (2013). 'Bodies and surveillance: Simondon, information and affect'. *Distinktion: Scandinavian Journal of Social Theory*, 14 (1): 31–40.

Tucker, I. M. and Goodings, L. (2014). 'Sensing bodies and digitally mediated distress', *Senses & Society*, 9 (1): 55–71.

Turner, R., and Killian, L. (1987). *Collective Behaviour* (3rd edn). Englewood Cliffs, NJ: Prentice Hall.

Van Wagenen, W. P and Herren R. Y. (1940). 'Surgical division of commissural pathways in the corpus callosum: Relation to spread of an epileptic attack', *Archives of Neurology and Psychiatry*, 44 (4): 740–59.

Vygotsky, L. (1934). *Thought and Language*, trans. E. Hanfmann and G. Vakar: Cambridge, MA: MIT Press.

Walkerdine, V. (2008). 'Contextualizing debates about psychosocial studies', *Psychoanalysis, Culture & Society*, 13 (4): 341–5.

Watson, S. (1999). 'Policing the affective society: Beyond governmentality in the theory of social control', *Social & Legal Studies*, 8 (2): 227–51.

Wetherell, M (2012). *Affect and Emotion: A new social science understanding*. London: Sage.

Whitehead, A. N. (1927-8/1978). *Process and Reality: An essay in cosmology*. D.R. Griffen and D.W. Sherburne (eds). New York: Free Press.

Wierzbicka, A. (1986). 'Human emotions: Universal or culture-specific?', *American Anthropologist*, 88(3): 584–94.

Zillmann, D. (2010). 'Mechanisms of emotional reactivity to media entertainments' in K. Döveling, C. von Scheve and E. Konijn (eds) *The Routledge Handbook of Emotions and Mass Media*. Abingdon: Routledge. pp. 101–15.

Zimbardo, P. (1969). 'The human choice: Individuation, reason, and order versus deindividuation, impulse, and chaos', in W. Arnold and D. Levine (eds) *Nebraska Symposium on Motivation, Vol.17*. Lincoln, NE: University of Nebraska Press. pp. 237–307

Index